Waste–Site Stories

Edited by

Brian Neville and Johanne Villeneuve

Waste-Site Stories

the recycling of memory

state university of new york press

Photographs by Stephen Bann and Bob Chaplin by kind permission.

Eduardo Paolozzi's *Lost Magic Kingdoms and Six Paper Moons from Nahuatl* copyright The British Museum.

The work of Gordon Bleach © is part of the private collection of Dr. Gayle Zachmann, 2801 NW 23rd Blvd., Apt. E39, Gainesville, Florida 32605.

Published by
State University of New York Press
Albany

© 2002 State University of New York

For information, address
State University of New York Press,
90 State Street, Suite 700, Albany, NY 12207

Production and book design, Laurie Searl
Marketing, Fran Keneston

Library of Congress Cataloging-in-Publication Data

Waste-site stories : the recycling of memory / edited by Brian Neville and Johanne Villeneuve.
    p. cm.
  Includes bibliographical references and index.
  ISBN 0-7914-5341-3 (alk. paper) — ISBN 0-7914-5342-1 (pbk. : alk. paper)
    1. Civilization, Modern—1950-   2. Memory—Social aspects.   3. Recycling (Waste, etc.)— Psychological aspects.   4. Refuse and refuse disposal—Psychological aspects.   5. Collectors and collecting—Psychological aspects.   6. Historic sites—Social aspects.   7. Historic preservation— Social aspects.   8. Material culture.   9. Postmodernism.   I. Neville, Brian, 1966– II. Villeneuve, Johanne, 1960–

CB430.W37   2002
901—dc21
                                             2002021041

10   9   8   7   6   5   4   3   2   1

In memory of

Gordon Bleach

1956–1999

Contents

Part II   Site

List of Illustrations

Acknowledgments

The publication of this book concludes a long collaborative effort involving the editors, the authors, and many of their colleagues and friends. What started years ago as a conference in Montreal, developed in time into two quite independent publication projects under our care. The first of these, a book in French entitled *La mémoire des déchets: Essais sur la culture et la valeur du passé*, has already appeared in Quebec (Nota Bene Éditeur). Our thanks go to the *Social Sciences and Humanities Research Council of Canada* and Quebec's *Fonds pour la Formation des Chercheurs et l'Aide à la Recherche* for their financial support. The editors are grateful to the British Museum for permission to reproduce the work of Eduardo Paolozzi, and to Gayle Zachmann for kindly allowing us to include works by Gordon Bleach. We would like to express our gratitude to all those who participated in the volumes; to the friends who read and commented on the project over the years; to loved ones for their forbearance and support, financial and otherwise; and to Alice van der Klei for generously donating her time in the preparation of the manuscript; and to Alain Biage for his assistance with the index. Thanks go to Dale Cotton for his interest in the project and his decisive influence in seeing it eventually published, as well as to Laurie Searl and everyone involved at SUNY Press.

In the development of this project, the editors were fortunate to make the acquaintance of Gordon Bleach. His eagerness to share ideas and his enthusiastic participation in the project were precious to its success. Sadly, Gordon passed away before seeing the fruits of our collaboration. We hope that, in however small a measure, this book and the sample of his diverse oeuvre it includes may help carry on his legacy. We dedicate this book to him.

Introduction

In Lieu of

Waste

for Bill Readings

Brian Neville and Johanne Villeneuve

> A society is not free to remain young. And even at the height of its
> strength it has to form refuse and waste materials.
> —Nietzsche, note from March-June 1888

WASTE REMEDIATION

Ours is a wasteful society, consumed with cares for its remains. That waste
matters today will not be surprising, especially in the wake of a century whose
career of destruction has irreparably altered our relation to the things and events
of the past. Whether it be the rapidly changing conditions of cultural memory,
the sometimes toxic ecological and social fallout from technological development, or the legacy of personal and historical trauma, the notion now seems particularly apposite. We live amid the decay of structures that once organized our
collective and individual experience: political orders and antagonisms, criteria of
value, categories of judgment (epistemological, ethical, aesthetic), traditions and
forms of collective expression, memorial and archival institutions. Meanwhile,
stories accumulate in which human beings scour the remains of experience for
vestiges of meaning. The waste book has now truly come into its own, not as
ledger for as yet unordered accounts, but as figure for the writing of disordered
experience. Heedful of the pervasive concern and care for remains of all kinds,
our lives are now taken up with routines of waste management. This has as much
to do with the proliferation of technologies for the recycling or disposal of waste,

as it does with the inescapable fact that the experience of catastrophe in the past century can only be articulated from its remains, our history sifted from among these storied deposits.[1]

Our age is by no means unique in its wastefulness, though it certainly has the dubious honor of creating waste of kinds and quantities as yet unseen. Indeed, ever since Nineveh was *laid waste* as a *gazingstock* for all ages, the specter of waste has shadowed historical sensibility. The waste of civilizations long since disappeared or devastated has always been the privileged site for archaeology. With the inception of "garbage analysis," the digging simply moves on to our "modern refuse 'middens,'" as the founders of Garbage Studies at the University of Arizona advertise.[2] Now, whether it be the nature of the waste we produce—the nuclear waste from medical, military, energy sources, and so on, whose intractability is notorious—or the manner in which waste has become integral to our economy,[3] our age cares for waste.

With Nietzsche the consequences of waste for culture take on a distinctly contemporary relevance. As we know, while culture is indeed seldom far from his concerns, it is hardly of mere historical interest but involves Nietzsche in the problem of valuation as such. The notes of Nietzsche's *Nachlass* (the literary remains recycled to such notorious ends by others) suggest a more refined treatment of waste than heretofore observed, one in which value and nonvalue commingle: "Waste, decay, elimination," it occurred to him, "need not be condemned: they are necessary consequences of life, of the growth of life."[4] This admixture of waste and life, of decadence and vitality, does much to render the representation of history as a progressive movement problematic. Writing ever with respect to the dominant historicism of his age, and the instrumentalization of memory within the institutions of Modernity, Nietzsche questioned our reified relation to the past and the transformation of culture into an accumulation of objects within the progressive determination of knowledge. Historicism's division of the past into the succession of discrete stages in the advance of knowledge effectively relegates "things from the past" to the category of waste, and with them a particular memorial efficacy (as many of the chapters included in this book show). In a lesson of consequence to subsequent cultural critique, Nietzsche instead proposed the *revaluation* of that which historicism disposed of as waste. The very "concept of waste," Nietzsche would go on to suggest, needed to be articulated in relation to life: "Reason," no less, "demands . . . that we do justice to it."

Picking up the thread of Nietzsche's argument, in the pursuance of his own critique of Modernity, Walter Benjamin concluded that true historical thought must involve, in the first place, overcoming the facile opposition of progress and decadence. In what he called a "modest methodological proposal for the cultural-historical dialectic," Benjamin opined that the "decadent" was merely the by-product of the system of representation itself, a system that produces knowledge only by separating the "'productive,' 'forward-looking,' 'lively,' 'positive,' part of the epoch" from that which it casts off as "abortive, retrograde, and obsolescent."[5] As in Nietzsche, it is significant that Benjamin neither espouses nor dispenses entirely with such categories; what we require, according to Benjamin, is a "displacement of the angle of vision," rather than any change in the "criteria." The negative component itself must be subject to the infinite evaluation of critique, continuously revised in the tension between value and nonvalue, until such time as everything that is waste matter to the present recovers an actuality, and past and present join in what he calls "a historical apocatastasis,"[6] or *restoration of all things*. Bringing this story summarily up to date, the legacy of Nietzsche and Benjamin is carried on in Peter Sloterdijk's recovery of the *kynical* moment in critique, or what he calls the different "liberating negativisms."[7] Here begin these *waste-site stories*.

That many, today, should develop a nose for waste is either an indictment of destitution in a prodigal culture or (and they are not mutually exclusive) an indication of this on-going recovery of negativity, where what is needed is precisely people, in Sloterdijk's words, "who do not get nauseated." As the variety of chapters in this book attests, discourses and disciplines from art history to anthropology to literature to media and film studies have discovered "the positivity of the negative," to borrow another of Sloterdijk's succinct turns of phrase. Meanwhile, the notion of waste has, likewise, been recovered in various artistic practices, conveniently and heuristically regrouped by Walter Moser under the heading "Aesthetics of Waste."[8] Here the notion of waste is redeemed for culture, a gesture that strikes at the very ontology of the work of art, leaving us what Gordon Bleach cheekily called "spurious artifacts." Within these different practices, we observe a growing concern for temporality and materiality, which guides artistic production to the heart of memory. Against the modernist myth of originality, such works recycle the historical avant-garde's penchant for the outdated, those waste-objects in the *desert of history*.[9] In a similar vein, Aleida Assmann draws our attention to the fact that, in the seeming absence of structures of cultural memory, twentieth-century writers comb the trash for vestiges of an authentic past. Ironically though, this same discourse of authenticity, itself so seemingly removed from the aesthetics of waste, is tributary to a kind of recycling—an irony not lost on Hans Ulrich Gumbrecht, who hypothesizes that authenticity, a notion dear to existentialist philosophy since Heidegger, may be no more than a "simulacrum of recycling."

Objects from the past concern us in curious ways. Were we to devise a nomenclature of objects on the basis of what distinguishes them through time, we would soon concur with David Gross that "only when they are degraded or discarded do they at last begin to reveal their true nature." Upon further consideration, however, the historian's preliminary distinction between "objects from the present" and "objects from the past" appears more complex, if not more perplexing, for only beyond such a nomenclature can we begin to appreciate the processes of valuation and devaluation that cast objects in with "fallen matter." At first glance, the texts collected here explore semiologies and epistemologies that subtend our notions of waste, of memory, and of recycling. Their concern is less with any putative contents of memory than with the efficacy of memory, there where modern and, for want of a better word, postmodern subjectivities contend with the global circulation of persons and cultural commodities. Many of the reflections collected here begin by examining the material infrastructures, the sites, if you will, that house memory: museums, monuments, commemorative practices, archives—the very architecture of memory—and their specific materialities. Susanne Hauser, early in the book, shows that while we observe the transformation of historical remains into works of art, we witness, at one and the same time, ironically, the transformation of historical institutions such as the museum into sites of resistance to the "dislocation and immateriality of the global economic process." At which point, we could conclude that these "materialized memories" consist, more than anything else, of collections of objects that tell stories. "Objects from the past" do not merely designate the past itself; they point to a process of transforming material composites into waste, a process in which disintegration and decomposition are constitutive factors. At the same time, the question imposes itself as to whether the use of waste in art can even be classified. As Christine Bernier argues in her contribution to the book, "Now that everything is considered part of culture, are we to assist the museumization of culture?" To which one might add, is culture doomed to being a culture of exhibition? From this vantage, we must recognize, as Bernier does, "the problematic erosion of criteria of relation and appreciation of objects." When waste is initiated into the museum of art, the border between archives and art exhibition becomes tenuous, to say the least. But to what extent does the archive still serve as mediation and memory? And why this accretion of "waste" in the contemporary study of culture and its modes of production?

Starting, as Moser does, from a semantic analysis, we discover in mulling over the origins of "waste" and correlate terms an aggregate of notions that includes purity, value, and memory. As an epistemological category, "waste" is fundamentally volatile; it is, Moser reminds us, "at once permanent and unstable, unavoidable and evanescent." Should we conclude from this that in contemporary critical discourse objects themselves must lose their outline and analytical value, at the very moment that waste acquires value and symptomatic status? When objects are no longer the vectors of historical discourse, and waste, reciprocally, becomes the vector of another discourse, what, we may ask, is its nature? Is the discourse of waste allied in some way with narrative, with history? Hauser points out the integration within myth of the things that have "fallen" into oblivion; Aleida Assmann, in turn, insists on the semantic significance of this "fall" for the notion of waste (and with it, the persistence of a sense of "sin"). Things that have fallen by the wayside, things we nonetheless try to consider both in their decay and recollection, acquire, it seems, an unforeseen value and status insofar as they lack contour—precisely because they are fluid as well as opaque and resistant to fixity, because they are at once fragile and incontestable for the particular pain that attends their possible reemergence into our world, a pain that commingles with memories buried deep. But their resurgence also can seem almost ironic, arising as they do in the temporal *in-between* that upsets the habitual way in which we look at things about us. From which memory do they arise? Not from history, which is precisely not memory, nor, rightly speaking, from that "collective memory," of which Maurice Halbwachs spoke, the supposed property of groups like guilds or families. The dissolution of these groups is, in some sense, at the heart of that dissolution of values that produces waste. For that matter, nor does it come from any so-called "personal" memory, which we know, and as Halbwachs argued, is always necessarily social. The disciplinary coup by which Halbwachs sought to wrest the study of memory from the grip of psychology, thereby instituting the sociology of memory, was mounted from the theory of the environmental a priori of memory, the necessary structuration of memory in social institutions or "frames," as he called them. While subsequently developing the ramifications of this insight, Halbwachs surmised that the concept of frame would necessarily expand to embrace "the society of things."[10] Pushing onward to the ground that is properly that of this book, he argued that personal memory could therefore only be conceived as a construction upon the site where individuals and things met in the realm of social relationship. In so doing, however, Halbwachs himself underestimated perhaps the important role of forgetting in this relationship—the role of oblivion in the mediacy of memory. To recapitulate, then, the "things" of which we speak, when we refer to the paradigm of "waste," come not so much from some locatable memory as they do from a forgetting whose efficacy we must assess. In other words, they derive from that *virtuality* which remains active in the heart of memory and which, for this very reason, is without direction or belonging, but out of which specters and figures arise. And what we here call "stories," moreover, refers to a quite particular narrativity (one we will consider shortly) that has everything to do with spectrality and figuration and little to do with historicism and teleology. Moreover, the problem with historicism is not so much the so-called "narrativity" of history—narrativity being so firmly bound to culture, as Paul Ricoeur has consistently reminded us in his reflections on time and narrative—but its teleological trend, its tendency to obliterate its own propensity to forget. History always tends to globalize reality into its own form, but as soon as the possibility of waste is taken into account, it seems that some sort of mediation becomes necessary, that some linkage and narrative desire are in turn produced. The result is a pro-liferation of stories, of narrativity without linearity, multiple narratives within singular voices and without ultimate agency.

It is when we reflect upon the relation between memory and forgetting that the notion of "recycling" becomes unavoidable. Recycling, it will be gathered from the chapters brought together in this book, has become the paradigm of cultural production today. If we thus recur to the notion of recycling, it is to address the necessary ambiguity that arises between value and void. Modernity, in Heidegger's influential definition, is the epistemological order grounded in the technological relation of the subject to the world of objects over which it holds sway, and among which it apportions the specific share of worth and waste. The subject ordains in valuation and in determining the use or obsolescence of things for the present. In this regard, we are inclined to agree with Wlad Godzich's contention that waste only exists with respect to the modern subject, as the waste matter of such an epistemological order. Conceived merely as an industrial process, recycling resembles just such a modality of means-oriented manipulation: the power the subject wields over the objects at its disposal, enabling it to exploit a further utility from waste, thereby consolidating its grip upon the world and its past. But with regard to the concept of recycling, we must inquire whether the problem of value and waste is not bound up with memory and the latter's processes of transformation and mediation. What is more, "recycling" affords us a further insight into what is at stake when we inquire into the "true nature" of those objects deemed waste. As Gumbrecht's and Wolfgang Ernst's chapters explore, introducing the notion of "recycling" opens a debate as to the precise meaning of "true nature." When what matters is to reveal the complexity of the paradigm of waste, to assess notions of memory and authenticity at specific sites (notions that are fundamental in the elaboration of that of culture), it is recycling, as a determinant process in our conceptions of culture and knowledge, that renders visible the potential inversion of value and nonvalue, of memory and oblivion, of end and origin.

To overcome the usual oppositions and demarcations between "authenticity" and "simulacrum," just as those between subject and objects at its disposal in cultural production, we must begin by examining, under the aegis of "recycling," various sites of resistance. This explains why "recycling" is inadequately comprehended within a positive or negative axiology.[11] Nature, to begin with, has always shown a proclivity to recycle, combining what it produces each day with what it decomposes. And the notion of recycling has long since moved beyond its initial industrial context to embrace a variety of practices—aesthetic, political, economic—that concerns not only the culture of obsolescence but equally so-called "developing" nations, those secondary markets where affluent societies have long sought to recuperate a further commercial potential from waste commodities, or simply and inexpensively dumped their unwanted, often toxic, waste.

Its technical aspects notwithstanding, the logic of recycling is rather singular: in a recycling economy, every "wastrel" holds value as potential resource material; at the same time, all things lose value insofar as they potentially become waste. Value—be it value *per se* or value-in-time—becomes inherently difficult to define, so it becomes necessary to recover the idea of virtual and potential value in order to overcome this difficulty, without thereby diminishing its complexity. We observe, moreover, that waste is defined by its own resistant materiality, by what we are tempted to call its "material memory." The overwhelming power of the modern subject, one capable of turning such a technology to its own ends, seems to coincide with the growing autonomy of a process of transformation that disposes of this same subject, simply because it no longer has need for it. It is this modern subject that in turn becomes the waste matter, so to speak, of technology, and therefore it is the remains of this subject that recover a new memory. Returning to the "origins" of the process, that is, to figures of authority and authenticity, brings us back without fail to the process itself. In seeking to understand recycling as a process, so Gumbrecht discovers, we wind up faced with the impossibility of accounting for origins without recourse to the idea of recycling. It should then come as no surprise that, where originality is indeed the result of "fake-recycling," something like a Nashville Parthenon would be designated an "original replica"—that is, as Éric Méchoulan puts it in his chapter, a site that "dissolves time in the immediacy or synchronicity of its presentation." Could recycling, then, not be seen as a mixing of temporalities? Things no longer appear throughout in a simple economy of time but within the economy of virtuality, and the acceleration of change leads to the extension of possibilities.

It has become commonplace to describe the logic of Modernity as one of anachronism. We live in heterogeneous temporalities in which past and present, the traditional and the technologically sophisticated, overlap (pastry dough is Hans Magnus Enzensberger's suggestive figure for this temporal predicament). As such, we deal as often with the "remnants of the past" as we do with the inventions of technical progress. We, our DNA, our cultural evolution, are all largely built out of older materials.[12] Agree as we may that Modernity deals with remains, with strands of past and present enfolded like pastry, we should nonetheless not mistake that Modernity never relinquishes the possibility, the necessity even, of separating out those folds of dough. Modernity preserves the illusion of the miraculous separation of the wheat from the chaff, to mix metaphors slightly. Furthermore, the very objectification that informs this operation of separating and demarcating transforms all loss into "lost objects." Freud himself, for instance, preserves this modern bias precisely where he conceives of both mourning and melancholia in terms of the ego's relation to an object. In the brief essay on "transience," Freud cast an almost mournful gaze upon the ruin of civilization in 1915, sympathizing with the despondent soul, bereft of the objects in which it was emotionally invested. The devastation of war, which only confirms the "proneness to decay" of all that is, had revealed the fragility of culture and nature alike and the sudden emptying of what seemed of changeless value. However, the temptation to mourn the loss of cultural "possessions" (Freud's words) is willfully shunt aside in the subject's undiminished capacity to recover the "riches of civilization." Just as suddenly as the subject leaves off mourning, so what was waste (the world consumed in the "losses caused by this war") becomes riches once more, and the subject is free "to replace the lost objects by fresh ones equally or still more precious."[13] Melancholia, which Freud approaches along the lines of his model of mourning, also is tributary to this process of objectification. Curiously enough, in the case of the melancholic, it is the ego itself that becomes object—some "thing." The subject, suddenly objectified, is confronted with its own loss, all the while preserving its unlimited power.[14]

Now Freud's melancholy has nothing to do with former conceptions, Aristotle's, for instance, which has only to do with movement, with the density, the power and gravity, of the humors. We know that within the framework of tradition, time can only be experienced in the combined influence of past and present. The very modern insistence on the agent who kneads the dough, to reprise Enzensberger's figure, does not obtain within tradition. The possibility, the necessity even, of separating, of distributing the elements, has in fact no bearing. Likewise, the individual and the collective are inseparably linked. They are inseparable, just as the artisan is inseparable from the material that he or she transforms, material that in turn transforms the artisan, transforms him or her into a craftsperson and not into the all-powerful force of origination. Separately, the object and its mediation are literally unthinkable. Otherwise put, the past itself and all objects within its precinct are ever alive in the feeling, seldom far removed, of the ascendancy of the dead over all things. Because for tradition, need we repeat, the dead are those who have gone before, those who have frayed a path, and whose figuration continues to throw light upon present hardship. The dead are not those who remain behind, in the folds of time. Modernity introduces the notion of such an unfolding in time. And if it likens ancestors in any way to precursors, it is only on the condition that they be seen not as the dead who prepared our way but as those that the present, in its absolute superiority, can summon at will, in period costume and under the spectacular lights of representation.

If the prospect of waste appears everywhere on the horizon of contemporary culture, the reason might just be that Modernity is now learning how to better recognize the difference between its dead and the dead of tradition. It seeks to acknowledge this difference, however, not from its own point of view but from the point of view of the dead themselves. Paradoxical though it may seem, Modernity adopts the point of view of that which has been doubly rejected: the vantage of oblivion (which has weighed heavily upon the dead, and which has formed the link between the living and the dead ever since human memory can recall) and, even more so, of the forgetting of this oblivion, which weighs heavily upon it, recalling it to its memorial responsibilities. For, in effect, Modernity must indeed recognize that by reflecting on this forgetting, it cannot return from whence it came; it will be perpetually compelled to fashion its own image in the reflection of the remains that are its own creation. Salvage from the deep has only the value that those who recover it accord. The latter may even see themselves as so much wreckage—like Freud's melancholic—but this does not release them from the salvage operation; even less does it remove the temptation to pillage, or the possibility of disaster.

LIFE, AND NOTHING BUT

As George Steiner compellingly argued, nineteenth-century Western culture harbored a "nostalgia for disaster" that found expression in sundry presentiments of catastrophe and figurations of global apocalypse.[15] That our century was indeed preceded by a "catastrophile complex" is no less clear than that it was succeeded, as Peter Sloterdijk termed it, by a sublimated "will to catastrophe."[16] As is so often noted, foremost here were the effects of the First World War. The latter, it bears repeating, witnessed the collapse of the European social order and its legitimation: "structures of decay," to quote Steiner, "are toxic."[17] Like the character Gödike in Broch's *The Sleepwalkers*—a man buried in the trenches, his mouth stopped with mud, who, though subsequently resuscitated, is no longer capable of communicating—the basic structures of experiential understanding were destroyed for those who survived the war.[18] Refusing to solve "the riddle of his life, the riddle of his death," Gödike survives between the two, in an infantile state—literally without language. With time, Gödike will painfully recover his soul in fragments until, finally, he manages to rebuild its bare "scaffolding." The postwar condition, in Broch's terrifying image, is likened to the postmortem: the war represents a descent into death, after which all, like Gödike, can say no more than that they are "arisen from the grave."[19]

The events of the war, as we read in account after account, would prove intractable to communication: one returned, Benjamin observed, poorer in communicable experience, precisely because such horrors could not be made comprehensible, that is, assimilated within the framework of experience. As with Gödike, there was an overwhelming sense of "interruption" in the continuity of a life, splitting it suddenly into a before and an after, casting one adrift. Experience had indeed "fallen in value."[20] This crisis of experience, a notion familiar to Benjamin's readers, was in part the result of a "technological gap": the disastrous first experience of modern technology by a historical imagination equipped for traditional warfare, a war in which technology was in advance of the ethical frames of society's conception of war. From this crisis of experience, a "poverty," as Benjamin termed it, descended on humanity. And this poverty of experience, while first felt so painfully in the trauma of war, would subsequently become common fare in technological society, where the speed and nature of change outstrip experiential understanding. Giorgio Agamben, in particular, has carried Benjamin's insights into the destruction of experience the furthest,[21] showing that this destruction no longer necessitates catastrophe; the conditions of contemporary life suffice. To cursorily summarize his well-developed argument: in the absence of appropriate frames of reference, the quick succession of novel events under conditions of modern technological society precludes their integration within experience. Experience is predicated on continuity, that is, on the individual's capacity to bring events in line with forms of the past, to reduce the shock of the new by calling upon the authority of tradition. Experience can only survive where no discontinuity between past and present arises. Where a gap does indeed open, tradition loses its vital force: events can no longer be integrated within a familiar structure of comprehension, nor communicated in their totality. This puts us, then, in a position to appreciate our radically changed relation to the past. What was keenly felt as the destruction of experience in the First World War—its sheer unfamiliarity, its incomprehensibility, and the incommunicability of its horrors—argues Agamben, following up on Benjamin's insights, is part of the more extensive "expropriation" of experience within Modernity. In retrospect, it appears already implicit in the validation of experimentation over experience in the progressive knowledge claims of scientific method, which remove knowledge from the realm of traditional experience and ground it in the cognitive activity of the modern subject. Today, however, the authority of the latter is no longer to be taken at face value and if something like life and culture are to be imagined anew, it is from their remains. For only when the subject is reconceived on the poor ground of this new concept of life can it begin to assume in some way the legacy of unassimilable experience that is its own. Here life is not what achieves a rationally determinate form accessible to the subject, a life drawn, in its entirety, within a circle of plenitude and integrated into a structure of comprehension (whether tradition or historical development). Rather, life is what remains, what leaves traces amid the ruins of experience, and it is precisely this concept of remains that can provide a new paradigm for questioning culture today.

Where technological society is concerned, speed and efficacy are alone what matter. Jack London's 1912 story "The Scarlet Plague" presents an elderly man recounting to his grandchildren the story of the end of his world, the plague-ridden world of the early twenty-first century.[22] What properly characterizes this disaster is not just the rapidity with which it struck (five minutes sufficed for the disease to carry off healthy individuals) or the quick decomposition of the corpses but the alacrity with which surviving generations forgot, so much so as to lose all interest in the past. The old man is a storyteller, in the true sense of the term, but his listeners can no longer follow him, incapable as they are of bridging the gap that separates them from this lost time. London's story reminds us to what extent the destruction of things and the destruction of life are swift and irrevocable, when compared to their emergence over time and the slow succession of generations. In modern Western culture, however, "advances" in technology do not obey this slow rhythm; technology, rather, seems to develop out of the profusion of violence and war. In "waste," as we see throughout these pages, we have a category that resists this phenomenon, bearing witness both to the *longue durée* of time and the suddenness of catastrophe—a category that, in today's "postwars" culture, is called upon to play a role much like that of London's old man.

As we have said, however, if the First World War left anything in its destructive wake, it was at once the gap between culture and experience, and the shared feeling that this war was no longer war, that war had henceforth become an obsolete notion insofar as the word could no longer describe such an event.[23] To put it another way, as both the last war of the nineteenth century and the first modern technological war—echoes of which resounded throughout the Second World War, confounding all reason in the events of the Holocaust and Hiroshima—World War I forever unsettles us. It resolutely ruined the criteria with which we define culture, and with it both progress and decline. Above all, however, it was from this wastage that began the long process of interrogation which led, ultimately, to the ethical horizon with which we are all familiar. This was a war without warriors; it prepared the way for genocide and blind destruction without rest or redemption, destruction without possible *history*. We are compelled today to recognize that in some sense we cannot really speak of what happened between 1939 and 1945 as a war. The many wars that have followed are hollowed by the same doubt: we are never truly dealing with men opposed in combat, but with the destruction of culture and its memory. With this memory and this culture reduced to remains, the destruction becomes that much more problematic.

In his 1989 film *La Vie et rien d'autre*, Bertrand Tavernier tells the story of an ephemeral yet miraculously lasting encounter between a man and woman in the absurd landscape of post–World War I life.[24] At war's end, Irène scours the devastated area in search of her missing husband, in the course of which she meets Delaplane, an officer in charge of retracing the whereabouts or identifying the bodies of missing soldiers. In his archives, Delaplane keeps drawings and photographs of unidentified corpses and missing soldiers, while across this wasteland, amnesiacs wander through sites left abandoned by the army and, here and there, an individual searches for a missing friend or fiancé. The wartime setting forms a palimpsest with neither a beginning nor an end. Meanwhile, the Estates General of France seems less concerned with the fate of the 350,000 missing than with finding the Unknown Soldier, the symbolic suture to wounded national identity—someone citizens can accompany to the Pantheon and the Arc de Triomphe. By the film's end, Delaplane's struggle with this monumental masquerade, his personal effort not to forget the dead, has turned up 51,000 missing individuals in just two months. In vain, he races against time and the film closes upon the vista of anonymous military crosses, extending as far as the eye can see. The encounter of an aging military man in search of *identities* and a young woman in search of a *body* is significant for the way in which the encounter both happens and does not: at the conclusion of two days spent together at the site where survivors looking for mortal remains are gathered around corpses, Irène insists that Delaplane declare his love for her: those words alone would convince her to follow him anywhere—"without a past." The man dares not answer; he will confess his love only three years later, in a letter that finds her in New York. There is no life without the past. Still, Delaplane writes: "You who are embarking on a new life, you who are the new itself, how little you need novelty!" In the film, the force of the new, a force figured in woman, has nothing to do with either the "New World" or progress. Rather, it concerns the generative power of women. Properly speaking, "woman" is the figure for the temporality of nature itself, a vital force that transforms suffering into hope, death into birth. The force of the new is greater than the force of destruction in war and has something ineluctable about it.[25]

In Tavernier's film, the masculine world, with its corpses, its military bureaucracies, its dashed dreams, and its madness, confronts the world of women and their singular memories, their living dead, their hopes and plans for the future. In the film, a sculptor everywhere accompanies this search for bodies; it is, he cynically allows, the golden age for monument makers such as himself, sculptors in the service of monumentalizing war and the representation of combatants. In spite of this, the sculptor dreams of figurations of hope, of the female form, which for this artist is the only material that gives shape to hope. While people file past, looking for lost loved ones at the site of a train explosion, objects, duly identified like relics, are laid out on tables in order to help identify the victims— photographs, wallets, flasks, canteens, pendants and chains, medals, lighters, bedside books, playing cards, objects that are just so many traces or supports for traces, with the inestimable value of life and the singularity of an existence amidst the anonymity of things. In ritual fashion, people touch these objects, trembling at once with fear and hope as they caress them. For many, the prospect of finding nothing is more daunting than the eventuality of recognizing something. In the midst of this ritual, the sculptor speaks of woman's body, "which we long to touch, to caress." The juxtaposition is not fortuitous: the caress of a woman's hand on one of these objects recalls the desire of the soldier who, in the trenches, dreams of a woman's body—a woman left far behind. It is as though such an attentive caress could bring back the man and with him a past whose irreversibility we only slowly come to accept. For the most part, though, such objects remain mute; they seem, at once, both insignificant and inestimable. When they do reveal their identity, and with it that of a world, we are surprised to find that it is not the object that becomes something dear but the dear one that becomes an object: "You're lucky," a soldier in charge says to one elderly couple, after they have found a canteen by which to identify their son. "We have a relic [the remains of a body] preserved in the mud, as fresh as a bottle stashed in a cellar." Upon seeing the cadaver of their son, the couple is astonished, but little more, to see the change in his appearance (now bearded and wasted away), as though this "thing" were no longer their son but only a brute factum.

Troubling as the dual status of the dead and the objects that they possessed may be, this commingling of value and nonvalue in a single, terrible, yet wonderful, and subsequently banal, anonymous moment reminds us that memory is read less as a narrative than as stories culled from the many deposits of experience. If history is a matter of "point of view," memory, we might say, pertains to materiality, which is why for history the question of value amounts to asking what is worth recounting, whereas memory (as in the example of those who come to identify the missing, in Tavernier's film) resides in the gap between the value and nonvalue of that which was and, as such, remains constantly endangered.

REFUSE OF HISTORY

As technological progress propels us toward a global future, we look back upon a past whose remains pile skyward like so much debris at a waste site. In this new world order, where the experience of space and time seems so altered, and where history as a discourse comes increasingly under suspicion (when it is not simply said to have ended), we are exposed to the idea of cultural exhaustion. Things past take on the aspect of waste, while technology labors in the development of new expertise in waste management. While mnemonic technologies increasingly take possession of the past, stocking it in ever-greater archives, the events, often traumatic, of this century actuate remembrance and charge with it those material forms that bear the marks of historicity. This predicament, which involves relinquishing a certain narrative history, opens up the present to the vitality and variety of stories that engage the past, the dead. In this way, the stories in this book emerge at certain sites of memory, from the ruins of experience, to explore the material infrastructure of memory, upon which such stories repose. The heterogeneity of memorial practices today recovers the value of the individual witness, site, object, which, relegated to waste, seemed destined for oblivion. It discloses the part of recycling in all memorial practices, while providing memory with new forms and functions.

Consider, for instance, the temple of Artemis at Ephesos. As Ernst shows, we enter here upon the ground of archaeology and the decomposition of sites, where the "memory of waste is being destroyed by the very act of recalling it to hermeneutic attention by excavation." If Ernst refuses to see narrative at work in the "aggregation of waste in archaeology," it is because the linkage of such data is not narrative but "hypertextual." This testifies to the ambiguity we find throughout the book: waste does indeed produce stories, but these have little in common with the linearity of a narrative thread that memory would supposedly follow. This "memory"—not history, not historicism, the consuming fever of which Nietzsche spoke and which prevents us from writing the history of this memory—resembles that discussed by Simonides in Cicero's *On Oratory* and refers to lived experience at a specific site. According to the Aristotelian distinction between memory *(memoria)* and recollection *(remimiscentia)*, mental images belong to memory, whereas recollection concerns "the recovery of a knowledge or sensation" one has had.[26] Recollection is an impulse of the faculty of images *(phantasia)* which, according to Aristotle, is the mediation between the sensible and the intelligible. This memory, then, is one of recollection, since it calls upon the lost sensation (think of Tavernier's characters caressing those objects). Today, however, recollection beckons toward history, as though history were no longer conceivable without respect to and memory of this sensation that is greater than everything. Even if we have not had firsthand experience of the events of the World Wars, we nonetheless bear the trace, a mark, a "feeling," the living legacy of that historical moment. At the least, we are indistinctly conscious and unconscious of it, at once terribly cognizant and oblivious. Thus in contrast to the distinction posed in classical thought, it appears that recollection is confounded with memory in two ways: in the first place, recollection constitutes a reaching out, certainly to a lost sensation, but to a sensation that never was: "we never lived through such and such." Consider the rhetorician's art of memory (or mnemotechnics), so well documented by Frances Yates, which sought to retain in images memories that were not their own. Stories act in part like these images, reaching out toward sensations from which they are cut off. But memory and recollection are confounded in yet another manner: despite the fact that "we never lived through such and such," and that the desperate effort to retrace the sensation is forever thwarted, knowing this, knowing that we are traces, marks, effects, consequences of that event, we are also aware that we cannot disown it. What we find, in lieu of the lived sensation, in lieu of the experience itself, is the sensation of the rift proper, and that which makes us living, remembering archives. For this reason, the question is not what kinds of use we can put the past to, as certain reifying views pretend.[27] The past can be as alive as we are and not simply regarded as *lieux de mémoire*. It may be that in probing our relation to the past, we become aware of a very tenuous rift, one that considerably alters the link between past and present. The past appears more efficacious than the present, variously modifying the latter in ways that no explanation can fully clarify.

In his contribution to these reflections on waste, Stephan Bann relates the stories of two stones, allowing him to address the question of the practice of collecting and the discourse (one is tempted to say the intrigue) of the *curiosity*, in which such things are taken up. Setting out to revisit John Bargrave's collection of curiosities, Bann winds up in a subterranean chamber in Toulouse, stocked full of desiccated bodies. Emphasizing the deliquescence of the fragments, Bann relates these qualities to certain cases in which the dead rise to haunt the living. The dead are a concern, explicitly as well as figuratively, in the book as a whole: reconsidering contemporary art on the basis of the function of the archive and the museum, Bernier recurs to the figure of the "cemetery"; while equally concerned with the notion of the archival, Assmann picks up the image of the "repository" of things, the site where things repose (as she says, archives and rubbish heaps can be interpreted as "emblems and symptoms for cultural remembrance and oblivion"). Focusing on waste and rubbish, Bernier and Assmann, like Hauser, are each led into the realm of "invisibility," where art "renders visible what is otherwise invisible—namely, the fundamental structures of cultural value production." Art then constitutes, in Assmann's words, a "counter memory," and sites (historical knowledge, the modern subject, etc.) quake under the pressure of invisibility. But what comes of this force? How is it that waste can produce *stories*? How do stories arise from *history in ruins*?

More than anything else, "refuse" and "waste" are categories that permit us to connect "nature" and humanly fashioned products; in the end, natural things, just as human beings, suffer a similar decline. But historical determination, as Benjamin pointed out, is not properly comprehensible within a model of "decline" or absolute "enlightenment." And while artifacts are always linked to human memory as "culture," nature has no memory as such: whereas "ending" holds no meaning for nature, it opens up a tremendous chain of significations for the one who is not only the "source" of humanly fashioned things but the sole interpreter of nature and memory. In this context, what is particularly telling today is the constant recourse to nature (as model for recycling, for temporality, and for an economy of resources) in order to comprehend, evaluate, classify, and finally to qualify the past. The past, the time to which the present remains indebted, thus seems caught in the pull of opposing forces: as nature itself, the past seems to enjoy an independence from interpretation and subjectivity, surviving without interpreters by its efficacy—the very efficacy that modifies the present, indeed, that "constitutes" our present. From this vantage, the present might be construed as the flat figuration of the past, its very visible and tangible surface, its "living map."

At the same time, however, the past appears as a mere object, one to be mastered, quantified, described, and evaluated, in order to produce knowledge. In the first instance, the past (the past as efficacy, as pure event) is inextricably bound to the problem of "memory"; in the second instance (the past as object of knowledge), the past appears before us in the traditional guise of historicism, which, to a certain extent, has less to do with memory than with archives.[28]

If what we call "the present" is but the sum traces of the past, then the problem of "cultural memory" ultimately becomes that of the present itself (which is to say, the problem of *being* with respect to the efficacy of time, or *being* in the process of change). In our role as interpreters, we can seize upon and measure traces rather than simply submit to their effect. We can "experiment" with them, if not "experience" them. As readers, we can pursue traces. But as products of the past ourselves, as well as of nature, we are part of the materiality of traces, and we are engaged in the natural process of devastation. Human beings decline, die, and are recycled. The conjunction of these two positions (on the one hand, seizing traces and experimenting, on the other hand, not being able to consciously and knowingly experience waste) defines the epistemological shift in contemporary cultural critique. The tension between the two is a matter for ethics, not only because the "present" is very much what is at stake (and with it, our share of *kaïros*), but because memory has begun to replace computable facts in the determination of historical knowledge and discourse. And memory, unlike facts, implies the necessity of a relationship between human beings.

If sensitivity to this shift is particularly acute today, it is by no means of strictly recent origin. It has been developing in the West since the emergence of a Modernity in which the singularity of experience gains upon universal history. As Reinhart Koselleck remarked, the Aristotelian dichotomy of history (as narrative of the particular) and poetry (as exemplary narrative) is reversed in Western Modernity: history would come to hold pride of place by the universality of its model, while literature would be left to recover the residue of singular experience.[29] In this regard, we could say that a process of recollection involving both history and literature has been underway since the utter destruction of experience with the First World War. Once decisively turned to the question of memory, literature carries on at the limits of history, right up to the contemporary epistemological crisis that spread in the wake of both wars. Admittedly, history has always borrowed from literature, especially where historical discourse is modeled on the rhetoric of narrative.[30] What it borrowed, however, were the "forms" of literature or, more precisely, that which Aristotelian poetics deemed universal or exemplary: the tragic form, the *peripeteia*, the epic model, in which temporality is made visible. What it discarded was the singularity of a historical moment, the unique features of an event that provide no basis for the ideal of the "good life." In the wake of the First World War and, more intensely, the catastrophes of the Second, the issue appears quite changed. Now wholly concerned with the substratum of individual experience and memory, literature becomes a precious guardian alongside historical discourse—the guardian of remains, of that which is unnarratable, unrepresentable. But unlike the Greeks, who found in poetry a form of ritual resolution for their obligation to the dead, our Modernity still grapples in a confused and paradoxical way with the dual incursion of historical and poetic discourse in the labor of mourning—a labor that remains as complex as it is insoluble. Once given over to the archaeological, history abandons its "form"; it cedes to memory the task of working through the layering of time, of researching the most singular traces: the history of the marginal, of the forgotten, the history, even, of historical oblivion. Having evacuated historicism from history—no longer trusting in its "forms" and "universality"—and having abandoned the model of "decline," "cultural memory" turns quite deliberately instead toward the singularity of experience and the uniqueness of events. The axiom that "there are no periods of decline"[31] inaugurates a new paradigm that regroups postmodern historians, cultural critics, and artists alike. Cultural studies and trauma studies provide fitting examples of this paradigm. The question arises soon thereafter, though, as to how the "cultural memory" paradigm, relying as it does on concepts such as "recycling," "waste," and "refuse," can avoid another "formal" determination—a form, in this instance, that is dependent on figures taken from the realm of "nature." Nature, as we well know, is determined: it lives, it dies, it rises once more from its remains, only to perish again. Does not all talk of the "cycle" of life and death, the mere reference to matter itself, which can neither be created nor destroyed, reintroduce the specter of a "form" into the discourse of cultural memory? And does this not simply substitute an epistemology grounded in the conceptual pairing of decline and progress for one anchored in the perishable and resurgent? What does it mean, in fact, to abandon universal history for an ethics of resurgence and loss, when the latter amounts to considering *things* and *being* in the absence of judgment? Ironically, this cultural memory returns precisely in the "form" of that which was cast off: in our attention to the residual, to "waste." It is subsequently fair to ask whether "waste" does not indeed draw within our purview—ever subjective, haunted, dubitative, and anchored to "stories" at a given site—*waste-site stories*. "Waste" produces stories inchoately— stories both multiple and singular, stories not without form, not without plot or puzzle, if often only the puzzle of an impossible story. The relationship between waste and stories becomes metonymical; stories emerge out of traces and refuse. The lost speak out, not in the Aristotelian form of *peripeteia* or the harmony of metaphor but within the *event* of the story itself, in a story opening out of a stone (Bann), a photograph (Grivel), an image (Villeneuve), or a lightbulb recycled by Ghanaian villagers (Godzich)—the things Benjamin called the *refuse of*

History, the "rags" and "refuse" that do not figure in historical representation.[32] What *incites* a story, finally, is the fact there is a story, that *from this* a story comes.

Emerging thus from the refuse of history, waste-site stories preserve the memorial efficacy of what, in conclusion, we might call "residual culture." In what was perhaps an effort to master his own mourning, as he took in the devastation about him, Freud anticipated humanity recovering possession of the riches of culture following the war, as though the things themselves and the manner in which they became objects of value were not thoroughly compromised in the ruin of civilization. Where Freud was seemingly unshaken in this high assessment of culture, we are more inclined to heed the seventh of Benjamin's testamentary theses: "There is no document of civilization which is not at the same time a document of barbarism."[33] What were "cultural treasures" to Freud sometimes seem more like "spoils" today. And though he cannot be wholly identified with the historicist conviction that the things carried along in the "triumphal procession" of historical progress consolidate the ascendancy of the present over the past, there is still the sense that culture, for Freud, remains untouched as an accumulation of inestimable objects. As we have argued, according to the historicist model of progress, the past exists but to confirm the superiority of the present, as the furthest point along the continuum of progress. To this ever-victorious present, things from the past are either left behind as waste or become spoils for us to inherit. The unquestioned belief in the progressive movement of history, from which the present draws its force, goes hand in hand with this unqualified esteem for the objects of culture. Each, in turn, disregards the social injustice at its base: not only does the historicist account ignore the experience of catastrophe, which undermines the legitimacy of the present as progress, but the high valuation of cultural objects effaces their participation in catastrophe. This is what Benjamin, rereading Nietzsche's critique of historicism and the conceptual pairing of decadence and vitality, would refer to as the imbrication of civilization and barbarism. The sudden devaluation that culture suffers at this point, unmooring it from its assured place on the linear chain that ties the "barbaric" past to the "civilized" present, grants its objects a status at once of value and nonvalue.

Shortly after Benjamin's death, at a time when the legacy of his friend's work on the Paris arcades and his intellectual heritage appeared threatened with oblivion, Adorno must have thought of Benjamin as he wrote: "Only the conscious horror of destruction creates the correct relationship with the dead: unity with them because we, like them, are the victims of the same condition and the same disappointed hope."[34] With Benjamin's *Theses* clearly in mind, Adorno attempted to articulate the cultural dialectic between what is waste and what is valuable. Historicism indeed presented, as Benjamin wrote, the succession of one victor after another; knowledge, Adorno would add, had followed a similar

design, and a more adequate conception of history would thus require compre-
hending the dialectic of barbarism and civilization, as Adorno called it. In other
words, it meant addressing precisely those things that fell out of the dynamic of
victory and defeat, the things that "fell by the wayside—what might be called the
waste products *[Abfallstoffen]* and blind spots."[35] To write history from the viewpoint of the vanquished, from the dead, would be tantamount to recovering
waste as a figure of thought.

As the critique of Enlightenment and the domination of nature through instrumental reason developed, Adorno's critique of culture would come to pivot
more and more upon figures of waste.[36] The subject's control over the world (the
past, in historicism) through reification littered this landscape with fungible objects. Nor could culture be secured from the creep of this devastation. On the
contrary, as Adorno confessed, the heritage of culture had "become expendable
to the highest degree, superfluous, trash *[Schund]*."[37] To insist on the transcen-
dent value of culture became, throughout Adorno's writings, as untenable as liquidating the concept completely. As the dialectic of civilization and barbarism
goes, culture remains precariously positioned between value and nonvalue; culture becomes waste with a thoroughly unstable significance. Nowhere is this
more fully played out than in Adorno's essay on Samuel Beckett's *Endgame*. Here,
the world of the elders (those who are most vital to the continuity of tradition)
is literally wasted. Having outlived their function by the criterion of social usefulness, the old are relegated to trash cans, while the "natural connection between the living," as Adorno provocatively wrote, becomes "organic garbage,"[38]
the progenitor as degenerate, as refuse. That they remain as mere torsos, reminds
us, as though it were necessary, that the past into which they threaten to recede at
each moment no longer survives like Rilke's archaic torso of Apollo—the symbol of the classical conception of the past as harmonious appearance and eternal
admonition to the present in its decadence—but in fragments, in stumps, as
waste. "Beckett's trash cans are emblems of the culture rebuilt after Auschwitz,"
insists Adorno, in what is probably his most brutal exposure of our cultural
predicament. In Beckett, Adorno finds a concrete expression of the impact of a
catastrophe that touches everything—the reduction of philosophy to "cultural
trash," the regression of language to "obsolete material" (clichés, fragments, "reified residues of culture")—and the decisive experience in which the "poetic
process declares itself to be a process of wastage *[Verschleiß]*."[39]

In the world of *Endgame,* everything "waits to be carted off to the dump,"[40]
but it is perhaps here, ironically, that culture recovers value, for it is only by this
wastage that art begins to adequately present historical experience. Henceforth,
culture can only appear residual; yet, though wasted, indeed by this very fact, it
remains weakly capable of summoning meaning, of preserving a force or an efficacy of critique. Our hopes may be historically disappointed, and culture shares

in that disappointment; but it preserves, at the same time, the vestiges of hope. "Culture is refuse, yet art—one of its sectors—is nevertheless serious as the appearance of truth."[41] With such shabby material Adorno sought to construct his unfinished *Aesthetic Theory*, and to provide the means for art to survive its own death. It is with the same residual aspect of culture that we continue today to articulate not just our aesthetics but our ethics as well. Waste is the figure, then, not for a redemption that recovers the wholeness of a fragmented experience in aestheticized form but a figure for what remains "possible" in the aftermath of catastrophe.

Looking back on the twentieth century, transfixed by the accumulated fragments of monumental memory—Verdun, Shoah, Hiroshima, and so many others, stumps of signifiers that barely recall the horrors they denote—and the vestigial remains of personal experience, the stories in this book map the local niches of history. They rummage amidst the ruins of Modernity in an effort to nuance the work of memory. Above all, by exploring the sites where history itself has passed over, where the ravages of war and ruin are scarred upon life, these stories feel out the texture of historical change, its silent deterioration as well as the silence of its victims. One may ask, as Valeria Wagner does with great insistence, "How [are] death and necessity articulated in our understanding of history?" And, if at this point the notion of waste presses upon us with increased force, it is no doubt because we can no longer afford to disregard our castoffs, our losses, what we forget and what we repress, as these pile up before us. We cannot acquit ourselves of the historical debt that at all times calls us to respond to the past and to take up its legacy in stories.

NOTES

1. Waste, as Don DeLillo has so compellingly depicted, has become our *Weltanschauung*. *Underworld* is suffused with the pathos of a twentieth-century experience that confronts us as waste, and now casts *the author as waste manager*. DeLillo's monumental book concerns waste of all kinds and the various discourses and practices, technical and cultural, that recycle it. The ultimate figure for that waste is none other than the bomb, emblem of the devastation of our time and our prodigious toxic legacy: "They had brought something into the world that out-imagined the mind. They didn't even know what to call the early bomb. It is merde. I will use the French. J. Robert Oppenheimer. It is merde. He meant something that eludes naming is automatically relegated, he is saying, to the status of shit. You can't name it. It's too big or evil or outside your experience. It's also shit because it's garbage, it's waste material." See Don DeLillo, *Underworld* (New York: Scribner, 1997), 77.

2. Established in 1973, the program sets out to "understand the relationship between mental, behavioral, and material realities that constitute human consumption and

disposal." See the University of Arizona's Garbage Studies Web page on the BARA (Bureau of Applied Research in Anthropology) site, http://128.196.139.105/gs.htm.

3. See David Gross' contribution to this book as well as Susan Strasser's recent history of waste-management discourse and practices. Strasser examines the changing significance of waste and the altered relation we have to our material environment, emerging with industrial society and its attendant construction of the subject of consumer culture. She identifies a growing threat in the shift from the nineteenth-century culture of "reuse" to today's "throwaway culture." As she shows, the equilibrium of the economic order in which waste functioned as resource, along with the various technologies and agents that invested it, has given way with the advent of consumerism and a commodity-based economy that perpetuates consumption through waste. See Susan Strasser, *Waste and Want: A Social History of Trash* (New York: Metropolitan, 1999).

4. Friedrich Nietzsche, *The Will to Power*, edited by Walter Kaufman and translated by Walter Kaufman and R. J. Hollingdale (New York: Random House, 1967), 25.

5. Walter Benjamin, *The Arcades Project*, translated by Howard Eiland and Kevin McLaughlin (Cambridge, Mass., and London: Belknap Press/Harvard University Press, 1999), 459.

6. Ibid., 459, 989.

7. See Peter Sloterdijk, *Critique of Cynical Reason,* translated by Michael Eldred (Minneapolis: University of Minnesota Press, 1987), 151.

8. In the modest gesture of the gleaner, Agnès Varda has found a compelling figure for contemporary aesthetic, economic, and memorial activity. A necessity for many, artists or not, gleaning in all of its varieties provides an allegory of individual survival within a culture of waste. In the poor who find matter for sustenance, in the artist who finds materials for recycling, in the filmmaker who gathers souvenirs, impressions, bits and pieces of lives, of her life, for stories, Varda depicts so many different practices of revaluating waste. Gleaning might just best describe aspects of the work of several authors in this book, whether they be combing through images, hypertextual arrays of information, or fragments of architectural discourse. Agnès Varda, *Les glaneurs et la glaneuse [The Gleaners and I],* Ciné Tamaris, 2000.

9. The expression is Manfredo Tafuri's, who has described in detail how not only in architecture but in other cultural forms as well "working with degraded materials, with refuse and fragments extracted from the banality of everyday life, is an integral part of the tradition of modern art: a magical act of transforming the formless into aesthetic objects through which the artist realizes the longed-for repatriation in the world of things." See Manfredo Tafuri, *The Sphere and the Labyrinth: Avant-Gardes and Architecture from Piranesi to the 1970s,* translated by Pellegrino d'Acierno and Robert Connolly (Cambridge, Mass.: MIT Press, 1987), 267.

10. See Maurice Halbwachs, *La mémoire collective* (Paris: Albin Michel, 1997), published posthumously in 1950 after the author's deportation to the camps.

11. Hans Magnus Enzensberger, for one, remains diffident in his disdain for cultural practices such as recycling: "In any case," he writes, "the industrial strength reprocessing of the past is a cheerless affair. 'Retro' and 'recycling' are names for strategies for cultural plundering and attrition. But there is no need to get overexcited about this ideological and artistic flea market. Commercial anachronism steers clear of anything truly

significant." See Hans Magnus Enzensberger, "Time As Pastry Dough: A Meditation on Anachronism," translated by Linda Haverty Rugg, in *Zig Zag: The Politics of Culture and Vice Versa* (New York: New Press, 1997), 50–51.

12. Ibid., 37. From the standpoint of evolutionary biology, Geoffrey Miller has argued, in fact, that waste is at the origins of all culture. Against those who would scorn prodigality, Miller contends that waste forms the "bridge" between natural selection and the semiotics of social interaction. More to the point, evolution is shaped not only by fitness for survival, by utility alone, but by the instinct for luxurious expense. It matters little what form that waste assumes, goes the theory, only that it be prodigious and thus serve as an indicator of fitness. As Miller has it, nature is necessarily wasteful: "Showy waste is the only guarantee of truth in advertising." This revaluation of waste recalls cultural anthropology's interest in economies of expense. By simply inverting the terms, however, the theory risks reproducing the same hierarchical order of values, when what is needed is to address the question of valuation itself. See Geoffrey Miller, *The Mating Mind: How Sexual Choice Shaped the Evolution of Human Nature* (New York: Doubleday, 2000).

13. Sigmund Freud, "On Transience," in *Art and Literature,* edited by Albert Dickson, in *The Pelican Freud Library*, vol. 14, edited and translated by James Strachey (New York: Penguin, 1985), 287–90.

14. Freud, "Mourning and Melancholia," in *On Metapsychology,* edited by Angela Richards, in *The Pelican Freud Library*, vol. 11, edited and translated by James Strachey (New York: Penguin, 1984), 247–68.

15. George Steiner, *In Bluebeard's Castle: Some Notes Towards the Redefinition of Culture* (New Haven, Conn.: Yale University Press, 1971).

16. Sloterdijk, op cit., 122–23.

17. Steiner, op cit., 55.

18. Figures of the crisis of experience can be chosen almost at random from contemporary literature, and not only from among inevitable European examples such as Ernst Jünger. What Broch called the "decay of values," which arguably reached its nadir in the First World War, speaks equally to the ruptured sensibility of Native Americans, for instance, returning to their traditional environment after the European wars: Abel, in N. Scott Momaday's *House Made of Dawn,* following the First World War, and Tayo, in Leslie Marmon Silko's *Ceremony*, after the Second World War—each returning to an impossible reintegration into tradition, each debilitated by their traumatic pasts. See N. Scott Momaday, *House Made of Dawn* (New York: Harper and Row, 1968); Leslie Marmon Silko, *Ceremony* (New York: Penguin Books, 1987). In Japan, literature has had to contend with the technological destruction of traditional structures of understanding in the fallout from Hiroshima. Tellingly, Kobo Abe, in *The Ark Sakura*, imagines a society that orients its daily life around waste: the eupcaccia, an insect that moves in circles, ever consuming its own waste, is Abe's figure for a society in which all aspects of life are negotiations with waste. See Kobo Abe, *The Ark Sakura*, translated by Juliet Winters Carpenter (New York: Vintage Books, 1988). African writers, in the aftershock of colonial destruction, have necessarily had to imagine their present anew on the basis of ruined traditions and ideologies, recycled for the present. As Valentin Mudimbe points out in *The Idea of Africa*, colonialism is perpetuated in the forced return to tradition, which effaces the memory of a colonial past. The memory of the colonized is woven instead of different

strands, ancient and colonial, and structured not around recovered tradition but the experience of discontinuity. As he shows, it translates, in aesthetic terms, into practices of recycling—what Mudimbe calls "*reprendre*"—which take up, in a critically reflexive way, both an interrupted tradition and the heterogeneous influences within an emphatically transformed colonial environment. See V. Y. Mudimbe, *The Idea of Africa* (Bloomington: Indiana University Press, 1984). For all of this, one is tempted to conclude that the shared reality which is still only virtual in today's political and economic order was presaged in the truly global reach of devastation of this century.

19. Hermann Broch, *The Sleepwalkers*, translated by Willa and Edwin Muir (San Francisco: Northpoint Press, 1985).

20. Walter Benjamin, "Experience and Poverty," translated by Rodney Livingstone, in *Selected Writings*, vol. 2, edited by Michael W. Jennings, Howard Eiland, and Gary Smith (Cambridge, Mass., and London: Belknap Press/Harvard University Press, 1999), 731.

21. See Giorgio Agamben, *Infancy and History: Essays on the Destruction of Experience*, translated by Liz Heron (London and New York: Verso, 1993).

22. Jack London, "The Scarlet Plague," in *Curious Fragments: Jack London's Tales of Fantasy Fiction*, edited by Dale L. Walker (Port Washington and London: Kennkat Press, 1975).

23. Jay Winter has eloquently argued how the sense of bereavement was universal in the aftermath of the First World War, and how remembrance drew its commemorative forms from the ruins of the prewar order. In his account, tradition could still effectively provide the framework within which to understand events. In his effort to substantiate the argument that remembrance could successfully work through mourning to an integration of the catastrophic events of the war within experience, Winter is compelled to situate the indubitable rupture in historical understanding after the Second World War. Only then, he contends, came the real caesura that precluded the integration of traumatic experience within traditional forms of representation. What goes unquestioned in his account, though, is the concept of experience itself. Following Benjamin and, in turn, Agamben, we are inclined to understand the destruction of experience as a more historically protracted phenomenon, concomitant with Modernity, and decisively accomplished in the events of the First World War. See Jay Winter, *Sites of Memory, Sites of Mourning: The Great War in European Cultural History* (Cambridge: Cambridge University Press, 1995).

24. The story is not unlike the one told by Marguerite Duras and Alain Resnais in *Hiroshima mon amour*, an impossible "love story" that takes place on the unique site, the only *common site*, that is, ground zero. For a discussion of their film along complementary lines, see Kyo Maclear, *Beclouded Visions: Hiroshima-Nagasaki and the Art of Witness* (Albany: State University of New York Press, 1999).

25. On a number of occasions, Tavernier's film remind us of that calibrated sequence from Jean Renoir's *La Grande illusion* (1937), in which French soldiers imprisoned in a German camp are permitted to stage a play. Suddenly finding themselves in the presence of a "female" body—one of their own dressed as a woman—they are dumbfounded. Their rapt attention weighs heavily at this point: it says more than any combat scene could about the memorial burden that these men repress. In looks that are at once terrible and wonderful, enchanting and suffused with melancholy, the transvestite draws

the collective gaze, arresting the passage of time in a figure, disfiguring though it may be, of utopian longing.

26. Frances Yates, *The Art of Memory* (Chicago: University of Chicago Press, 1966), 34–35.

27. See Tzvetan Todorov's *Les abus de la mémoire* (Paris: Arléa, 1995).

28. The chapters in this book share many of the concerns of cultural studies for what has been overlooked or effaced in historical representation, but they go further in problematizing the labor of recollection. Where cultural studies speaks of a crisis in historical representation, it never wavers in its certitude of the appropriate reading of the past. It is an ultimately ideological reading that insufficiently recognizes the difference *in* the past. We might ask whether the past only interests cultural studies, generally speaking, insofar as it serves the present.

29. Reinhart Koselleck, "Geschichte," in *Geschichtliche Grundbegriffe. Historisches Lexikon zur politisch-sozialen Sprache in Deutschland*, vol. 2, edited by O. Brunner, W. Conze, and Reinhart Koselleck (Stuttgart: Ernst Klett and J. G. Cotta, 1975), 647–717.

30. The nineteenth-century novel being a case in point. See Hayden White, *Metahistory: The Historical Imagination in Nineteenth-Century Europe* (Baltimore: Johns Hopkins University Press, 1973).

31. Benjamin, *The Arcades Project*, op cit., 458.

32. Ibid., 460–61.

33. Walter Benjamin, "Theses on the Philosophy of History," in *Illuminations*, translated by Harry Zohn and edited by Hannah Arendt (New York: Schocken, 1969), 256.

34. Theodor Adorno and Max Horkheimer, *Dialectic of Enlightenment*, translated by John Cummings (New York: Continuum, 1988), 215.

35. Theodor Adorno, *Minima Moralia*, translated by E.F.N. Jephcott (London: NLB, 1974), 151.

36. The figures of waste in Adorno's writings merit a study of their own. Waste and related terms—garbage, trash, scrap, rubbish, refuse, dead inventory, etc.—recur throughout the postwar writings, shouldering the brunt of negativity and alone capable of shattering the appearance of harmony in a commodified world. This is not the place to inventory all occurrences or the varied significance of "waste" in Adorno's work; the following exemplifies Adorno's conviction that culture has assumed the form of a *heritage of waste*: "All post–Auschwitz culture, including its urgent critique, is garbage *[Müll]*. In restoring itself after the things that happened without resistance in its own countryside, culture has turned into the ideology it had been potentially—had ever been since it presumed, in opposition to material existence, to inspire that existence with the light denied it by the separation of the mind from manual labor. Whoever pleads for the maintenance of this radically culpable and shabby culture becomes its accomplice, while the man who says no to culture is directly furthering the barbarism which our culture showed itself to be." See Theodor Adorno, *Negative Dialectics*, translated by E. B. Ashton (New York: Seabury Press, 1973), 366–67.

37. Theodor Adorno, "Cultural Criticism and Society," in *Prisms,* translated by Samuel and Shierry Weber (Cambridge, Mass.: MIT Press, 1981), 34. Despite often

strained relations with Bertholt Brecht and fundamental reservations about his work, Adorno shared Brecht's sense of the fundamental culpability of culture in its continued existence. Fondly, he would quote Brecht's line to the effect that culture abhors stench "because its mansion is built of doghshit." See Adorno, *Negative Dialectics*, op cit., 366.

38. Theodor Adorno, "Trying to Understand *Endgame*," in *Notes to Literature*, vol. 1, translated by Shierry Weber Nicholsen (New York: Columbia University Press, 1991), 266.

39. Ibid., 241–43.

40. Ibid., 252.

41. Theodor Adorno, *Aesthetic Theory*, translated and edited by Robert Hullot-Kentor (Minneapolis: Univesity of Minnesota Press, 1997), 310.

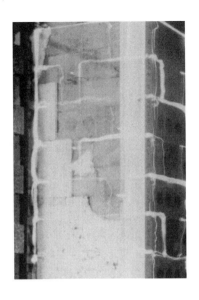

I

Objects from the Past

David Gross

WE ARE, COLLECTIVELY SPEAKING, SURROUNDED BY "THINGS," many billions if not trillions of material objects of every kind. The number of these things is so great, in fact, that it is difficult to gain a conceptual hold on the almost infinite multiplicity of objects that constitute our world. One way to begin mentally ordering what we encounter, though, is to establish a rough taxonomy that distinguishes between what might be called "natural things," on the one hand (trees, rocks, plants, etc.), and humanly made or humanly fashioned things, on the other hand (shoes, chairs, books, etc.). My concern in what follows is only with the second order of things, which from now on I will call "objects."

Objects are always products of human intentionality, even when they are made by machines. Because they are shaped by human will, usually to meet some need or want, they are social products from the beginning. And they are social, too, because once they are created, they exist and circulate in a social world. (It is true, of course, that natural things also can be brought into the social world. They can be given a certain amount of value—for example, rocks can become "precious stones"—and then be made to circulate as commodities. Nevertheless, because they are not products of human labor or design, I exclude them from my discussion here.) We interact with these man-made objects and become socialized through them, and they in turn become humanized through us as a result of the social uses we give them. Objects, for instance, become "goods." They are utilized and exchanged; they are "owned" by someone; they become possessions, commodities, gifts—and all of these kinds of things that happen to objects tend to humanize them, but more importantly, they also so-cialize us as we interact with them.

Now with regard to these humanly made objects, it is important to make yet another distinction, this one between objects made in the present and those made in the past. By objects made in the present, I mean those produced during the last few years, perhaps the last ten or fifteen years at most. These would include a great number of the objects we encounter in any given day, including the clothes we are wearing at the moment, the pencil and paper lying on our desk, or the newspa-per we read this morning. By objects from the past, I mean those made a genera-tion or more ago that still survive into the present and continue to be used and valued (e.g., furniture passed down from our parents or grandparents, old tools that remain functional, and the like). What is particularly interesting about the lat-ter kind of object is that they were present and part of the everyday experiences of people living in, say, 1940, or 1900, or even earlier, and they are at the same time present and able to be experienced by us today as well. Someone in 1900 could say of a chair or desk in their home, "This object is contemporaneous with me," and someone in 2002 could say the same thing of the same object, even if, by 2002, the object becomes visibly more time-worn than it was before.

My concern here is only with objects from the past, not objects made in the present. And, as just indicated, the past will mean for our purposes that long span of time beginning about two or three decades ago (i.e., about a generation) and stretching back from there, if we want to go that far, to the Paleolithic Age or even earlier, when human beings first began to fashion objects for their own use. Obviously, there are very few objects more than several centuries old that have survived, and those that have are likely to be found in a museum. Most of the objects from the past that I will refer to in what follows would fall into the range of being perhaps thirty or forty to about 150 or 200 years old. The farther back one goes, the fewer the number of objects that have persisted intact into the present.

In approaching objects that have survived from earlier times, one of the first things to be noted is that some of these objects are said to be valuable, while others are not. Whole classes of objects from the past, in other words, have come to be described as "worth something," while whole other classes of ob-jects that survive are designated as "worth-less"—as junk. The valuable objects, such as antiques, heirlooms, or certain works of art, are likely to be displayed in a prominent place in one's home, while the things deemed to be without value are usually confined to one's attic or basement, and from there they are period-ically gathered up and thrown out as trash. Though we need not pursue this point here, it should be noted that the differences in value do not necessarily have to do with the condition the object is in, for an antique can be in fairly bad shape and still be an antique, while an old hat or a suit from the attic can be in good condition and yet be considered almost rubbish. Rather, the worth of an object is determined primarily by either the market value that the object has or the sentimental value that it holds for some particular individual. In the latter case, some things, such as mementos or souvenirs, could have virtually no market value and yet still be deemed valuable for personal reasons, that is, because of nostalgic feelings that they might evoke when one comes into contact with them.[1] But though it might be important to understand how an object's market worth is determined, as compared to its merely subjective or sentimental worth, it would take us too far afield to pursue this line of thought here. Instead, I want to focus on the apparent opposites that I have just set up between those objects from the past that are said to have value and integrity and those that are said to "lack value." The former are cherished and treasured, while the latter are dismissed as waste or rubbish.

A quick judgment suggests that these two very different kinds of objects from the past are so unlike one another that they have to be considered for all practical purposes incommensurable. But in fact both types of objects exist on a single continuum. They are not dichotomous, but rather over time they can and often do merge and meld into one another, sometimes being deemed valuable and at other times valueless. This is so because every humanly made object, no matter how grand or trivial—and regardless of what happens to it at some later point in its life history—starts out as something "genuine," something possessing at least a minimal degree of worth. Every object, for example, has its own form, its own aesthetic, its own integrity, and its own identity, and every one contains some amount of human expressivity, even if mediated by a machine. Furthermore, when objects of any sort are produced socially, they necessarily contain some degree of value simply by virtue of the labor that went into fashioning them. Nevertheless, every genuine object that enters the world is subject to the same natural depredations, the same ravages of time, that befall all material things. Objects get used or used up, worn or worn out. Usually their fate is to move steadily and inexorably from the status of objects to the status of waste *unless* or until something intervenes to slow or even reverse this process, in which case the object does not become junk but rather just the opposite: it retains or even increases in value.

What intervenes? Nothing intrinsic to the object itself, but always something outside of it, for instance, the increasing *rarity* of the object, which will normally lead its owner to take special care to preserve it and in this way hinder or halt the usual processes of deterioration. Of course, every object simply is what it is, and no more. It is what happens to *other objects* of the same type or genus that determines whether or not an object becomes rare and hence suddenly increases in value for no other reasons than extraneous ones. Another factor that could intervene, as already mentioned, is sentiment, the sentiment that is sometimes attached to objects in such a manner as to instantly increase their personal value, thereby preventing them from being treated as waste. Or finally, the vagaries of the market could intervene, causing some things to increase in worth not despite but because they survived long enough to be recycled or refunctioned in the present.

But these examples of objects keeping their value or increasing in value over time do not represent the norm. The norm for perhaps 95 percent of the objects made is to move relentlessly from being things that initially contain value to being things emptied of value—in other words, rubbish, or what Louis Aragon aptly called "fallen matter."[2] To be sure, different objects have different life expectancies, just as people do. Some things deteriorate relatively quickly, while others endure for a long time. A finely crafted desk would be expected to last longer than a well-made pencil, so it should take several decades or even several generations before it is ready to be scrapped as junk (unless, as I say, some other process intervenes), but only some weeks before a pencil loses its use or exchange value and is finally disposed of as worthless.

Put briefly, some things have relatively short and others relatively long natural lives: the natural life of a loaf of bread is about three or four days before it becomes waste; the natural life of a pair of shoes might be two or three years; an overcoat maybe ten years; a house 100 years or more; a church or a castle possibly several centuries. But in time these objects wear out, erode, or become degraded, and when this happens they lose their status as useful or worthwhile things. In so many words, they become waste, which is a handy term to describe the normal terminal state of an object.

Now I want to take this point and *historicize* it. In premodern times, most objects were made to last as long as possible. When objects approached the point where they were on the verge of disintegrating into waste, great care usually was taken to repair or refurbish them to sustain their existence and keep them available for use. For an ordinary individual living centuries ago, to discard something, which in effect was to declare it of no value, was not only a difficult act to perform, it also was considered a destructive act, because it was disrespectful of the person or persons in the past who had originally made the object. Unnecessarily jettisoning something that someone had fashioned amounted to a kind of dismissal of the time, energy, and skill that went into the making of the object in the first place.

If, however, the decline or disintegration of an object was unavoidable, then it often happened that a particular social function was given to each stage of its decline. By this strategy, the object continued to retain some value, even though the value attributed to it as it neared its end was different than the one attributed to it at the beginning of its existence. The idea that an object, as it aged, had to be assessed on a sliding scale of value appears to have been a widely accepted one in premodern times, and it is an idea that persists as well among primitive peoples today. For the Suku of Zaire, for instance, a newly built hut is expected to last, on average, about ten years. At first the hut's value lies in the function for which it was initially built, namely, to provide housing for a couple or an extended family. After a while, when the hut has endured a certain amount of wear and tear, it changes its function and assumes a different value: it then becomes in turn a guest house, a gathering place for teenagers, a kitchen, and finally, when it has exhausted all of the human uses to which it can be put, it is turned into a goat or chicken house.[3] In this particular case it is not only the function of the hut that changes with its changing physical state but also its personal and social value. Only when the hut loses its last bit of utility does it finally lose its last bit of value.

When we come to the modern period, especially the industrialized West in the twentieth century, what I have just been describing changes considerably. Most objects produced now are not only not expected to last very long, but many are actually designed to become waste as rapidly as possible—so rapidly that often there is virtually no time for an object to go through the kinds of value stages I mentioned with reference to the Suku hut. Today, the process of waste making has been enormously accelerated, because there is now a greatly foreshortened time span between an object's initial entry into the world and its exit as trash. At times it seems that some objects become waste almost immediately after coming into being, and hence they have no life history to speak of. One can see, even at the moment the object comes into being, the approaching end state that is never far off. In fact, what we have in the present age is not only shoddily made things, which quickly become waste, we also have *premature waste,* that is, the discarding of things when they are only about halfway through their natural life spans, or in some instances, even less than halfway. The act of discarding objects today is nowhere near as difficult to do as it was in earlier times, for our culture now encourages—even actively promotes—the rapid consumption or using up of objects. It does so for reasons with which we are all by now acquainted: as soon as one object becomes waste, there is another allegedly "better" one that can be made to step in and take its place, and when that better object eventually becomes waste, there are still more "new and improved" ones waiting in the wings to replace it as well.

Today, then, most objects produced become junk very quickly, including those objects which, in premodern times, were made on the assumption that they would be kept in existence for as long as possible. Not only is the phenomenon of planned obsolescence new in our era, but we also have something else that seems not to have been present before, namely, the tendency to regard waste as not always and under all circumstances a negative thing but rather as something that can have positive aspects as well.

What is there that can conceivably be positive about waste? Briefly, I think, two things. The first is that it can reveal something about the nature of the society that both defines *what waste is* and determines just when and why and how certain objects come to be declared worthless. Just as a study of what is considered deviant can help illuminate what a particular society might think is normal or healthy, so too the study of what is called waste can reveal a great deal about what that same society views as valuable and therefore worth preserving from the corrosive effects of time. Archaeologists, of course, understand how to approach waste in this way. For them, the refuse of the past—including both the things that were deemed to be waste at some earlier point in time *and* the things that have unavoidably *become* waste by being buried for centuries (e.g., broken shards of formerly valuable pottery)—is the chief medium through which they gain insight into the life conditions of some distant historical or prehistorical period.

The second positive function that waste can have goes well beyond its role in providing clues to the norms, codes, or categories of some previous epoch. If deciphered correctly, waste may also make visible certain larger "truths" that transcend any particular era of the past and consequently have the capacity to shed some light even on our own present and possibly our future as well. For this higher order of understanding to occur, waste has to undergo a metamorphosis. It has to become not simply rubbish (thought it may still be that on *one* interpretive register) but also a new kind of object and hence valuable once again, though now for reasons that were *not* present in the minds of those who originally made or consumed these objects in the past (that is, *before* they became the "fallen matter" they seem to be to us today).

This second, and to me more interesting, conception of what makes waste valuable was most thoroughly articulated by German critic Walter Benjamin. For Benjamin, writing in the 1930s, waste was important not just because there is something about it that propels the mind backward, leading one to reflect on certain earlier points in time when the object was fully what it was intended to be and not the meaningless historical debris it eventually became for later generations. Rather, waste also was important for Benjamin because it gives one a glimpse of something that shoots beyond the past as such and calls out to be recognized and responded to in the present. To get a clearer picture of what this something is, we need to look more closely at a notion that informed Benjamin's massive *Arcades Project*, which occupied him on and off for the last thirteen years of his life.

According to Benjamin, when someone in the past made an object, that object expressed at least three things. First, it expressed (as Marx had said as well) a part of the worker's human essence, for in fashioning an object either in a preindustrial or an industrial setting, the worker drew on his or her own skill and creative energy and then externalized these in the thing produced. Second, and without this being any single individual's conscious intention, the object expressed something of the historical character of the age in which the object was made. Hence, objects produced in the fourteenth century unavoidably reflected certain aspects of that period due to the peculiarities of their form, style, or design, just as objects made in, say, the early or mid-nineteenth century, which was the period that most interested Benjamin by the time he undertook to write his *Arcades Project*, reflected a very different tone and style. Third, and hardest of all to see, Benjamin also believed that objects contained something he called "wish images" *(Wunschbilder)*. These images were projected into objects by the people who made them, but this was done more at the unconscious than the conscious level of awareness, for according to Benjamin, the true source of wish images lay not in an individual's mind or even in his or her expressive will-to-form but instead in a much deeper mental substratum (something close to but distinguishable from Jung's "collective unconscious") that has been present in the psyche of all human beings since virtually the beginning of the species. This substratum, he thought, contains some of the deepest and most profound longings and dreams of humankind—for example, the yearning to be in harmony with nature or to overcome the subject-object split, or to at last achieve real happiness and wholeness here on earth. These longings stemming from the "primal past" have, according to Benjamin, always lingered in a dormant state, but they also can sometimes emerge and become externalized in material objects as a result of the creative activities of *homo faber*. When this externalization takes place, the wish images are attached to, or fused with, the things created. The result is that objects become something more than mere physical artifacts; they also become things suffused with utopian visions and "dream images" *(Traumbilder)* of a "better world," which had long been imagined but had not yet come to be.

Writing from the perspective of the twentieth century, however, Benjamin believed that these images had either been forgotten or else radically distorted, almost beyond recognition, by the processes of capitalist commodification. For Benjamin, capitalism is driven by its very nature to turn objects into commodities and then to fetishize these commodities by associating them with magic qualities that capitalism promises each individual can acquire by consumption. But by commodifying and fetishizing objects to serve the end of profit, capitalism simultaneously strips away the *true* wish images in things. The utopian element in objects is thus obscured or even apparently replaced by fake and glitzy "magic images," which falsely reenchant the objects of modern life. As a consequence, material things acquire a new aura, one devised by the newly emerging advertising and marketing industries to mystify and delude a population rather than point the way toward fulfillment. Hence, in the process of buying and consuming objects, people mainly see only the phantasmagoric side of things, which is that side conjured up by the bewitching power of commodity fetishism. Commodities, due to their dazzling and mesmerizing effect, ingeniously hide from people the authentic "dreaming forward" that objects do in fact contain, all the while indicating that no loss, no forgetting, has taken place.

It was just because of this deception that Benjamin thought the masses in the modern era had fallen into a deep "dream sleep" *(Traumschlaf)*, the dream sleep of false consciousness. But since, as Marx had pointed out, capitalism does not stand still but on the contrary moves forward only by revolutionizing its own means of production, it cannot help but undermine the value of the very things it creates, thereby making its own commodities obsolete. Sooner or later almost all of the objects that capitalism touts as "purchasable" or "worth something" fall in status, becoming second-class or third-class objects that are then said to be both unusable and uninteresting. In other words, capitalism produces a plethora of things that have some amount of exchange value for a while but then become junk. Benjamin was fascinated by this "junk," especially by an assortment of early nineteenth-century gadgets, toys, out-of-date illustrated magazines, and the like, some of which he collected himself, that had become *passé* by the 1920s and 1930s. But in becoming *passé*, these objects also lost the aura previously invested in them by the market forces of capitalism. As a result, the spell cast by fetishization fades, and as it does, the original wish images contained in those same objects can begin to come forward and make their presence felt. Paradoxically, objects have to be deserted by capitalism; they have to fall into desuetude at one level in order to come more fully into their own at another. Only when they are degraded or discardable (in market terms) do objects at last begin to reveal their true nature: a nature that is not only richer and deeper than anything imagined by those who merely fetishize commodities, but also, according to Benjamin, one that is at the same time potentially subversive of everything false in modern life.[4]

It would be hard to conceive of a more positive evaluation of waste than that offered by Benjamin in his *Arcades Project*. For most people today, waste is simply waste. It contains no hidden dimension. There is nothing in it that can be or deserves to be rescued. It is not surprising then that it has become so easy to throw things away, and to do so in a quantity and volume that would have been unimaginable to our forbearers. The loss that accompanies this flat, one-dimensional view of things is that we perhaps never see (or see through) objects in the way we might, nor do we allow most objects to stay with us long enough to establish a fraternal relationship with them. In this respect, our world may be more empty than it was in earlier times, for even though we have far more material objects around us than our ancestors did, most of these things live shorter lives and then disappear forever, whereas in the past, objects lingered long enough to become familiar to and cherished by those who used or interacted with them.

NOTES

1. See Susan Stewart, *On Longing: Narratives of the Miniature, the Gigantic, the Souvenir, the Collection* (Baltimore: Johns Hopkins University Press, 1984); Jonathan Culler, "Junk and Rubbish: A Semiotic Approach," in *Diacritics* 15 (1985): 2–12.

2. Louis Aragon, *Treatise on Style*, translated by Alyson Waters (Lincoln: University of Nebraska Press, 1991), 89.

3. See Igor Kopytoff, "The Cultural Biography of Things: Commodities As Process," in *The Social Life of Things: Commodities in Cultural Perspective*, edited by Arjun Appadurai (London and New York: Cambridge University Press, 1989), 66–67.

4. On Benjamin's view of objects from the past, see the material collected in, *The Arcades Project*, translated by Howard Eiland and Kevin McLaughlin (Cambridge, Mass. and London: Belknap Press/Harvard University Press, 1999). Also see Susan Buck-Morss, *The Dialectics of Seeing: Walter Benjamin and the Arcades Project* (Cambridge, Mass.: MIT Press, 1991); Max Pensky, *Melancholy Dialectics: Walter Benjamin and the Play of Mourning* (Amherst: University of Massachusetts Press, 1993), esp. pp. 211–39.

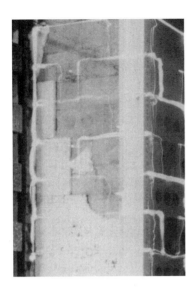

2

Waste into Heritage

Remarks on Materials in the Arts, on Memories and the Museum

Susanne Hauser

MUSEUMS ARE THE MOST PROMINENT INSTITUTIONS that care for the material culture we consider heritage. We do not expect museums to exhibit or store waste. In this respect, our expectations are still more traditional than recent, avant-garde museological approaches to materials and memories. This chapter will present some of the many ways in which the arts, the museum, and collective memories are intertwined with waste of many kinds. Such links join what is most disgusting with what is most valued. They cross symbolic lines, open criteria of selection, and, finally, function as eye-openers for the state of our concepts of matter or materials, memories, and the museum.

MUSEUMS

Museums function as archives of material culture. Things, artifacts stored in museums, originate in the world of everyday practices and functions, economic processes, and ordinary consumption. Museums are places immune to the usual reactions to the passage of time. Ideally, anything stored in a museum will be kept indefinitely. Museums still provide a space which—by its mere existence—resists dislocation and immateriality, while locality and materiality are marginalized in a global economic process. Museums shelter testimonies of events deemed worthy of preservation. These institutions also care for those very precious things called works of art. In this sense, museums are materialized memories. In Western societies, where memory is tied to matter, museums guarantee the possibility of returning to the material basis of identity and the consideration of cultural heritage.

Even after years of didactic re-definitions of the museum, it is still possible to hear solemnity spoken of as the appropriate attitude toward these institutions and their exhibits. This solemnity dates back to the first *mouseion* in Alexandria, founded around 280 B.C.E., which, if nothing else, left its name to the museums of today. In its hall, topped by the famous cupola, were statues of the muses, including Clio (muse of history) along with all of the others embodying and inspiring the arts—epic and lyric poetry, dance and music, comedy and tragedy, religious music, and astronomy.

Museums, especially the national museums of the eighteenth, nineteenth, and twentieth centuries, presented the treasures of culture and the achievements of Western civilization. They also were based on a lofty idea of the importance of the museum. They showed a selection of the most valued and valuable things from the past, and they represented developments up to the present, hopes for continuity, and progress for tomorrow. Nothing that any cultured person might have thrown away would have been accepted in a national museum. Of course, certain objects did suffer the vicissitudes of burial, neglect, destruction, and misinterpretation before they entered the treasure houses of European nations, but this is true for most archaeological finds.

On the whole, eighteenth- and nineteenth-century museums cared for and preserved eternal values materialized in objects of different kinds and made these values accessible to the public. These institutions showed highlights of culture, science, and national heritage and embodied the memory of the very history that was the foundation for the self-image of Western nations, those that perceived themselves to be the most civilized of this world.

WASTE

Precisely the opposite is true for waste, garbage, rubbish. As long as it is considered as such, waste is cast out of any order and system of values. There is no relation of any kind to history, culture, or memory. Waste is worthless, beyond, aside, and even against culture. Waste tends to be chaotic, unstructured, repellent, or even toxic. The only attention that waste, garbage, or rubbish garner is during their destruction or hygienically safe disposal. Otherwise, waste is usually neglected.

But waste is not a stable category; the word signifies different things and depends on notions of order and systems of value. The separation of useful and functional things, of valuable and precious things, on the one hand, and useless, nonfunctional, worthless and dirty things and materials, on the other hand, depends on categories that change historically and differ from one culture or group to the next. The means of production and consumption developed in

Western industrialized countries, however, seem to be heretofore the most effective and impressive ways to turn matter of all kinds, including nonmaterial
resources, into waste.

The excess in waste production is quite a recent phenomenon. Environmental historians coined the phrase, the "50's syndrome" (Christoph Pfister), to
refer to the change in mentality from one of economization to one of accelerated
consumption occurring shortly after the Second World War. But decades before,
industrialization, urbanization, and the differentiation of products, combined
with the global integration of more and more economic activities, were already
setting the stage for the patterns of waste production today. Some of the organi-
zational and conceptual groundwork had already been done during the nineteenth century.

It was at this point that "garbage" was invented—when most urban adminis-
trations in Europe and in countries colonized or otherwise influenced by European mentalities and cultural patterns reacted to economic development,
growing urban populations, and the mounting problem of refuse. Urban systems
of waste collection and disposal were then established. These systems secured the
clean, orderly, and beautiful space of culture within cities and relegated waste
sites to areas beyond their limits. This established a generalized practice defining
a generalized object called garbage, rubbish, debris, déchets, Müll, a definition that
led to the well-organized concentration and removal of unwanted, unused, and
nonreusable matter.[1]

A PIONEER

At that time, anything even faintly reminiscent of waste was foreign to museums.
Neither did artists usually show any interest in this newly defined type of matter.
Successful European artists were just as far removed from reflections and practices
related to the newly created waste disposal sites as were the art museums that
bought or exhibited their works.

But artists began to discover waste sites toward the end of the century. This
discovery is one of several developments marking the slow progress of waste and
garbage directly into the safe sphere of the houses of collective treasure called
museums. It also marks the beginning of a process of liquidating the categories
used to segregate those materials honorable enough to appear in the arts from
other materials. Artists' acceptance of waste challenged the criteria of value and
created a sphere in which any material could rightly become an appropriate
material for the arts.

Vincent van Gogh was one of the first artists who took an interest in waste.
In 1883, he made an expedition to the site of a garbage dump. Upon returning
home, he wrote an enthusiastic letter to his friend Anthon von Rappart:

Well, today I went to visit the place where the dustmen dump the garbage. Lord, how beautiful that is. . . . Tomorrow I shall get some interesting objects from this Refuse Dump—including some broken street lamps—rusted and twisted—on view—or to pose for me, if you like the expression better. The dustmen will bring them around. That collection of discarded buckets, baskets, kettles, soldiers' mess kettles, oil cans, iron wire, street lamps, stovepipes was something out of a fairy tale by Andersen. . . . Whenever you come to The Hague, I shall be greatly pleased if you will allow me to take you to this and some other spots, which, though they are commonplace in the extreme, are really an artist's paradise.[2]

Clearly this is the record of an expedition to a foreign and an exotic place, a report of discoveries in a newfound wilderness. The artist is an explorer and a pioneer, bringing back trophies, which will be carefully examined and serve as models for studies and drawings. Here, in 1883, the rubbish dump turns out to be a very special and stimulating place, beyond the usual conception of the dump. Van Gogh was not at all scandalized. He shows neither disgust nor nausea, nor any repression. His reaction reveals a clear, aesthetic view of a new type of object and model. Crossing the border between ordered spaces and their wastes is not described as a transgression into the sphere of refuse but as the adventurous discovery of a new kind of exoticism, of a paradise for the artist.

INTEGRATION AND PROVOCATION

Since van Gogh's time, there have been many different approaches to waste and rubbish in the arts. These have established widely varied relations between waste and museums. There are exhibitions of garbage as such, works of art that do not betray that they consist of materials found on rubbish dumps, and works that clearly indicate and even underscore their origin. Some artists challenge the norms of refined taste by explicitly presenting the ugly and disgusting. Some of their works have caused scandals, while others have been forthwith accepted as avant-garde art. There also are precious waste, spolia, or symbolic surplus materials, such as the lead taken from the roof of the cathedral in Cologne and used by Anselm Kiefer in his work. In other cases, freshly manufactured materials are crushed in a way that makes them look like scrap.[3]

Joseph Albers' early work offers one possible attitude toward waste. In the early 1920s, Albers collected sheet metal, wire gratings, lead, broken bottles, and shards from windows of *Gründerzeit* houses at rubbish dumps in Weimar. Inspired by medieval stained glass windows, Albers produced small and very delicate pictures made of glass. In this case, the rubbish was transformed into a material that did not reveal its origins in the dumps of Weimar. The history of the raw materials was obliterated by the very process of their artistic use. They became material, traditional material—colored glass, lead—in works of abstract art showing effects of light and color achieved by assembling different qualities of glass, with different grades of transparency and coloration. In their lead frames, they are much more reminiscent of jewels than broken glass and used wires.[4]

Kurt Schwitters had a rather different approach. He revealed the process of integrating waste materials in a much clearer way. In 1927, he described his choice of materials and the intention behind his work as a way to develop new colors and forms, adding new materials to the traditional ones used in painting. He aimed, as he said, to enhance and improve the spectrum of paints and colors at the artist's disposal. Found objects, tickets, pieces of driftwood, wires, and parts of wheels became "colors," a new kind of "paint." Schwitters strictly denied any provocative intention and wondered why the public reacted so emotionally to this way of dealing with the found relics of everyday life.[5] But he admitted that the new materials had to undergo a special treatment in that they had to be "evaluated, one against the other" *(Wertung gegen einander)*. In the process, found materials would lose their specific quality and everyday context. Schwitters insisted that they be stripped of their history. To be useful as a new kind of paint, they had to be semantically "cleansed." Their ability to indicate former processes had to be obliterated. Schwitters called this process, none too precisely, "dematerialization," a process that culminates in "material for a painting." Schwitters banned from his art the history of his materials; for him, his material was "new," regardless of what his provoked viewers might see.

A scandal of quite another type was caused by John Chamberlain's use of the crushed metal parts from the bodies of old cars. Chamberlain claimed to have first had the idea when he spotted an old car in the yard at a friend's place. Although the car represented "other peoples' idea of waste," its forms and colors were interesting and struck him as the right material. Chamberlain used the car as material to create his first sheet-metal sculpture, and only afterward did he discover that he had inadvertently taken parts from an antique car. Mistaking a museum piece for waste, however, did not occasion the scandal in question; the latter arose when the public felt challenged by Chamberlain's first sculptures of this kind and those in the same material—scrap taken from old cars—that followed. His use of this material reminded the public of the dangers of traffic and stirred up repressed and hidden fears of vulnerability and mortality.

Since this was not what Chamberlain had in mind, he began working with other materials, which did not prove satisfactory however. In 1974, he returned to sheet metal but decided this time to change how he gathered his material. He started to select his supplies of various qualities and colors of metal directly from car-body producers, and he deformed these parts in his own private press. The finished product still looked like "other peoples' idea of waste," but only because people were mistaken in their assumptions about the material.[6]

DISGUST

The confrontation between waste and order may be provocative, sometimes even frightening. But today, the effect of the artistic presentation of glass, paper, scrap, and other types of trash does not produce the same reverberations it did before and shortly after the Second World War. This is partly explained by the fact that waste of all kinds is now a frequent topic of discussion. The traditional recycling and reuse of materials, which seemed on the verge of dying out in industrialized countries during the 1970s, have once more become routine on the household and municipal levels, as well as on the national and international levels. Categories have changed, perhaps mentally more than materially. Reuse and recycling have even come to represent responsibility—highly developed ecological standards that often are confused with morality. Today, waste materials have undergone a second "desemanticization."

The fact that waste now tends to be perceived as a resource does not completely explain its current failure to provoke. No one is shocked any longer by the use of rusty metals, broken glass, or train tickets in works of art. But there is one remaining way to shock and scandalize by using waste in art: to use organic, foul, stinking, decaying, and decomposing materials, possibly behind a protective pane of glass.

These processes made their entrance into the fine arts in the 1950s, with Arman's *Poubelles*, or garbage cans, for example. Arman declared that garbage, as such and just as it was, had an enormous expressive potential. He objected to Schwitters' idea of aesthetic production based on waste materials used as colors, and he proposed the direct and unformed presentation of refuse.[7] In 1959, Arman's first *Poubelle* showed "*Petits déchets bourgeois.*" He then created the "*Poubelle ménagère*" and the "*Poubelle des enfants,*" and he went on to make *Poubelle* portraits dedicated to Yves Klein, Eliane, and others (1960–1961). In 1960, at the Galerie Iris Clert in Paris, Arman showed "*Le Plein,*" a showroom filled with waste and refuse of all kinds. The original plan had been to put the contents of a garbage truck into the gallery, but this turned out to be too difficult of an undertaking, so the project was cancelled. Instead, Arman carefully composed a heap of assorted garbage, including, among other things, a hula hoop and a violet-colored paper bag with three pieces of Camembert cheese inside.[8]

This is when garbage made its debut in the lead role on the fine arts stage. Arman showed garbage as garbage, merely transferring it from the dustbin to the gallery and obstinately putting it on display. This act, however, was related to several other concurrent ways of exhibiting waste, garbage, and compost. The remains of meals, unwashed but dried plates and glasses, cigarette stubs, and used tablecloths and napkins were fixed in assemblages by Daniel Spoerri during the 1960s. The process of the production of the meals, as well as their consumption, was also part of Spoerri's work. Cooking, eating, assembling, and fixing belonged together.[9] Processes of decomposition, molding, maturing, and other forms of organic development have been presented by many artists: Joseph Beuys produced his "Friday Objects," made of herring; Arman created marzipan accumulations; Dieter Roth showed his sculptures made of chocolate and bananas and molding heaps of various organic materials.[10] All such organic materials and processes which, outside of the sphere of art, produce mere garbage and compost made up the fascinating objects and subjects of art in the 1960s.

The process of dealing with organic materials was anticipated early on by the *Wiener Aktionismus*. Its acute commentary on cleanliness and order elicited strong reactions, public uproar, and occasionally even brought in the police. Otto Mühl perceived himself as an artist who, by transgressing and destroying boundaries marked by strong feelings of disgust, could unmask the repressed truth behind them. As Mühl said, "The sight of decayed, rusty, dirty materials arouses my religious feelings"; "cleanliness is extremely suspicious; it is the camouflage of dirt and impotence."[11] Some years ago art historians regarded the *Wiener Aktionismus* as a "stress-phenomenon" caused by the particular situation in postwar Vienna. They claimed it was a commentary on the relation between superficial cleanliness and political and social developments.

Yet the themes of disgust, nausea, bad taste, and the materials—the blood, excrement, hair, and fingernails reminiscent of the *Wiener Aktionismus*, as well as Georges Bataille's erotic stories—are still important today, as an exhibition called "Abject Art," held at the Whitney Museum of American Art in 1992, demonstrated. Andy Warhol's *Piss Paintings*, Kiki Smith's carcasses made of beeswax, and some of Cindy Sherman's photographs already played with taboos and the repression and disgust underlying them, so an exhibition of art using these types of materials did not take the public by surprise. But a provocative and unsettling event did take place at the Whitney Museum the following year, when Mike Kelley presented his exhibition "Catholic Tastes." He succeeded easily in the old avant-garde ploy to "*épater les bourgeois.*" The public was shocked by his materials and themes alone: Kelley showed deformed, ugly, and dysfunctional forms and objects; his sculptures, especially, made of used and dirty stuffed animals performing an uncanny play with childhood images and reality, were deeply hated.[12]

BEYOND CLASSIFICATION

This is just a very small selection of the different guises in which waste, garbage, and certain organic materials appeared on the art stage. Museums and other institutions sustaining the system and discourse of art were able to absorb

and integrate these materials and processes without trouble. Use of waste became accepted, widening the range of potential materials, qualities, techniques,
and effects in the fine arts. All of these examples, and many others, now belong
to the canon of twentieth-century art. Following initial emotional resistance, it
soon became evident that these shocking events and presentations belonged to
avant-garde practices. They were recognized as having a functional role within
the system, because they challenged and broadened its limits and boundaries.
Practices and materials turned out to be familiar; the works merely pursued
what Carl Einstein and art theorists at the beginning of the twentieth century
considered the most important and prominent function of art—to teach the
senses, awaken sensitivity, and sharpen perception.

Thus it is logical that some artists object to the very idea that there might be
anything in the world that merits being called "Art Made of Waste," "Art Made
of Garbage," or "Art Made of Compost." This was sculptor Tony Cragg's argument when, in 1992, he was asked to talk about these topics at a conference of
the *Internationales Forum für Gestaltung* in Ulm, Germany. Cragg denied any relation between art and waste. He insisted on the artist's freedom to choose whatever material necessary without regard for classifications of the kind proposed by
the organizers of the conference.[13]

Simply denying a relation between art and waste, however, is not conceptually promising; but Cragg may be right to a certain degree: dealing with waste
materials is not an end in itself but is related to different programs and concepts.
Schwitters was looking for new "colors" or "paints." Arman showed things as
they were. Spoerri fixed moments of time. Kelley challenged sentimentality and
bigotry, and so on. These programs are not based on concepts of waste but concepts of artworks and practices. They keep a well-defined distance from any kind
of "Art Made of Waste." But, as the examples above have shown, this distance is
not absolute. In any case, there is a specific and characteristic attitude toward the
materials. Most of these attitudes are related to customary classifications, and
some of the practices observed even rely on concepts of waste or garbage to produce their effects. In this respect, they are connected, however carefully and distinctly, with the most common and habitual everyday classification of materials.

MUSEUMS AND TIME

Another common trait is that all of the works discussed so far deal with questions of memory, tradition, and history, in one way or another. Albers returned
to the traditional processes of glass art without concerning himself with the
source of his actual materials. Schwitters claimed to broaden the range of materials after having destroyed the traces recalling specific historical contexts or certain everyday events. Chamberlain first used a material that was reminiscent of

the everyday context of traffic and accidents, and he unintentionally raised the repressed idea of mortality. To prevent this from happening again, Chamberlain continues to use the same material, though no longer using "real" scrap.

When Arman exhibited "garbage," he exhibited "a reality" that was considered obscene. He pointed to a quite "normal" process of expulsion, along, perhaps, with its conditions. When decay or maturation becomes a theme and object of art, traditional ideas governing its relation to time are challenged and abolished. If images and projections are questioned by pointing to their repressed aspects, they become uncanny. And when it is the human body—its parts or secrets, its destruction, mutilation, or annihilation—that is the object and material of art, the questions raised become even more pointed. Artistic views of what is human can be extremely provocative if they expose the sheer materiality of the human body. This cuts to the very basis of Western ideas about humanity and the central principles sustaining Western images of the self. They are deconstructed right at the heart of the institutions which, by their mere existence, continue to produce the tradition, history, and collective memory of Western society.

Questions of life and death are integral to the work of many twentieth-century artists; they exist or disappear within the work itself. This contests a system that is set up to store, keep, maintain, and save material objects. Happenings, along with decaying or evaporating materials, have caused plenty of conservation problems. Some objects cannot be preserved, because their materials are not suitable for eternal preservation and repose in the archives of material culture. This is true for Angelika Tippel's fragile sculptures in cotton. Other artists have chosen to keep their works out of the reach of museums and collections in order to control the effects of time on their work. Wallace Berman, for example, installed his trash sculptures on the streets of San Francisco: it was left to the weather and passersby to further combine them with other waste—an idea that can be regarded as a true and consequent confirmation of a concept of cyclical time, as well as a profound statement on tradition and history.

SANCTUARY AND MEMORY

The next two examples highlight another aspect of the relations entertained in the twentieth century between art, its museums, and waste. They show the museum as a special place with specific functions and organize the concept of art around this idea of the museum: the museum is a site where anything worthy of protection finds sanctuary, once it is introduced by an artist.

In the 1950s, François Villeglé described the practice of a group of fellow artists, in which he and others walk around the city looking for the remains of worn-out placards on walls, on doors, or on advertising pillars. With the well-trained eye of the true artist, identifying and choosing the most beautiful among them, he takes them away to safe places, meaning private or public art collections. Villeglé explained that he was not interested in painting or any other traditional means of producing art but in the coincidences manifested in the destruction of placards, brought about, for instance, by the incidental actions of passersby. He contends that coincidence and the unintentional are the true and inexhaustible sources of art. For Villeglé, research and choice are artistic interventions that are necessary to save "beauty" and prevent its disappearance. A tribute to bourgeois conditions must be paid to ensure the permanence and special treatment of the rescued object. The artist must sign the rescued object and in doing so transform it into art. The future buyer is asked to share the artist's merits by signing as well, thereby returning at least part of the anonymity to the found object, which is then made available to collectors and museums.[14]

The artist's eye can see what must be saved and has the power to choose and open a sanctuary for what is chosen. It is a place where neglect, destruction, or wastage is not expected to affect the object. In the early 1980s, Raffael Rheinsberg surveyed the site of the Anhalter railway station, in the center of Berlin, a station that was bombed during the Second World War and finally torn down during the 1960s, leaving a small part of the facade to be preserved as a monument. On the surrounding grounds, Rheinsberg collected fragments of artifacts and put them into two large boxes. He then presented them as the result of archaeological research, evidence of the history of a century, and as "diagnosis" and "testimony" to it. He wrote, "First, resolute steps towards progress, soon followed by condensations, knots; countless arrivals, departures; later on, flights and slow good-byes, at last; now, everything covered, rolled into the ground a long time ago. On top, the chaff of the age of plastic. A mere arrangement of things and remains of things that leads back to the exact reality of the mythic."[15] The finds are identified as documents associated with and somehow embodying German history. They are interpreted as traces and evidence of a historic imagination leading directly into "the exact reality of the mythic." Rheinsberg performs a very complex play on rubbish, material, places, memories, and history, alluding to discussions about history and its material substrate, historicity, and historiography. The remains are waste transformed into a work of art, which testifies to the fact that historic materials have become "aesthetic" materials. As such, they may be rescued and left to reside in a gallery or, in this case, in the Berlin Museum.

THE MATERIALITY OF MEMORY

Hannah Arendt has argued that things or artifacts are the crucial precondition for memory, because remembering requires material support. Claude Lévi-Strauss also proposed that material remains are the only means to understand that "something" occurred between people in the past.[16] Hermann Lübbe and others have diagnosed the large number of newly founded museums as a reaction to the accelerated rate of change in industrial and postindustrial societies. Lübbe argues that the founding of museums is a response to the perpetual revision of conditions, habits, customs, ways of life, and rapid wear and tear of objects and materials involved in practices that are now obsolete.[17] These developments turn nearly any object into potential waste. Taken from this point of view, diversification, fashion, and permanent renewal spur the founding of stabilizing institutions. Collective memory and the individual feeling of continuity seem threatened, needing the reliable solidity of material things for support. Saving and exhibiting "the past" and "identities" are thus pinpointed as the driving force behind the expanding number of museums in the 1970s and 1980s.

Such arguments and views are an important interpretation of the function of the museum, in this case, the museum of everyday life—museums of local or regional traditions—more so than the museum of art. The local history museum seemed to be the solution to the problems of accelerated change. One of its functions was to archive the outmoded, degraded, and no longer functional things that were once part and parcel of normal, everyday life. The museum of everyday life appeared capable of coping with the accelerated appearance and disappearance of objects.

Although these arguments still play an important role in museological theory and influence museum policy, the New Museology deconstructed most of these traditional premises. It pointed out the various ways in which the historical museum, the museum of the past, was a far cry from true evidence of any kind of a past. On the contrary, the New Museology showed the museum to be a construct comprising concepts and objects that are the components of newly created models of the very past that these museums claimed to present. Critiques of traditional museology emphasize that one precondition of any museological work is that its objects are removed from their original context, becoming quite different objects within the walls of the museum.[18]

The idea of preserving any past for the present and future has become more and more dubious. On the one hand, criteria for selecting what is to be saved no longer appear available. Everything is potentially waste or evidence, depending on the context, so everything must be saved, which is, of course, impossible. The very idea of a complete collection of things representing common and everyday life exceeds museum capacities. This is the source of questions directed at museology and the arts today. Villeglé's and Rheinsberg's works address precisely this point.

MEMORY AND ACCELERATION

Museums of daily life have sought their objects in abandoned factories. They have saved office furniture and kitchen equipment; they have shown, among other things, plastic bags, umbrellas, and canned mackerel. Flea markets became an important source of objects and were thus visited by museum experts, all of which has brought potential waste, and things that otherwise might have ended up at the dump, into the museum.

The motives do not necessarily coincide with the artistic concepts presented here, although they are tied to discourses of history, memory, and the desire to preserve the means of anchoring remembrance of things past. Collecting items that are on the verge of being lost, however, has its parallels in the approaches artists have had and still have to trash and junk of all sorts. This is true especially in one respect: although they are collected to tell stories—the story of the development of products, the history of design, the history of practices, or the history of ways of life—the collections also heighten sensibility.

Another problem could not and cannot be easily solved. Any collection of the everyday objects of today has to deal with a process that runs at high speed. The rescue and documentation of everyday objects require a trained sensitivity for things that are characteristic, special, typical, normal, and vanishing. The curator's choice has to be fast and sensitive enough to grasp a normality that is perpetually vanishing. This perception and the creation of heritage become more and more exhaustive, as things become waste or a piece of history within a very short time. The saving of everyday things is a task dependent on a trained and specialized eye, capable of anticipating the future strangeness of normal things and saving them before they are lost to the dump. One museum of daily life indeed forgot to save its own first-generation Apple computer.

WASTE, ART, MEMORY, AND THE MUSEUM

Some years ago, museological work and artistic concern with materials and objects began to overlap. Reflection on materials and matter and the conservation potential of museums converged and began to be challenged. Some famous exhibitions and works of art attest to this development: Claes Oldenburg's "Mouse Museum" should be cited as a forerunner of this development, as should Andy Warhol's boxes filled with sorted materials. Other artistic collections contributed as well,[19] but new forms of communication between art and museums of daily life tore down the barriers more thoroughly. Take Ursula Stalder's installation "*Gefunden an den Stränden Europas*," a collection of items found washed ashore on several European beaches and exhibited in 1994 at the Kunsthalle Zürich, and in 1997, in the exhibition space of the Werkbund Archiv, a museum of everyday things in Berlin.[20]

An even closer connection between art, the museum and reflections of daily life is the "Museum of Garbage," launched in Sweden in the mid-1990s. This is a recent form in which waste, garbage, trash, organic materials are brought into the museum and intimately associated with the latter. The project is designed as a traveling exhibition that puts garbage as such on display. This is not exactly what Arman did in the Galerie Iris Clerc, for this time garbage is not a fact in itself; rather, it is exhibited, by the organizers of the exhibition, Monika Gora and Gunilla Bandolin, as a didactic as well as an artistic object.

The exhibition is installed in a truck and includes well-lit showcases containing objects found at dumps, supplemented by animation. Some of the cases are filled with "real," fresh garbage, and visitors are invited to don protective gloves and touch it. The thirty objects in the other cases are finds, trophies of an archaeological expedition into dumps. The exhibition may have been inspired by the professional archaeological research on dumps undertaken at Texas University mainly during the 1980s. Gora's and Bandolin's objects, however, are the result of an excavation that reached layers produced during the 1970s, historic garbage, so to speak. The finds, among them a broken refrigerator handle, a diaper, and a headless, one-legged Barbie doll, have been carefully selected. Artists were asked to interpret the finds and to think about the past and present of the objects that they were working with, in addition to the role they played in the lives of their designers and users. The imaginative results have been transformed into an interactive computer animation and supplemented by musical interjections. The holistic perception is enriched by garbage odors blown into the truck. Commenting on their project, the organizers contend that dumps are the graveyards of the Western unconscious; they represent our feelings, our guilt about the past, and our anxieties about the future. The usual way of dealing with dumps—that is, sowing grass and integrating them into the landscape—is stigmatized as an irresponsible illusion, a repressive way of forgetting, a way of being pardoned, a ritual.[21]

RESCUE AND SALVATION

Personally, I do not think that Western attitudes toward materials and the past can be exclusively understood on the basis of individual morality, guilt, fear, and a menacing unconscious. The project does, however, raise some state-of-the-art questions about materials, waste, and the museum. A sensitivity is created that guides perception directly into the sphere of the overlooked. The strange, the chaotic, and the expelled are exhibited. The project espouses a concern for disgusting objects and materials; it also suggests the necessity of keeping anything ever made, used, or perceived in the realm of perceptible things. Nothing ever perceived should be lost, and whatever has been lost must be regained.

This implies an enormous expansion of attention and an infinite obligation to perceive. I call it an obligation, because whatever has been introduced into the sphere of the museum, the exhibition, and the arts cannot be easily ignored;

it has become part of what demands to be remembered, what claims to be heritage. Following the proposition of the Museum of Garbage, the expelled, the no longer functional, the disgusting, and the decaying must be publicized and made manifest. In this respect, the design of the Museum of Garbage presents a true parallel to the universal consumption of resources—and a reinterpretation of a deep-rooted, Judeo-Christian concept of salvation.

BEYOND CAPACITIES

Today, museums and exhibitions function as eye-openers (nose-openers), in ways that were once the exclusive purview of avant-garde art. They shock and play on the limits of the tolerable. There are obviously tireless researchers and prosecutors pursuing what is on the verge of being lost. The consequences and the future development of their attitudes and practices with regard to memory and heritage cannot be predicted.

One of several possibilities is that the idea of a comprehensive collection and publication will die from the most terrible fate that can befall the arts, exhibitions, and museums—boredom.

It also is foreseeable that, although profound criteria may not be available, restrictions will be applied to which materials and objects may be institutionalized and rescued and moved into the sphere of the timeless, at the public's expense. Saving objects already creates problems, because the sheer number of objects to be stored and classified exceeds capacity. This is a problem that museums of everyday life face when they must cope with nontraditional, industrial societies and their production of objects.

To a certain degree, these are problems the museum of everyday life shares with the art museum. Some must store their treasures in huge warehouses, which may serve as a welcome opportunity to use otherwise useless industrial buildings or wastelands. Sometimes reports of discussions concerning the usually concealed selling practices of museums reach the public and undermine the idea of the function of the museum. Questioning this situation from a general point of view, however, will have as a consequence the explicitation of museum choices and the necessity of discussing what really belongs among the treasures to be stored.

Another scenario is that the potential of the goal of hierarchically ordering materials and objects will not be exhausted at all but will be renewed by free and different combinations profiting from an abundance of options. This would be a felicitous and promising prospect for the archives of material culture. If the abundance of materials, artifacts, things, or objects exceeds all available capacities, if the ways of ordering and selecting them cannot be grasped or defined anymore, the objects may be lost—a phenomenon well known to respectable and even venerable libraries and museums. This, however, leads to delightful occasions of the sudden, incidental, and unexpected finding of lost or unknown items, which could result in the same freshness, happiness, and intensity that Vincent van Gogh felt when he discovered the dumps of The Hague.[22]

NOTES

1. See my "Garbage, Waste and Boundaries," in *World of Signs—World of Things/Welt des Zeichen—Welt der Dinge*, edited by Jeff Bernard, Josef Wallmannsberger, and Gloria Withalm (Vienna: ÖGS, 1997), 73–86.

2. Vincent van Gogh, *The Complete Letters of Vincent van Gogh*, vol. 3 (Greenwich, Conn.: New York Graphic Society, 1959), 365–66.

3. See my "'Die Schönste Welt ist wie ein planlos aufgeshütteter Kehrichthaufen': Über Abfälle in der Kunst," in *Paragrana* 1 (1996): 244–63.

4. See *Glass, Color, Light—Josef Albers* (New York: Guggenheim Foundation, 1994), 3–5.

5. Kurt Schwitters, *Kurt Schwitters 1887–1948: Der Künstler von Merz* (Bremen: Graphisches Kabinett Kunsthandlung Wolfgang Werner, 1989), n.p.

6. See Julie Sylvester, "Auto/Bio: Conversations with John Chamberlain," in *John Chamberlain: A Catalogue Raisonné of the Sculpture, 1954–1985* (New York: Hudson Hill, 1986), 15ff.

7. See Pierre Restany, "Fünfundzwanzig Jahre als Erfolg," in *Arman. Parade der Objekte: Retrospektive, 1955–1982* (Hannover: Kunstmuseum Hannover, 1982), 22.

8. Alison de Lima Green, *Arman, 1955–1991: A Retrospective* (Houston: Museum of Fine Arts, 1991), 2.

9. See Otto Hahn, *Daniel Spoerri* (Paris: Flammarion, 1990).

10. See Milena Scheibert and Maria Wegener, *Dieter Roth: Unikate Multiples Skulpturen Graphik* (Berlin: Wolgang Werner, 1994).

11. Veit Loers, "Als die Bilder laufen lernten/When Pictures Learnt to Walk," in *Von der Aktionsmalerei zum Aktionismus: Wien, 1960–1965/From Action Painting to Actionism: Vienna, 1960–1965*, edited by Dieter Schwarz and Veit Loers (Klagenfurt: Ritter, 1988), 18.

12. Elisabeth Sussman, *Mike Kelley: Catholic Tastes* (New York: Whitney Museum of American Art and Abrams, 1993).

13. Tony Cragg, "Kunst aus Müll," in *Gemeinsam nutzen statt einzeln verbrauchen: Eine neue Beziehung zu den Dingen* (Giessen: Anabas, 1993), 76–81.

14. See François Villeglé, "Die kollective Realität," in *Dufrêne, Hains, Rotella, Villeglé, Vostell: Plakatabrisse aus der Sammlung* (Stuttgart: Staatsgalerie Stuttgart, 1971).

15. Raffael Rheinsberg, "Zeit-Brüche, Zeit-Schicten, Interferenzen," in *Daidalos* 3 (1982): 90–91.

16. See Hannah Arendt, *The Human Condition* (Chicago: University of Chicago Press, 1998); Claude Lévi-Strauss, *Look, Listen, Read,* translated by C. J. Singer (New York: Basic Books, 1997).

17. Hermann Lübbe, *Zeit-Verhältnisse: Zur Kulturphilosophie des Fortschritts* (Graz, Vienna, and Cologne: Styria, 1983), 9ff.

18. See the arguments in *Interpreting Objects and Collections,* edited by Susan Pearce (London and New York: Routledge, 1996).

19. See *Deep Storage. Arsenale der Erinnerung: Sammeln, Speichern, Archivieren in der Kunst,* edited by Ingrid Schaffner and Matthias Winzen (New York: Prestel, 1997).

20. See Ursula Stalder, *Gestrandet an den Rändern Europas* (Zürich: Museum für Gestaltung, 1994).

21. See Monika Gora and Gunilla Bandolin, "Das Müllmuseum, Schweden," in *Topos* 14 (1996): 66–71.

22. I thank Taryn Toro for her help in revising my English in this chapter.

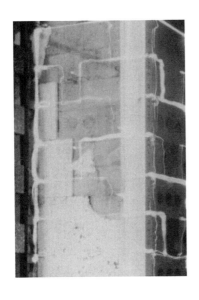

3

Art

and Archive

The Dissimulation Museum

Christine Bernier

THE METAPHORS USED TO DESCRIBE THE MUSEUM often enough evoke the notion of memory: "reservoir of the past," "mausoleum of culture," "temple for the Muses, daughters of Mnemosyne, goddess of memory," "cultural cemetery," "burial chamber of the past"—to name just a few.[1] But in most cases, such metaphors belong to a modernist culture that conferred upon the museum a relatively stable definition, one that made it part of tradition and history.

Today it is hard to deny that museums have changed considerably and now exert a new attraction, both in the field of theory and over various sectors of the public that previously paid them little attention. In recent years, there has been a spectacular increase in museum-related activity: museums themselves have increased in number, their space and collections have expanded significantly, and their programs have become ever more diversified. At the same time, we have seen the proliferation of new museums, created to accommodate a variety of cultural objects and practices hitherto kept outside of institutional walls. Yet as the museum-going public grows, responding to the latest mass-media strategies, we find that the success of a museum is increasingly determined by the quality of its marketing, and that the structure of these cultural institutions is shaped by economic principles. This phenomenon has in turn triggered a number of theoretical and critical studies of the museum institution, confirming it as the new paradigm of contemporary cultural activity. Indeed, all museums define their mission as exhibiting a particular facet of culture, now that everything is considered part of culture, and all cultures are put on display in museums. Such a rapid expansion on a number of fronts has led to what we could call the "museumification" of culture.

THE CASE OF ART MUSEUMS

Some believe that what we are now faced with is the museumification not only of the past but also of the present. Are we witnessing a frenzied obsession with the archive, or an unprecedented craze to ennoble the object, rooted in a phobia of waste? Or are we dealing, rather, as Andreas Huyssen suggests, with a new form of memory, conceived as "the attempt to slow down information processing, to resist the dissolution of time in the synchronicity of the archive, to recover a mode of contemplation outside the universe of simulation and fast-speed information and cable networks, to claim some anchoring space in a world of puzzling and often threatening heterogeneity, non-synchronicity, and information overload"?[2]

The special case of art museums is an ideal site in which to examine the current status of the object of historical and aesthetic interest, especially the value of an object as an artwork. Major changes in the type of objects exhibited in art museums have considerably altered the role of aesthetics and art history as the theoretical frameworks that provided the selection criteria and principles for organizing museum works—so much so that the hegemonic function of these disciplines is now being fundamentally questioned. At the same time, the significance of the work is explored from the perspective of the cultural conditions obtaining in both its production and reception, and ethical questions often wind up taking precedence over aesthetic ones. This has been the source of some rather obvious reevaluations of museums of history, anthropology, and ethnography. As for art museums, and particularly contemporary art museums, the decline in interest for the object's aesthetic status results in an epistemic catastrophe when it coincides with the problematic erosion of criteria of selection and appreciation of objects.

THE OBJECT TRANSFORMED

The art museum, in its modern form (as it first emerged toward the end of the eighteenth century), established itself as an institution open to the public, one which, as far as possible, excluded from its exhibitions objects that were not considered works of art.[3] What initially led to the creation of the museum was the desire to extract objects from their original context and continued circulation in society in order to settle them in a purportedly neutral site that would endow them with new meaning and apparently preserve them in a permanent state of physical and epistemic stasis.

We now realize that museum walls are not as impermeable as the modernist discourse claimed, and that a number of changes have been triggered by contemporary practices in the fields of both museology and contemporary art. It is therefore important to examine the objects being exhibited, for today the work itself is subsumed in a new and broader definition of culture, one that entails a number of major transformations, not only in the relative democratization of access to the work but in the very nature of the objects being shown.

Two types of transformation, brought on through the agency of museum personnel, are manifest in the fact that cultural objects other than artworks now appear inside the museum, and sometimes even inside exhibition galleries themselves. The first case, for which administrators are generally responsible, involves the creation of replicas and "spin-off" products offered for sale in museum boutiques and lobbies.[4] This practice often is a source of heated controversy, and whatever our attitude toward it, we must acknowledge that it reflects a powerful incursion of consumer society ideology into the museum sphere. And when the "universally accessible" museum program is regularly sponsored by the private sector, the situation becomes even more complicated: the democratization of art teaching is vitiated by the parasitical strategies of consumer society, while mass culture, with its endless array of consumer objects, gradually penetrates the museum, threatening to supplant the artwork. Here the museumification of culture means not simply that "good," "living" culture will be mummified before our eyes but also—owing to the confusion between democratization and consumerism— that the museum, now more open, less hermetic, will henceforth accept within its confines the waste products of mass culture.

Another transformation of the exhibited object is currently being brought about by art exhibition curators who conceive projects with themes that are more museological than aesthetic in nature.[5] Studies seem to indicate that the public generally appreciates this type of transformation,[6] probably because it effectively replaces traditional chronological display practices with a rapidly readable space in which works are compared according to *symbolic systems.*[7]

There also is a third and rather different type of transformation, rooted in the practices of artists themselves. Following the example of Marcel Duchamp, early in the century, the primary goal of certain artists' work was to bring the museum as institution into question. Through their work, the social and material conditions surrounding the production and reception of the artwork in a public place are disclosed. By such practices, the museum can no longer be seen simply as the physical space sheltering the work; it becomes the actual site of their work's conception, a discursive space that the work inhabits in a decisively critical way.

Of course, the museum was never really a neutral space, in spite of the pretensions that accompanied its creation in the eighteenth century. But it was not until the early 1970s that certain artistic practices focused critically on the museum itself, illuminating the various strategies of what was in fact a discursive space. These productions often are site specific, conceived especially for a particular space that becomes an integral component of the work. This approach, a growing trend in contemporary art, can be adapted to a wide range of sites (urban or rural) other than the museum. But what I wish to concentrate on here is, above all, the fact that works created in and for the museum institution throw into relief two important characteristics of the contemporary art museum: first, most of the objects it contains do not wind up there after having been in circulation with other cultural objects; second, the museum has become, both literally and figuratively, the *frame* of the work. Contemporary artworks and the museums that exhibit them thus reveal yet another change in the structure of the museum: art is now framed and museumified from the very moment of its conception.

These contemporary works come to the museum without a cultural past; they are, *ipso facto*, titled, catalogued, archived, and conserved from the outset, never having experienced the art market round of collectors and galleries. This is perhaps not true of all of the works in a contemporary art museum, but it is of many, and as Krzysztof Pomian has shown, the phenomenon signals something new.[8] For surely it has the effect of turning artworks into objects from the past. At the least, does it not redefine the whole notion of historical value? The fact is, these cases represent something very different from the functional changes (and semantic modifications) that objects underwent when they entered the modern museums of the eighteenth and nineteenth centuries. We can take the situation that prevailed in most museums during the last century and examine just how a historical object moved from its original function toward its new aesthetic function within the institution. We can look, for example, at how the function of a statue taken from an ancient Greek temple shifted from the religious toward something new, determined essentially by the visual interest it aroused in the Louvre, because it embodied the canons of sculptural beauty. This change was effected largely by the passage of time. We can see now that contemporary artworks reveal a fundamental difference, for the change of function does not occur, in today's museum, with the passage of time. It happens immediately, the moment the work enters the museum. Of course, the seeds of the phenomenon lie in the last century, with the emergence in Paris of exhibitions devoted to living painters and the resulting development of the retrospective exhibition. But the temporality seems qualitatively different when the artist produces the piece specifically *for* the museum, knowing that from the moment it is created, the institution will be its first exhibition site, for in this case the work is totally dependent on the contingencies of its display.

There is therefore a tension in today's art museum, created by the simultaneous operation of two symbolic spaces: on the one hand, there is the persistence of the traditional discursive space, founded on permanence (and often nourished by the ideology of the transcendental power of the masterpiece), and on the other hand, the emergence of the real physical space, experienced from the spectator's perspective and determined by the conditions of display.

THE VALUE OF THE OBJECT

So a brief look back shows us how this different temporality can have a direct impact on the value accorded to the museum object. The criterion of historicity, long considered essential to an evaluation of the work, seems to "disappear" in contemporary art, giving way to a sense of doubt that increases in direct proportion to the degree to which the work lacks a historical existence, however brief, outside of the museum. Traditionally, a work was exhibited in a museum *after* having been recognized for its historical value and aesthetic quality; the museum represented the culmination of the object's life in circulation among other cultural commodities. This, indeed, has been part of the modern museum's discourse since the late eighteenth century: there was nothing arbitrary about the way in which a collection was built up; specific meaning was attributed to each art object, and its place in an exhibition corresponded precisely to the position assigned to it by art history. A judgment of "taste"—based on an aesthetic outlook that was more or less Kantian, depending on the period—led to the establishment of a set of criteria according to which works could be selected.

Today museums still undertake the task of establishing selection standards, principally for the purpose of building their collections, and they still organize (more than ever, in fact) exhibitions of works using criteria that they determine and that are only revealed to the public through the medium of the museum visit.[9] These criteria are founded on predictions about what the historical value of each work will prove to be, predictions themselves based on the artist's previous exhibitions. Such selection methods do away entirely with any notion of the work's ontological value, without offering the public any theoretically developed criteria for judgment. Spectators are thus left without the "keys" that would guarantee them a certain autonomy in their appreciation of the artwork. Today's object, then, is always already potentially waste, its actual status being determined by the conditions of its display. But despite this "nihilistic" state of affairs, and its erosive effect on the criteria of appreciation, the art museum continues to draw a public and seems to fulfill the visual needs of the "new technologized and fragmented subject."[10] If interest persists, regardless of the problem of appreciation, is it because we have now arrived at a culture of exhibition, in which any object inspires interest so long as it is exhibited? Or is it rather that the art museum is a place whose classification system still reassures us, in spite of all the changes? Granted, it still seems to possess a certain reality, embodied in and treated as a physical corpus. And what is more, we are assured that this corpus finds in the museum all of the necessary guarantees for its protection. Seen thus, the museum offers the advantage of being, on the one hand, a place where the object can be conserved and stored in accordance with all of the most well-established principles and, on the other hand, a place where the relationship with art can be experienced through state-of-the-art technologies fully adapted to visitors' needs.

The inherent paradoxes that handicap the museum thus form the basis of its strategy of persuasion. We might ask whether, in the gulf that separates High Art from the general public, the museum is not playing the role of mediator, imbuing its works with historical value by treating them as "archives." Is this not the way the notion of historical value gets redefined? But this idea discloses yet another paradox: although the museum gathers an imposing quantity of archived documents, it remains a fact that the display conditions of certain recent works undermine the traditional notions of "archive" and "historical value." A closer look at a work by Christian Boltanski can help us grasp the paradoxical situation in which any recent work exhibited in a museum must find itself, especially one conceived specifically for the museum site.

Boltanski's installation, *Les Archives du Musée d'art contemporain de Montréal*,[11] is a site-specific piece, set into the architectural structure of the museum space. Its title, moreover, makes direct reference to a particular museum institution. Finally, it is an installation conceived for the museum in question, at its request (a form of commission).[12] It is one of those works that, through its critical dimension, reveals the social and material conditions surrounding the production and reception of art in a public place. But in this particular work, it is no longer a question of subverting or resisting the principles of the institution and its market-economy ideology. Its aim is rather to *merge* with the institution, to give itself over to recuperation by the museum, and in so doing to reveal the fragility of the two systems—the cultural institution and artistic practice. A study of this piece allows us to move on from the heroic works that, during the 1960s and 1970s, aimed to challenge the system—not that these efforts were in vain, but their repetition would have little impact in the postindustrial museum.

NON-REVOLUTIONARY RESISTANCE

Boltanski's work does engage a certain resistance to traditional exhibition policies and current museum structures. But above all, it complicates critical approaches of the past few decades that perceive the museum as a space of exclusion or as the vehicle for ideologies of control in a society of entertainment and cultural massification. Disclosing the discourse apparently concealed by the institution's "neutrality" is not the aim of this work, for the work is clearly grafted upon the museum. We therefore cannot call an installation such as this one "revolutionary" in Douglas Crimp's sense of the word, that is, something "altogether incompatible with the museum's space."[13] In fact, such an approach no longer has the critical impact that it might have had twenty or thirty years ago, for we are no longer at that point in history when the museum represented a public space embodying the principles of "an independent market economy striving to instill in the establishment a respect for individual freedom."[14] Individual autonomy has since been considerably restricted and weakened, even in the realm of art appreciation.

Boltanski's installation is therefore neither "revolutionary" nor avant-garde. Like the rest of the artist's work, it denounces nothing in particular; as he himself says: "I don't think it is any longer art's aim to influence life; art is just art, painting is ruled by the world but has very little effect on it."[15] Nevertheless, this work—in spite (or rather because) of its discreetness—resists the spectacle effect, since the museum conceals the work from the gaze rather than forces us to look at it "attentively."[16] Moreover, the installation avoids the hegemony of a certain form of logocentrism by escaping the notice of those who possess the knowledge that is normally useful in identifying works.[17]

An examination of this work can lead us beyond the pessimistic critique of the museum, which leaves us no options save for abandoning art, or the traditional postures of Marxism and nihilism, denounced by certain critics of so-called postmodern theories.[18] It opens the way rather to freeing ourselves from traditional ways of contemplating a collective memory that is structured by the parameters of a modernist, progress-oriented ideology, by forcing us to rethink accepted notions of "public space" and "archive."

CHRISTIAN BOLTANSKI

Les Archives du Musée d'art contemporain de Montréal is a piece consisting of the "archives" of 336 construction workers involved in the building of the museum.[19] First the artist obtained from the museum the names and photographs of the laborers who worked on the construction site. Subsequently, a series of gray cardboard boxes,[20] each bearing a label with a worker's name and his photograph, was laid out on metal shelves. The ensemble was then installed in a very small room illuminated only by the dim glow of a few desk lamps placed at regular intervals atop the shelves.

The piece illustrates the full presentational device characteristic of Boltanski's work,[21] which includes references to memory, death, the body, and disappearance. A number of essays have explored in depth the relations between body and memory in Boltanski's work, showing how the collective memory of the concentration camps operates within installations that often are composed of childhood memories. As Christian Boltanski has said:

The reconstructions of the early seventies . . . all appeal to the memories of those who are supposed to look at them. They leave spectators free to imagine, remember, identify. The goal of a biographical work is to prevent the artist from dying: to surround him with so many details that we know everything about him, so that finally he is not dead. In fact, it never quite works . . . I've often thought, but I'm not sure about this, that it [the contradiction] was rooted in my Jewish background or lack thereof.[22]

DISSIMULATION AND PUBLIC SPACE

Boltanski initially intended the work to be located in the basement of the museum, outside of the usual exhibition galleries. It was ultimately installed out of the way, as the artist wished, in a cramped space next to the stairway leading down to the basement. It is interesting to note that this spot is actually very close to the busiest area of the museum (the stairway in question leads off the main lobby and is on the circumference of the traditional rotunda) and that the site, paradoxically, dissimulates the installation. In the traditional art museum, whether ancient or modern, the exhibition galleries represent a space that creates the museum's characteristic "aestheticist and historicist effects."[23] However, an object located outside of the galleries of a traditional art museum can still be recognized as an artwork by the frame (in the case of a painting) or base (in the case of a sculpture) that identifies it as such. Site is an important guide in identifying contemporary works, works often consisting of fragments or accumulations of objects whose shape and function are uncertain and often lack the conventional "attributes" of the museum work. A contemporary installation that is placed outside of the traditional display spaces offers none of the usual clues that help the visitor recognize it as a work of art.

In *Les Archives du Musée d'art contemporain de Montréal*, we must ask ourselves why the expert eye of the art aficionado (as much as the uninformed gaze) is unlikely to recognize it as a *work of art*, unless encouraged to look more closely. If Boltanski's installation goes entirely unnoticed it is, in the first place, because it is dissimulated within the "entry" space *(hors d'oeuvre)* of the lobby, usually reserved for commercial establishments (boutiques, bookstores) and functional activities (receptions, security, coat check). This dissimulation is made even more effective by the artist's effort to camouflage the piece. The work looks like a room, sealed off behind a locked grillwork door that prevents any clear view of what it contains. The door, furthermore, has a functional look: made, at the artist's behest, "of metal grillwork, like that found in reserves,"[24] it blocks access to the objects inside of the room. But more importantly it quells any desire to go closer, since it fails to identify the room as an artwork. The installation mimics areas normally accessible only to museum personnel; it is simultaneously displayed and concealed and so confounds the visitor's codes of orientation that it becomes invisible.

The work was created for a temporary exhibition organized by the museum and from which only Boltanski's work, completely integrated into the museum's architecture, would be permanently kept. The dissimulation of a work within an architectural site often is temporary, as Andreas Huyssen has pointed out.[25] It is therefore even more surprising that visitors to the museum, including those alert to such issues and interested in Boltanski's work, should see the space without recognizing the "work," in spite of its permanent installation. The work's deliberate discreetness and permanence lead us back to its title, and the key word in it: *archive*.

WORK AND ARCHIVE

Like museums, archives consist of collections of objects and documents. In archival departments, as in cabinets of curiosities, people have for ages assembled and preserved items considered, according to various criteria, to hold a certain interest (current and future). Every archival document aims to be a "guardian of memory," and the archive, like the museum, forces us to consider the notion of an object's value: what deserves to be archived?

Let us first look at the question of the location of archives which, in a public space such as a museum, must always be taken into account.[26] In speaking of the *archontic* function of the archive, Jacques Derrida addresses issues of both place and law, of the privileged site wherein resides the power of the archive.[27] Site is thus not without significance; and Boltanski's, which renders it at once accessible and invisible, leads us to wonder about the consequences of such dissimulation. Boltanski's work destroys the spatial order normally associated with the power to construct history, traditionally represented by a space that is organized according to certain classifications and a certain use of the archives. For this organization to make sense, it has to create an impression of continuity within a homogeneous whole that presents the distinctions inherent to the corpus. On this subject, Hubert Damish is succinct:

> The architecture of the museum is not just destined to reinforce the image of the institution itself, endowing it with a monumental appearance. Even if it stood in a potato patch . . . the museum would still remain a *monument* in the etymological sense of the term, i.e., an instrument of the memory, its support. Mnemosyne, the Mother of the Muses: one can't help instituting a parallel between the architecture of this "temple of the Muses" and the architecture of the places where the classical art of memory taught how to arrange mentally the *images* corresponding to the content of the various parts of speech, places that in their orderly sequence are like tables

on which is inscribed the text which one intends to commit to
memory. . . .

By analogy, the museum does not merely display objects but displays them in a certain order and in a certain context, prompting the
visitor to go through the rooms in sequence, just as the orator passes
in review the "places of memory."[28]

In a museum, memory is organized in a deliberate fashion, and the archive
supports the museum's legitimizing, ordering function by employing a system of
classification. Boltanski's installation blurs the boundaries and distinctions that
permit the employment of classification systems; it destabilizes the *archontic* power
of the archive, its capacity to ascribe value, by ignoring the linear history that
normally determines sequence.

Evidently, it is not Boltanski's aim to rewrite history. As Bernard Marcadé
writes: "History is not the perspective adopted by Boltanski, because History in
fact came to a standstill, stopped, around the middle of the century, somewhere
between Auschwitz and Treblinka."[29] Nor is it a question of blotting out memory: "The reference to this dark chapter of Western civilization is particularly
clear in a piece like the *Archives* shown at Documenta VII in 1987."[30] Rather,
the impressions created by Boltanski reinvoke what his archives seem to have repressed. But is not repression, in spite of appearances, indissociable from the
archive? Does it not often bespeak—even when associated with the archive and
its retroactive gaze—a possible return of whatever has been suppressed or repressed? This at least is what Jacques Derrida suggests when speaking in *Archive
Fever* of the archives of psychoanalysis:

It follows, certainly, that Freudian psychoanalysis proposes a new theory of the archive: it takes into account a topic and a death drive
without which there would not in effect be any desire or any possibility for the archive. But at the same time, at once for strategic reasons and because the conditions of archivization implicate the
tensions, contradictions, or aporias we are trying to formalize here,
notably those that make it into a movement of the promise and of the
future no less than of recording the past, the concept of the archive
must inevitably carry in itself, as does every concept, an unknowable
weight. The presupposition of this weight also takes on the *figures* of
"repression" and "suppression," even if it cannot necessarily be reduced to these.[31]

Boltanski's work puts us in a peculiar temporality by presenting people (the
subjects of his photographic portraits) as archived, by inscribing their memory in
a time yet to come, by anticipating the advent of the monument in their name:
he suggests a memory that pushes us toward the future—a future already archived
before it has passed. Not an apocalyptic vision (which would be too totalizing,
insufficiently differentiated, overly determined by a linear notion of history) but

a fragment, of variable temporality: "Everything happens as if Boltanski had begun at the end, as if the development of works (their aging, their deterioration) led, retroactively, to their conception and their execution."[32] The archive now no longer refers systematically to the past; rather, it has to be taken to implicate the present and refers first and foremost to the contingencies of exhibition. This triggers a major reversal: if the archive seems to "point toward the past to refer to the signs of consigned memory, to recall faithfulness to tradition,"[33] how is it that Boltanski presents us, in the form of archives, with photographs of people whom history has not consigned to memory? The unsettling effects of the installation are caused in part by its evocation of the Holocaust but mostly by its upsetting of chronological order: it does not represent an event that we can comfortably assign to the past but an archive of the present and the future. Let us look more closely at this idea.

To effectively fulfill its traditional role as the guardian of memory, the archive must be conservable and accessible for possible consultation (and this is equally true of the electronic archive). But the "archive" in Boltanski's installation can never be examined. When the work was executed, the artist invited each person who had submitted a photograph to put some personal objects in the box bearing his or her name. Moreover, the invitation stipulated that he or she would be allowed permanent access to the box and could place other objects in it at any time. Did the construction workers respond to this invitation? Are there any objects in the boxes? Because we spectators do not have access to the boxes behind the locked door, we can never examine the items therein. It will never be possible to put "behind us," in time, the objects they contain (or could contain). In other words, they can never be treated as archives. At this point, dissimulation verges on secrecy.

But as Derrida points out, "of the secret itself, there can be no archive, by definition."[34] The order of the institution—of the museum, but also of history and the archive—is disturbed by Boltanski's "archives," for they are composed of secrets, and their being gathered together is of such little value (in the sense that the people "archived" remain unknown to us and are not judged "worthy" of being remembered by history) that it cannot serve as the basis of a homogenous principle of gathering. Derrida adds:

> The archontic power, which also gathers the functions of unification, of identification, of classification, must be paired with what we will call the power of *consignation*. By consignation, we do not only mean, in the ordinary sense of the word, the act of assigning residence or of entrusting so as to put into reserve (to consign, to deposit), in a place and on a substrate, but here the act of *consigning through gathering together signs*. It is not only the traditional *consignation*, that is, the written proof, but what all *consignatio* begins by presupposing. *Consignation* aims to coordinate a single corpus, in a system or a synchrony in which all the elements articulate the unity of an ideal configuration. In

an archive, there should not be any absolute dissociation, any hetero-geneity or *secret* which could separate *(secernere)*, or partition, in an absolute manner.[35]

It is important to note the paradoxical association, in this work, of forget-ting with the archive. How are we to approach the archives of those we can for-get, since their action is "without value" for a collective cultural memory? Andreas Huyssen, for one, does not see forgetting as a negative function—on the contrary:

> Via the activity of memory, set in motion and nurtured by the con-temporary museum in its broadest and most amorphous sense, the museal gaze expands the ever shrinking space of the (real) present in a culture of amnesia, planned obsolescence and ever more synchronic and timeless information flows, the hyperspace of the coming age of information highways.
> In relation to the increasing storage capacity of data banks, which can be seen as the contemporary version of the American ide-ology of "more is better," the museum should be rediscovered as a space for creative forgetting.[36]

Traditionally, the archive serves as a clue by which to recognize what de-serves to be remembered; it has the power to produce value (notably its own) by determining what will become history. But what happens when we archive documents—whether the boxes in Boltanski's installation are empty or full mat-ters little—about people who do not inspire the desire to remember?

> There would indeed be no archive desire without the radical finitude, without the possibility of a forgetfulness which does not limit itself to repression. Above all, and this is the most serious, . . . there is no archive fever without the threat of this death drive, this aggression and destruction drive.[37]

The archive reassures—to unveil the archive, to make it public, is to offer citizens a guarantee that they are participating in the culture so transparently re-vealed. Boltanski's work emphasizes the archive in order to reveal its inherent paradox: memory disappears, the traces are unclear, and history is not valued—the absence of the archive is disquieting.

The archives of the construction workers will always remain secret. The content of the boxes will never be known to us. The museum is not conserving the private stories of these individuals in order to subsequently make them pub-lic.[38] We are not concerned with these people's lives as recorded in a history of the museum according to certain criteria of evaluation and classification. Mu-seum visitors have no desire to see inside the boxes; they take for granted that the objects they contain are absurd, meaningless scraps. It is this acceptance of for-getfulness that makes the work disturbing.

I don't really know myself. We are all so complicated, and then die. We are a subject one day, with our vanities, our loves, our worries, and then one day, abruptly, we become nothing but an object, an absolutely disgusting pile of shit. We pass very quickly from one stage to the next. It's very bizarre. It will happen to all of us, and fairly soon too. Suddenly we become an object you can handle like a stone, but a stone that was someone.[39]

For Boltanski, the work with photographs leads to a reification of the individual: "In my use of photos of children, there are people about whom I know nothing, who were subjects, and who have become objects, that's to say corpses. They're nothing any more, I can manipulate them, tear them apart, stick things in them."[40] The artist's vision is, admittedly, a pessimistic one: the subject, the work, memory, art—everything becomes a relic, and perhaps even waste, in this reliquary of dereliction. But for the time being, at least, this piece by Boltanski can put an end to the sterile debate that opposes "revolutionary" art and the institution as cemetery, for it becomes clear that both are caught in the same trap—the one in which the value of the archive is suddenly glimpsed as precarious.[41]

Translated from the French by Judith Terry and Brian Neville.

NOTES

1. Some of these terms have been employed recently in works by Hubert Damisch (the reference to Mnemosyne), Bernard Marcadé ("cultural cemetery"), and Andreas Huyssen ("burial chamber of the past"), references for which are given below.

2. Andreas Huyssen, *Twilight Memories: Marking Time in a Culture of Amnesia* (New York and London: Routledge, 1995), 7.

3. Objects of a more ethnographic nature were sometimes included in exhibitions, however, the definite desire to distinguish themselves from the "cabinets of curiosities" that preceded them led these museums to exhibit objects as artworks, or at least as objects representative of the canons of artistic beauty.

4. It even happens that consumer products (such as cars) are exhibited not only in the "general" spaces (such as the lobby) of a museum but in the galleries in place of artworks.

5. For example, the current taste for mournful retrospection: (1) exhibitions inspired by the cabinet of curiosities or including reconstructions of period rooms, in which artworks are shown alongside cultural objects that provide them with a "context"; the additional objects possess a powerfully discursive dimension that lends connotative value to the artworks by evoking ethnographic, historical, or industrial issues; (2) exhibitions with a museological theme, in which the installation of the works is defined by a concept and by a display plan focusing primarily on museographical questions; (3) commemorative

exhibitions, in which museums make their own history the central subject of the project, and where the installation alternates artworks with photographic documents and didactic panels.

6. But the positive reaction to the hybridization of the exhibition is not restricted to the general public, nor an exclusive effect of *masscult*. The writings of certain critics had already paved the way for some of these changes by questioning the assumption that exhibitions had to remain "pure" and free of any objects other than artworks; it was pointed out that artworks had not always been created to be shown exclusively inside "the white cube" with which the *habitués* of American formalism had made us so familiar. For more on this subject, see Brian O'Doherty, "Inside the White Cube," in *Artforum* (March 1976): 24–30; (April 1976): 26–34; (November 1976): 38–44.

7. Catherine Millet, "L'Art moderne est un musée," in *Art Press* 82, reprinted in special issue 15 (1994): 151–58.

8. Krzysztof Pomian, "Le musée face à l'art de son temps," in *Les Cahiers du Musée national d'art moderne*, special edition (1989): 5–10.

9. I am not talking here only of the general public; artists, critics, and specialists of all kinds recognize the power of the museum to establish a reputation, while they have become accustomed to an international contemporary art exhibition culture that determines the fashion of the moment. This culture is perpetuated—and even created—not only by museums but also by the major fairs (Basle) and biennials (Venice, Johannesburg) and Kassel's *Dokumenta*.

10. This is the expression used by Rosalind Krauss in "The Cultural Logic of the Late Capitalist Museum," in *October* 54 (1991): 3–17.

11. *Les Archives du Musée d'art contemporain de Montréal*, metal shelves, 336 cardboard boxes, 336 labels, 16 electric lamps, 196 photographic prints. Work acquired by the Musée d'art contemporain de Montréal in 1992.

12. For the exhibition entitled *Pour la suite du monde* (1992).

13. Douglas Crimp, "The Postmodern Museum," in *Parachute* 46 (1987): 61–69.

14. Michel Freitag, *Le Naufrage de l'université, et autres essais d'épistémologie politique* (Québec: Nuit Blanche, 1995) (my translation).

15. Christian Boltanski, quoted by Bernard Marcadé in "La vie impossible de Christian Boltanski," in *Parachute* 55 (1989): 5 (my translation).

16. According to Svetlana Alpers, the effect the museum produces is one that enables us to look attentively at an object, even if this means isolating it from its cultural context. See "The Museum As a Way of Seeing," in *Exhibiting Cultures: The Poetics and Politics of Representation*, edited by Yvan Karp and Steven D. Lavine (Washington and London: Smithsonian Institution Press, 1991), 25–32.

17. Jacques Derrida writes: "[I]t is within a certain experience of spacing, of space, that resistance to philosophical authority can be produced. In other words, resistance to logocentrism has a better chance of appearing in these types of art." See Derrida, "The Spatial Arts: An Interview with Jacques Derrida," in *Deconstruction and the Visual Arts*, edited by Peter Brunette and David Wills (Cambridge: Cambridge University Press, 1994), 10.

18. Pierre Bourdieu, for example, in his lecture "Pour un historicisme rationaliste," presented at the Université de Montréal on March 30, 1996, attempted to offer

alternatives to an attitude he qualifies as nihilistic and associates with postmodernism and deconstruction.

19. It is worth noting that these workers form a particular social group, most of them members of Montreal's Italian community.

20. The artist requested that these boxes be "very ordinary, everyday, similar to shoe boxes."

21. For example, the work entitled *Détective* also takes the form of "archives" and is composed of shelves, cardboard boxes, photos, and lamps. Moreover, the very titles of the works (from 1973 to 1991) make frequent reference to the notions of memory, archive, archaeology, and death: *Monuments, Reconstitution, Lessons of Darkness, La Réserve des suisses morts.*

22. Boltanski, quoted in Marcadé, op. cit., 5–7.

23. This idea is discussed by Donald Preziosi in *Rethinking Art History: Meditations on a Coy Science* (New Haven, Conn.: Yale University Press, 1989) and especially in "Modernity Again: The Museum As Trompe-L'Oeil," in *Deconstruction and the Visual Arts*, op. cit., 145.

24. The artist's request was perfectly in keeping with the title of the work, since it usually is the archival department of the museum that manages the reserves (the work storage areas). Needless to say, this type of written request ends up in the archives of the museum.

25. He made this comment during a lecture entitled "Monumental Seduction," while discussing Christo's wrapping of the Reichstag. The lecture was presented during the *Modernist Utopias* conference, held at the Musée d'art contemporain de Montréal on December 9 and 10, 1995. Unfortunately, I do not have the space here to address the interesting question of the disappearance of the work in relation to the acceleration of museum activity. See Paul Virilio, *The Aesthetics of Disappearance*, translated by Philip Beitchman (New York: Semiotext(e), 1991), and Andreas Huyssen, *Twilight Memories*, op. cit.

26. In a museum, the management of archives involves not only the preservation of documents but also the monitoring of the circulation of objects and the immediate inputting of data concerning everything that enters the institution.

27. Jacques Derrida, *Archive Fever: A Freudian Impression*, translated by Eric Prenowitz (Chicago and London: University of Chicago Press, 1996), 13.

28. Hubert Damish, "The Museum Device: Notes on Institutional Changes," in *Lotus International* 35 (1982): 6–11.

29. Marcadé, op. cit., 6.

30. Ibid., 7.

31. Derrida, *Archive Fever*, op. cit., 29–30.

32. Marcadé, op. cit., 6.

33. Derrida, *Archive Fever*, op. cit., 33.

34. Ibid., 100.

35. Ibid., 3.

36. Huyssen, *Twilight Memories*, op. cit., 34.

37. Derrida, *Archive Fever*, op. cit., 19.

38. In museums, information about an artist is first catalogued and then made available to researchers. The assembled objects and documents may later be presented to the general public as part of an exhibition. With Boltanski, this order no longer holds, and the temporality is reversed: the public exhibition of the "archives" is the starting point.

39. Christian Boltanski, from an interview by Georgia Marsh, "The White and the Black: An Interview with Christian Boltanski," in *Parkett* 22 (December 1989): 36–41.

40. Christian Boltanski, quoted in Marcadé, op. cit., 6.

41. This work has been made possible by the financial support of the Musée d'art contemporain de Montréal.

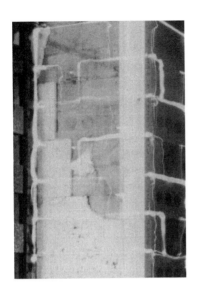

4

Beyond

the Archive

Aleida Assmann

ARCHIVES ARE REPOSITORIES FOR THINGS PAST THAT ARE DEEMED, however, worth preserving. As such, they have a reverse affinity with rubbish dumps, where things past are accumulated and left to decay.[1] Archives and rubbish are not merely linked by figurative analogy but also by a common boundary, which can be transgressed by objects in both directions. Objects that are not confined to archives end up on the rubbish dump, and objects occasionally cast out of archives, due to shortages of space, likewise end up there. Furthermore, as Krzysztof Pomian has pointed out, certain objects stored in archives today were at some stage classified as rubbish. According to him, the sequence, "object—waste product—object with symbolic value," applies to most objects "which constitute the repository of our cultural legacy."[2] In order for waste products that have lost their primary context of use to have any chance of an afterlife in an archive or a museum, they must possess something of the relic, which resists the ravages of time by its robust materiality. Moreover, archives and rubbish dumps can be interpreted as emblems and symptoms for cultural remembrance and oblivion. In this capacity, they have attracted the growing attention of artists, philosophers, and scientists over the past few decades.

Objects considered rubbish are those that have "fallen out" of the cycle of utility, once they are worn out, destroyed, or replaced by newer objects. Upon closer scrutiny, the German word for certain kinds of waste, *Abfall*, reveals metaphysical connotations—to wit, the original *Ab-fall* from the Edenic state of perfection and union with God. *Abfall*, in this sense, connotes law and hierarchy, as well as separation and Original Sin; in fact, the word is virtually synonymous with sin. In common usage, of course, the word has a different meaning. It refers to what falls from our hands or off the table and is carelessly left on the floor, that is, in a more general sense, to objects that have lost their commodity value and become obsolete. With the loss of commodity value, an object also loses its function and meaning. Waste, consequently, consists of objects no longer valued or cherished by society. What remains is their sheer materiality. Art, however, having always kept a certain distance from the utilitarian, subscribes to a rather different economy than business, allowing it to take an interest in waste. By incorporating waste into their works and installations, artists achieve two different objectives. They create an alternate economy and compel the observer to look beyond the external boundaries of his or her symbolic sensory world and recognize the cultural system with its mechanisms of (de)valuation and exclusion. This type of art is not mimetic but structural. It does not represent or copy anything but renders visible what is otherwise inconspicuous—namely, the fundamental structures of cultural value production.

As recording facilities, especially in the audio-visual field, become increasingly sophisticated, and storage becomes technically ever more optimal and economic, consciousness simultaneously becomes more sensitive to what is not and cannot be recorded. What applies to human consciousness and memory applies as well and to a greater degree to the archive: not everything can be included, and structural exclusion mechanisms exist that cannot be circumvented. Or can they? The vision of a universal archive of humanity is bound up with the view that history has reached a standstill, at which point the feeling grows that everything has happened before and can be quoted at will. Such a melancholic suspicion can give rise to paranoid feelings of claustrophobia. It creates an urge to transcend the boundaries of this archive, to perforate the stifling totalization of memory, and thus in turn to pave the way for the new. Boris Groys, Russian theorist of the museum and historian of the avant-garde, raised the issue in an interview, when he spoke of the periphery or outskirts of the archive as the most vital resource for cultural innovation:

> The question is whether our archives, museums, galleries, libraries, and film archives, etc. encompass everything that has historically been produced. It is certainly not the case; on the contrary, outside of this actually finite archive, there is an ocean of unhistorical, everyday, irrelevant, maybe insignificant, unremarkable objects which have not been historically recorded. This is a potential reservoir for the new. In my view, the new is not the development dictated by time, but the interplay between what is known and has been recorded in the archive, and what remains outside the archive: the inconspicuous that has passed unobserved. And this level of the unhistorical, the unrecorded or non-archived, the merely quotidian, cannot disappear.

Each society and individual has this unarticulated, perhaps inexpressible dimension of the merely extant.[3]

For Groys, the "inexpressible dimension of the merely extant" is still the
most essential, inextricable, and inexhaustible resource for artistic endeavor. It
does not interest him in its material structure but as a medium of artistic innovation. Art, which is committed to the task of permanent innovation, must permanently operate on the boundary between the archive and the unclassifiable,
creating the new by continually incorporating new areas from beyond the
archive. Innovation is the act of permanently replenishing the archive, and yet,
according to a certain law of cultural economy, the resource of the "profane," of
asemantic and desemanticized objects, remains inexhaustible.

    In the following, I will look at certain artists who also work with waste but,
unlike Groys, who approaches it from the perspective of artistic innovation, do
so from the vantage of personal and cultural memory, or to be more precise, from
counter-memory. Drawing on literary texts and artistic installations from the
1960s to the 1990s, I shall illustrate how, in a variety of media and in both the
West and the East, art has become a remembrance of things lost and forgotten.

RAGPICKERS—THE RELATIONSHIP
BETWEEN ART AND WASTE

In the nineteenth century, waste acquired new value in the process of industrial
production. Certain materials were collected as raw materials to be recycled by
new industries. This applied particularly to the increased production of paper, for
which large quantities of rags were reprocessed. This gave rise, in the words of
Walter Benjamin, to a kind of cottage industry lying on the side of the road.
"The ragpicker fascinated his epoch. The eyes of the first investigators of pau-
perism were fixed on him with the mute question as to where the limit of
human misery lay."[4] Benjamin's view of the ragpicker was above all influenced by
Baudelaire, who saw the *chiffonnier* as a product of the modern city and described
him in the manner of a Theophrastian character:

> Here we have a man whose job it is to pick up the day's rubbish in the
> capital. He collects and catalogues everything that the great city has
> cast off, everything it has lost and discarded, and broken. He goes
> through the archives of debauchery, and the confused array of refuse.
> He makes a selection, an intelligent choice; like a miser hoarding
> treasure, he collects the garbage that will become objects of utility or
> pleasure when refurbished by Industrial magic.[5]

Baudelaire explicitly creates an analogy between the archive and rubbish as
he classifies the *chiffonnier* as a type of collector. The latter fascinates him as a

kind of inverse counter-image of the archivist who, in the realm of rubbish, se-
lects, collects, sorts, classifies, and guards his stock like a treasure. Baudelaire's
chiffonnier reemerges with similar characteristics in contemporary American literature. Here, however, he is not primarily a figure of social misery but the
agent of a cultural counter-memory. In *Ceremony*—Leslie Marmon Silko's
novel about a Native American soldier, Tayo, who is traumatized by his experiences in the Second World War—medicine man Old Betonie manages to invent a ceremony that initiates the healing process. At one point in the novel,
Tayo gets a chance to enter the old man's hut which, in traditional style, is half
buried beneath ground level. To Tayo's astonishment, the circular, open-
ceilinged room is stacked to the roof beams with cardboard boxes, untidily
piled one on top of the other. Old articles of clothing and rags burst forth from
some boxes, while dried roots and rushes are visible in others, along with
Woolworth bags full of dried mint and tobacco leaves wrapped in unspun yarn.
Other stacks consist of years of newspapers and telephone directories from
large American cities. Looking around the room, Tayo swoons, a reaction that
does not surprise Old Betonie in the least: "The old man smiled. His teeth
were big and white. 'Take it easy,' he said, 'don't try to see everything all at
once.' He laughed. 'We've been gathering these things for a long time—hundreds of years.'"[6] Tayo is relieved to see the traditional ceremonial tools of the
medicine man on top of a heap of waste paper, but his memory is jolted when
he sees a series of old calendars hanging one on top of the other, dating back
to the years 1939 and 1940.

> "I remember those two," he said.
> "That gives me some place to start," Old Betonie said, lighting
> up the little brown cigarette he had rolled. "All these things have sto-
> ries alive in them." He pointed at the telephone books. "I brought
> back the books with all the names in them. Keeping track of things."
> He stroked his mustache as if he were remembering things.[7]

The collector culture of the Native American medicine man is the exact
counter-image of the modern culture of waste. It envelops it like a shadow, in
which the discarded is collected and the forgotten remembered. The tools,
packed like sardines in the medicine man's waste archive, are not indifferent
waste but the material props of personal histories. Like the tobacco leaves
wrapped in wool, these objects are enveloped in stories, objects that when
considered in isolation seem like stray, irrelevant rubbish, transformed into a
mysterious cosmos of knowledge, once fleshed out with anecdotes and cere-
monies. But since the white man has changed the world so profoundly, the traditional knowledge of the shaman no longer suffices for an effective ceremony;
new stories have to be narrated and new elements invented for the ceremony.

A new cultural memory also must be developed to support the anecdotes and actions: an archive of waste.

City of Glass, the first novel in Paul Auster's New York Trilogy, recounts how a man named Quinn winds up taking on the role of detective shadowing a stranger called Stillman. Stillman's behavior is indeed peculiar, if not necessarily criminal. Day after day, he leaves his hotel and wanders within an exactly circumscribed area of the city. The routes he takes have no recognizable pattern or goal, and he meanders slowly, without raising his eyes from the ground. Occasionally, he stops, picks up an object from the ground, and inspects it carefully. Sometimes he throws it away, but more often the objects end up in a bag, at which point he takes a diary out of his pocket and makes a note, like an archaeologist marking the location of an important shard at the site of a prehistoric ruin. Stillman, it turns out, is yet another avatar of Baudelaire's chiffonnier, just like Old Betonie.

> As far as Quinn could tell, the objects Stillman collected were value-less. They seemed to be no more than broken things, discarded things, stray bits of junk. Over the days that passed, Quinn noted a collapsible umbrella shorn of its material, the severed head of a rub-ber doll, a black glove, the bottom of a shattered lightbulb, several pieces of printed matter (soggy magazines, shredded newspapers), a torn photograph, anonymous machinery parts, and sundry other clumps of flotsam he could not identify.[8]

Like Silko, Auster is interested not in the poverty but in the mysteriously metaphysical aspect of this character. Quinn, who manages to interview Stillman, asks him to explain the strange excursions: "You see, the world is in fragments, sir. And it's my job to put it back together again."[9] In presenting his metaphysi-cal project, Stillman ironically assumes the air of a certain Hamlet of Denmark who, if you recall, bore the responsibility of repairing a world out of joint. His project, however, is even more closely allied with another fictional character bearing the initials H. D., the figure from an English nursery rhyme, fictionally immortalized by writers such as Lewis Carroll and James Joyce: Humpty Dumpty, the egg which, once broken, could never be put back together again. Stillman's explanation sounds like a postmodern commentary on Genesis:

> For man is a fallen creature—we know that from Genesis. Humpty Dumpty is also a fallen creature. He falls from his wall, and no one can put him back together again—neither the king, nor his horses, nor his men. But that is what we must all now strive to do. It is our duty as human beings: to put the egg back together again.[10]

For Stillman, there is only one way to cure the basic ills of the world, namely, to invent a new language, a sort of prelapsarian lingua adamica. Since the

Fall, language is no longer a transparent image of the world; a veil has been spread over words and objects, distorting the perfect original pattern and leaving mankind with a heap of unrelated fragments. The only means to triumph over this fallen state is through a true language that restores the proper correspondence between words and objects.

> "My work is very simple. I have come to New York because it is the most forlorn of places, the most abject. The brokenness is everywhere, the disarray is universal. You have only to open your eyes to see it. The broken people, the broken things, the broken thoughts. The whole city is a junk heap. It suits my purpose admirably. I find the streets an endless source of material, an inexhaustible storehouse of shattered things. Each day I go out with my bag and collect objects that seem worthy of investigation. My samples now number in the hundreds—from the chipped to the smashed, from the dented to the squashed, from the pulverized to the putrid."[11]

What he does with these "things" is give them "names," "new words that will correspond to the things." Old Betonie collects rubbish for a shamanistic ceremony designed to cure a soldier of a war trauma. Stillman collects waste in an attempt to cure the primal trauma of mankind, to restore prelapsarian humanity. This primeval waste also deformed language, thus obstructing humanity's true access to the world. The renaming of the world through waste is intended to reverse the effects of the mythical *Ab-fall*, known as the Tower of Babel, which afflicted mankind with the confusion of tongues.[12] In the postmodern novel, according to the erudite Auster, this once powerful piece of metaphysics has itself become a fragment, the shattered relic of a lost intellectual history that gets recycled in literature. As a carnivalesque-cabbalistic showpiece of bewilderment and mystification, it creates an atmosphere of playful but unsustained suspense.

Leaving the literary aside and turning our attention to the visual arts, we see that a relationship between art and waste exists here as well, one that is constantly redefined due to the mounting waste of industrial mass production. As Susanne Hauser has shown in her examination of the relationship between waste and art, one can identify various phases in the history of artistic concern with waste.[13] This development began in the second half of the nineteenth century and reached its peak in the 1920s. The early phase is exemplified in quotations by two particular artists. The first comes from a letter by Vincent van Gogh to Anthon van Rappart, already cited by Hauser: "Tomorrow I shall get some interesting objects from this Refuse Dump—including some broken street lamps—rusted and twisted—on view—or to pose for me, if you like the expression better."[14] The other quotation comes from Kurt Schwitters, who writes: "I don't see why the used tickets, driftwood, cloakroom numbers from attics and rubbish dumps couldn't be used as painting materials just like factory-produced paints."[15] Van Gogh plans to inspect the trophies of the rubbish dump, with a view to using them as "models." These patented objects, whose expressive force has been shaped by extensive use, serve as props that he incorporates into his paintings. Schwitters' interest in rubbish differs from this mimetic approach. He does not collect old street lamps or stovepipes but smaller objects such as buttons and used tickets, which he integrates as objects into his paintings. Van Gogh paints old junk, while Schwitters paints with old junk. The collage breaks the homogeneous surface of the canvas, rendering it jagged and uneven. Representational art is succeeded by an art based on miscellaneous objects, involving the assortment, assemblage, and composition of heterogeneous components.

Meanwhile, there is yet another considerable leap from painters using waste materials as motifs or artists integrating them as objects to works of art that exhibit the waste material per se. In the *objet trouvé* or, indeed, the ready-made, artistic composition becomes secondary. Objects once discarded and forgotten are recovered by the artist and, if necessary, forcibly brought to the attention of the viewer. Arman, as Hauser has mentioned, began in 1959 to exhibit packed trash cans, placing them in museums in order to achieve a shock effect. He maintained "that the expressive quality of rubbish and redundant objects has an immediate, intrinsic value of its own, rejecting any aesthetic classification which would blur them and emulsify the palette of colors."[16] He never sought to value rubbish in aesthetic terms and his work is a paradoxical gesture in the monumentalisation of rubbish. It reminds us of the precarious nature of the boundaries that culture creates between art and rubbish, archives and waste. Furthermore, it is clear, and graphically so, that rubbish, which should but cannot be disposed of, can itself assume a monumental shape.

A SMALL MUSEUM FOR THE REST OF THE WORLD—ILYA KABAKOV

Boris Groys deemed the private rubbish collection of Russian artist Ilya Kabakov "the only museum of modern art in the Moscow of the seventies and eighties."[17] In the recent history of our affluent and wasteful society, rubbish has increasingly captured the interest of artists, who see in it the repressed side of consumerism, a symbol of our waste economy, a signal of imminent ecological catastrophe. These obvious associations are not foremost in Kabakov's work. He does not see rubbish as the emblem of the postindustrial social system but more as an emblem of the system of the Soviet Union: "[E]verything is deliberately destroyed, or is missing a part. Rubbish is a good metaphor for such a dys- or non-functional civilization."[18] More fundamentally, however, rubbish is a metaphor for life itself in its ephemeral nature, life in thrall to the fury of extinction. Loss, oblivion, and transience are the monotonous teleology of all living things. Even this rather neobaroque perspective on *vanitas*, *mutabilitas*, and *memento mori* is linked to a paradoxical vision of eternity. In religious meditations of the Baroque period, it was possible to face the prospect of universal decay because of the certainty of an afterlife. For Kabakov, however, rubbish and eternity belong to the same category: "[I]t is discarded, turns gray, and disintegrates in order to fulfill its destiny as rubbish. For me, however, rubbish is as eternal as life itself. Thus I already see the brightly colored poster in shreds on the ground. It transforms itself into rubbish and will exist eternally as such."[19]

Precisely speaking, Kabakov distinguishes between two eternities: the eternity of rubbish as the inescapable, enduring permanence of waste and the eternity of art and museums as the other form of permanence, the "sphere of immortality." He does not, however, set these two eternities in opposition to each other but, as we shall see later, he transforms and interweaves them.

How did Kabakov develop his interest in rubbish? He himself has given a detailed account of how rubbish gradually and peremptorily became the main focus of his attention.[20] In Moscow, he owned an apartment in the attic of a large tenement. To reach it, he had to make his way each day through several patches of rubbish—past the rubbish bins at the gate, through all kinds of dirt and litter in the yard, up the stairs to the fifth floor, past the rubbish bags in front of the various apartment doors, past the janitor, who heaved heavy iron bins of rubbish down the stairs (something that had left its mark on the stairs over the years), and finally past the refuse in the loft, before entering his apartment. Instead of returning to the canvas or writing desk, Kabakov began to look at his own rubbish with new eyes, saving waste paper perfumed by the scent of memories, the last precious tokens of so many memories.

Kabakov worked his collection of personal waste paper into various artistic forms, according to archival designs. His cardboard box arrangements remind one of the setup of the Native American medicine man, Old Betonie, in Silko's novel. The boxes contain stacks of personal papers in no particular order, as though hastily gathered and stuffed into boxes before relocating. He packs souvenir chests with all kinds of objects that fix the memory of things normally forgotten. Some objects are arranged in bunches, each part affixed by string to a label. Indeed, Kabakov considered classifying, ordering, and labeling the most important forms of processing rubbish. The so-called "life books" are cardboard files containing papers and rubbish produced on a day-to-day basis. Each file ends with a neatly written, fastidious inventory of the contents, thereby transforming the unsorted contingency of life, the authentic, random flow of papers, into the bureaucratic system of the archive, which inevitably envokes associations with "state memory" as well as "state control." The certificates, invitations, sketches, recipes, newspaper articles, and other scraps of the "life books" document paradigmatically day-to-day human contact with reality, the reality of lived life. The most striking and daring example of this practice is surely the contents of a dust cloth, whose every detail and grain Kabakov meticulously analyzes and records.

Kabakov is clearly not interested in organic rubbish, consumer waste, or industrial debris but rather in biographically relevant cultural waste that bears traces of human handling and use—only this waste intersects with the archive. A flexible boundary between value and nonvalue runs between cultural waste and cultural archive, and it is a constant topic of discussion and renegotiation. The artist is less concerned with the wholesale dismantling of the boundary between value and nonvalue, the total "museumification" of life, than with shifting this boundary, in order to reveal the individual and official act of decision involved in remembering and forgetting, between permanence and transience. In contrast to Arman's *Poubelles*, Kabakov's rubbish is not anonymous; it consists of relics from his own personal life, ordered and preserved as memory aids and evidence. He writes:

> Of course, that's exactly it: a small museum for the rest of the world. I collect nothing for the sake of collecting, but for the benefit of the visitor. Perhaps even for the auditor, the inspector, who may demand an explanation of what I did on this or that day, for example. I can then open file no. 8 and produce the necessary documentation. It's a bit like self-denunciation or confession.[21]

Memory is a reliable counsel in the vacillation between waste and conservation, between rubbish and (private) museum. In Kabakov's view, the value of an object is "dictated by a specific memory." Confronted with a stack of papers, consisting of "receipts, used cinema or travel tickets, presents or purchased reproductions, old newspapers and journals, and memos on things to be done or that have been done," a familiar instinct is awakened.

> It is an intense feeling for the events associated with each single paper. Each scrap of paper jolts our memory: it evokes a particular moment in our lives. To part with all these punctuations, these paper marks and credentials would be to part with one's memories. In our memories and minds, everything is equally important and significant. All these sentimental items are interconnected and form chains and connections in our memory, which ultimately constitute the sum of our lives, the history of our lives.[22]

On the one hand, this classification of rubbish is for the purpose of collecting evidence for a trial where individual existence is at stake and must be justified before a higher authority. The bureaucracy, already powerful in Gogol's Russia, became an instrument of compulsion under Stalin. Confronted by such powers, the individual is under constant pressure to account for herself or himself.[23] However, the self-reliance of individual identity also includes the ancient desire for self-perpetuation, the artistic transformation of the ephemeral into the permanent. Kabakov's work effects a mysterious transubstantiation of rubbish into archival objects and archival objects into art. His art organizes the move from the world of transience into the museum, the sanctuary of eternity. This too is a metaphysical project in which self-justification and self-denial converge. Juridical and soteriological metaphors express the sinner's desire for approval and justification: "In fact, it is the desire to become part of culture with all my junk, all my dirty laundry—without any fear whatsoever."[24]

But Kabakov's project concerning rubbish is not simply personal. Rubbish also becomes the warrant of collective utopia. This is made evident in a text that describes a tour of Moscow's rubbish dumps:

> And so, the world which I saw already with a "backward" glance, seemed to be a gigantic dump. I have been to a few real dumps—near Moscow and in Kiev—they are sorts of smoking hills reaching to the very horizon of the most diverse things. On the whole, this is junk, crap, the refuge of an enormous city, but as you can see, wandering around them, that the whole of it sort of majestically breathes, it breathes as though with all of its past life, this dump is full of sparks similar to stars, stars of the cultural realm: you see either books of some sort, or a sea of some kind of magazines in which there are even photographs hidden, and texts and ideas, or things which were used by some people. That is, an enormous past rises up behind these crates, bottles, sacks, all forms of packages which have ever been needed by man, they haven't lost their forms, they did not become something dead when they were thrown out, they somehow howl about that life, they preserve it in themselves.[25]

This utopia promises that life is stronger than death, and that human articulation is more robust than the powers of destruction. However, Kabakov first discovers the power of this life under the pressure of its negation. A counter-memory chrysalises under this pressure and from which the new can emerge. Seen from this perspective, it is possible to understand why the artist, living as he was in a totalitarian state, devoted himself so passionately to the work of rememberance through rubbish. The following sentences summarize his credo:

> A sensation of an enormous, cosmic nature, of actual existence seizes you at such dumps. It is not at all a feeling of abandonment, of the death of life, but just the opposite, of a return, the revolution of life, because as long as there exists a memory of life, everything will live, being involved in life; the memory "remembers" everything that has lived.[26]

In both the West and the East, in literary texts and artistic installations alike, modern art has discovered rubbish. We have seen that there are three distinct economies involved, that of the market, that of art, and that of memory. The economy of the market is grounded on the functional value of practical use; if this is no longer given, an object is considered obsolete and is replaced by a new one. The economy of art is grounded on cultural values such as truth, beauty, and meaning. Like the economy of the market, it is organized in terms of old and new, the artistic innovation, however, does not aim at ever new modes of technical function but at new forms of human expression and perception. A third economy is personal and cultural memory, which is grounded on an identity value that provides the criteria of relevance for what is remembered and what is forgotten. As Krzysztof Pomian and Boris Groys each have pointed out, industry and art, which both operate on the principle of innovation, have a common boundary with the possibility of a transference: what has become old in the system of the market may be recovered as new in the system of art. The artists who we have examined in this chapter, however, have explored yet another borderline that separates and connects the system of art and the system of personal and cultural memory. In focusing their attention on garbage, these artists have explored the margins of personal and cultural memory and stressed the possibility of counter-memories and a new vision of culture. In the totalitarian context, the dump becomes an emblem of a subversive counter-memory that cannot be controlled by the institutions of political power, figuring as a perpetual resource of creative energy. Thus through their waste archives, authors and artists have created various forms of cultural counter-memory, their refuge for the forgotten and rejected. Their memorial art resembles the *ars memorativa*, whose methods it faithfully copies in the neat archival systems of collecting, ordering, and arranging its materials. But it also includes the *ars oblivionalis*, since it is constructed on the paradoxical act of remembering what is forgotten.

Translated from the German by Linda O'Riordan.

NOTES

1. On trash in general, see Michael Thompson, *Rubbish Theory: The Creation and Destruction of Value* (Oxford: Oxford University Press, 1979); William Rathje and Cullen Murphy, *Rubbish! The Archaeology of Garbage* (New York: HarperCollins, 1992); Volker Grassmuck and Christian Unverzagt, *Das Müll-System: Eine metarealistische Bestandsaufnahme* (Frankfurt: Suhrkamp Verlag, 1991).

2. Krzysztof Pomian, "Museum und kulturelles Erbe," in *Das historische Museum: Labor—Schaubühne—Identitätsfabrik*, edited by Gottfried Korff and Martin Roth (Frankfurt: Suhrkamp Verlag, 1990), 43.

3. Boris Groys and Wolfgang Müller-Funk, "Über das Archiv der Werte. Kulturökonomische Spekulationen: Ein Streitgespräch," in *Die berechnende Vernunft: Über das Ökonomische in allen Lebenslagen*, edited by Wolfgang Müller-Funk (Vienna: Picus, 1993), 175 (my translation).

4. Walter Benjamin, "The Paris of the Second Empire in Baudelaire," in *Charles Baudelaire: A Lyric Poet in the Era of High Capitalism*, translated by Harry Zohn (London: Verso, 1983), 19.

5. Charles Baudelaire, *Artificial Paradise: On Hashish and Wine As Means of Expanding Individuality*, translated by Ellen Fox (New York: Herder and Herder, 1971), 7–8. Cited in Walter Benjamin, *The Arcades Project*, translated by Howard Eiland and Kevin McLaughlin (Cambridge, Mass. and London: Belknap Press/Harvard University Press, 1999), 349.

6. Leslie Marmon Silko, *Ceremony* (New York: Viking Press, 1977), 120.

7. Ibid., 121.

8. Paul Auster, *City of Glass* (New York: Penguin Books, 1987), 95.

9. Ibid., 119.

10. Ibid., 128.

11. Ibid., 122–23.

12. See my "The Curse and Blessing of Babel; or, Looking Back on Universalisms," in *The Translatability of Cultures: Figurations of the Space Between*, edited by Sanford Budick and Wolfgang Iser (Stanford: Stanford University Press, 1996), 85–100.

13. See her "Waste into Heritage," chapter 2 of this book.

14. Vincent van Gogh, *The Complete Letters of Vincent van Gogh*, vol. 3 (Greenwich, Conn.: New York Graphic Society, 1959), 365–66.

15. A note dated April 3, 1972, *Kurt Schwitters, 1887–1948: Der Künstler von Merz* (Bremen: Graphisches Kabinett Kunsthandel Wolfgang Werner, 1989) (my translation).

16. See Pierre Restany, "Fünfundzwanzig Jahre als Erfolg," in *Arman. Parade der Objekte: Retrospektive, 1955–1982* (Hannover: Kunstmuseum Hannover, 1982), 22 (my translation).

17. Ilya Kabakov and Boris Groys, *Die Kunst des Fliehens. Dialoge über Angst, das heilige Weiß und den sowjetischen Müll* (Munich: Hanser, 1991), 110 (my translation). I would like to express my thanks to Schamma Schahadat for introducing me to the work of Kabakov and to Tomàs Glanc for his paper on Kabokov, "Hierarchie und Verdoppelung" (Constance: MS., 1996).

18. Ibid., 115.

19. Ibid.

20. Ilya Kabakov, *Söppelmannen/The Garbage Man* (Norway: National Museum of Contemporary Art, 1996), 122–25. My thanks to Natalia Nitikin and Boris Groys for sending me a copy of this book.

21. Kabakov and Groys, op. cit., 107.

22. Ilya Kabakov, *SHEK*, vol. 8, edited by Günter Hirt and and Sascha Wonders (Leipzig: Reclam, 1994), 111 (my translation).

23. Kabakov may have been influenced by the Russian philosopher Fedorov, who developed a theory of rebirth via memorial practices. See Michael Hagemeister, *Nikolaj Fedorov: Studien zu Leben, Werk und Wirkung* (Munich: Sagner, 1989). I owe the hint to Alexander Etkind.

24. Kabakov and Groys, op. cit., 115.

25. Kabakov, "The Apology of Personalism in the 1960s," in *The Garbage Man*, op. cit., 141–43.

26. Ibid., 143.

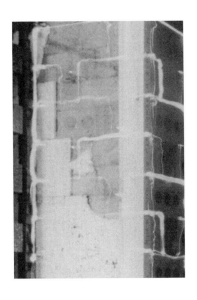

5

The

Acculturation

of Waste

Walter Moser

As RECENT HISTORICAL APPROACHES TO THE QUESTION HAVE SHOWN, the reality of waste is intrinsically tied to the very existence of human society throughout its history. But the novel development that interests us here is not the existence of waste per se but rather its accession to culture. So in what follows I too will speak of the "acculturation" of waste, all the while taking this term in its most literal sense, one that falls short of its specifically anthropological and sociological acceptations. Because, for the longest time, waste has been relegated to the fringes of culture, if not expelled altogether, and has thus stood as a term opposed to culture. Such exclusion is being reconsidered, even repudiated, within today's society; a new relationship between waste and culture is in the midst of emerging: a less negative, more ambivalent, and certainly more complex relationship.

The new perception of waste results from a particular constellation, which depends upon several concomitant developments. Among these, we should mention: the spread of industrialization, which has radically changed the quantity and nature of waste produced; the advent of a new ecological awareness and its resulting practices; the emergence of an economy of recuperation and recycling; the recognition of waste as an artistic resource; and, finally, the expanding scope of "waste" (and more or less synonymous terms) by analogy. The challenge is to comprehend the cultural transformation being brought about by the new multiform presence of waste, as both discursive and material reality.

Because it is a process of considerable historical and cultural complexity, a thorough examination of the "acculturation" of waste can hardly be embraced here. This chapter, therefore, forms only one moment in a more comprehensive ongoing analysis. It should be preceded by a symptomatology of sorts, which will inventory and describe the various signs attesting to the existence of the phenomenon on a global scale—signs ranging from our fears of smothering beneath an avalanche of refuse, through the sundry techno-economic solutions devised to rid ourselves of it, all the way to the increased application, by analogy, of the notion of waste across the entire range of discourses. It would then be followed by the presentation and analysis of various "aesthetics of waste."[1] Within this larger ensemble, we undertake the beginnings of a philological and conceptual analysis of "waste."

THE SEMANTICS OF WASTE

Let us begin with a brief foray into the linguistic landscape of waste, or, more precisely, let us explore its semantic field and the relations that this field maintains with its lexical compass. These explorations will draw on vocables from different languages, to point out contrasts or bring out certain regularities occurring between them. I employ "waste" as a generic term to designate the semantic field in question. But for all that, "waste" is never more than one vocable among many making up the full lexical range of this field in English. Among other words, more or less synonymous with "waste," the most frequently encountered are debris, detritus, dirt, dreck, garbage, junk, leavings, leftovers, litter, refuse, remains, rubbish, scraps, smut, and trash.

A number of isotopics emerge within this field, allowing us to bring out certain structuring distinctions:

Organic and inorganic. Inorganic waste derives most often from an artisanal or a manufacturing process, though it can just as well occur naturally (as in geology, for instance). Most of the above words partake of both isotopics. Some have an inclination one way ("detritus" is organic on the whole) or the other ("debris" is rather inorganic). In general, all of the words designate something that remains partially at odds with respect to this distinction: no vocable belongs exclusively to one or the other isotopic.

Fragment and totality. Waste is often fragmentary, partial, residual in relation to a totality that would have preexisted it. The French *déchet*—singular, nominative— conveys this sense better perhaps. This separation of part from whole is usually one of the genetic preconditions for the existence of waste. In many languages, these words have both a singular and a plural, thus permitting us to designate either one element alone or a pile of fragments or particles resulting from a process of disintegration. Nevertheless, we observe a tendency, notably in French, to use most of these words in the plural. The words thus often comprise a narrative potential that refers to the process of waste formation:

- *mere persistence:* waste is what remains after the use or consumption of a product, what is left of a whole that has disintegrated or deteriorated: remains, residue, or leftovers, as we say in English.

- *decay:* waste is that part which passively detaches itself from a whole by a falling off or away. The French *déchet* (cognate of decay and rendered indiscriminately in English as waste, refuse, or rubbish) comes in fact from the Latin *de* and *cadere.* In German, the same construction is found in the word *Abfall,* that which detaches itself in falling away. This isotopic cannot help but evoke a moral connotation by its association with the whole family of words derived from *cadere* and the biblical myth of the Fall.

- *rejection:* waste is that part which has been actively detached (torn, ejected, expelled) from a whole and subsequently cast off and excluded: refuse. In French, *rebut;* in Italian, *rifiuti.* This isotopic applies above all when waste is produced in an artisanal or industrial process, where the product is obtained by the removal and rejection of the surplus parts of the material, or when a desired substance is extracted from a plant, whose remains are then discarded: "trash" designates, among other things, the remains of sugar cane, once the juice has been extracted.

Aggregate and magma. When we refer to decayed fragments in the plural, a heap of rubbish, say, we can distinguish between two states of consistency: either an aggregate of particles or heteroclite objects, whose origin in a disintegrated whole remains recognizable, or an amorphous mass, a magma in which the constituent particles have undergone a process of homogenization. The French *gadoue* and *immondices* belong, on the whole, within the sphere of undifferentiated magma, as does the German *Müll,* whereas obviously *débris* and perhaps less clearly *déchets* and *ordures* belong within the sphere of aggregates. English seems to prefer words used in the collective singular form (garbage, litter, rubbish, trash, waste), which nonetheless does not necessarily imply a choice between the two terms of this semantic opposition.

Negativity. This last isotopic is a constituent of the whole semantic field. Already on the level of their semantic content as lexemes, and thus even prior to their discursive elaboration, most of the words used to designate waste comprise a constitutive semantic negativity. This negativity is coupled with other polarizing dichotomies (high—low; good—bad; appetizing—disgusting) and easily takes on a moral valuation. In the first instance, however, it refers to degradation in the form of a loss of value that is at once material (degraded, corrupted), practical (useless), and semantic (insignificant and nonsensical). This negativity is more or less virulent depending on the word. In French, the vocables with the strongest negative association are *ordure* (cf. the personal invective *quelle ordure*, and the morally connotative adjective *ordurier*) and *immondice* (as in the moral evaluation *ceci est immonde*). In English, "rubbish" is found in idiomatic expressions such as "this is rubbish!" (this is something worthless, meaningless), whereas "trash" can take on the verb form "to trash" (to destroy something by devastating criticism).

At this moment, a general remark on this linguistico-philological approach is in order: The words of a given language, as defined in the dictionary, present us with a certain semantic stability. Their discursive elaboration, on the other hand, is by nature event-like; consequently, such elaboration is likely to bring about certain transformations, however infinitesimal, in the semantic structure of the words. One must therefore postulate a dialectical relationship between semantic structure and discursive event.

Nevertheless, our objective of describing the historical process behind the "acculturation" of waste obliges us to privilege the event aspect of this dialectic. In what follows, therefore, we are above all concerned with questioning, not so much the words as such, but how they are taken up in discourse. In their variety and repetition, discourses provide one way of gaining an understanding of the cultural transformation that we are exploring.

CONCEPTUAL ANALYSIS OF WASTE

Several discourses on waste have common currency today: a technical, an economic, an ecological, a historical and, more and more, an aesthetic discourse. But theoretical approaches to this semantic field are rare, as are attempts to define it conceptually.

The "acculturation" of waste is a troubling phenomenon. Consequently, all kinds of discursive logics and conceptual apparata have been called on to explain it. Peter Sloterdijk, to give just one example, devotes a brief section to the phenomenon in his *Critique of Cynical Reason*. In a single page, Sloterdijk proposes no less than three ways to tackle the problem, though he does not pursue it further. Employing the phrase "to unlock the positivity of the negative," he appears to relinquish the issue to the logical machinery of the Hegelian system. He equally ascertains that one legacy of ecology will be "to transform the phenomenon of refuse into a 'high' theme." This would appear to align it with the postmodern concern for the inversion or, at least, the confusion of the hierarchies of cultural production and diffusion (high/low culture). Finally, in speaking of an "anal culture," he also points out the Freudian and psychoanalytic perspective.[2]

I will rely upon more developed propositions as I endeavor to provide "waste" with the conceptual articulation necessary to reflect upon and explore the phenomenon that I have called the "acculturation" of waste. I shall distinguish three conceptual stakes which, if only for heuristic reasons, I will address individually. It goes without saying, however, that in order to deal with concrete objects and phenomena, one must consider them in light of the interaction of all three elements. The stakes are those of *purity*, *value*, and *memory*. By picturing the interaction between at least these three, we shall be in a better position to attend to the complexity of the phenomenon of the "acculturation" of waste.

PURITY

The problem of waste arises in the context of all sorts of systems: domestic economy, manufacturing, an ecological system, a village, a city, a country, the planet. Despite the diversity of these systems, attitudes toward waste and its treatment—its management, as we like to say nowadays—betray certain constants. In order to draw these out, anthropologist Mary Douglas opts for a structuralist approach. As the title of her book indicates, she has chosen the notion of purity, along with its opposite, pollution by impurity, as the basis for exploration.[3]

In her book, Douglas explores attitudes toward the category of "dirt."[4] Dissatisfied with what she calls "piecemeal explanation," she proposes, by way of alternative, "a systemic approach,"[5] which implies three things: in the first instance, she conceives of society as a system presupposing the distinction between an interior and exterior space. Next she postulates that we should consider all of the aspects of such a system (the ritual, symbolic, economic, medical, hygienic, social, etc.) in an integrated manner, so that we may understand, for example, a ritual, the object of which is the impurity of the sacred, or a dietary interdiction. Finally, she postulates that all systems are consequently equivalent regarding their capacity to cope with whatever threatens their continuity and integrity—particularly so-called primitive societies (from which she draws most of her examples), but also "our society," as she calls it.

In any given system, "that which is not in its place"—that which has lost value and utility and, having become "impure," upsets the order of the system to a dangerous degree—will be branded with the semantic negativity contained in the category "dirt" and will be rejected. For Douglas, then, the distinction between positions inside and outside the system, giving rise to gestures of inclusion and exclusion, is fundamental. At one point she offers the following narrative of these structural laws:

> In the course of any imposing of order, whether in the mind or in
> the external world, the attitude to rejected bits and pieces goes

through two stages. First they are recognizably out of place, a threat to good order, and so are regarded as objectionable and vigorously brushed away. At this stage they have some identity: they can be seen to be unwanted bits of whatever it was they came from, hair or food or wrappings. This is the stage at which they are dangerous; their half-identity still clings to them and the clarity of the scene in which they obtrude is impaired by their presence. But a long process of pulverizing, dissolving and rotting awaits any physical things that have been recognized as dirt. In the end, all identity is gone. The origin of the various bits and pieces is lost and they have entered into the mass of common rubbish. It is unpleasant to poke about in the refuse to try to recover anything, for this revives identity. So long as identity is absent, rubbish is not dangerous. It does not even create ambiguous perceptions since it clearly belongs in a defined place, a rubbish heap of one kind or another.[6]

The two stages here distinguished, by which things become rubbish, correspond almost exactly to the isotopics "aggregate" and "magma." It is a process of "pulverizing, dissolving and rotting"—thereby including material transformations that are as much organic as technical—which will usher things from the first to the second stage. In the prevailing system, "purity" would then correspond to an ordered state, prior to the appearance of waste, or after its orderly transformation and disposal. Between the two is that "dangerous" moment when order is disturbed, which is due, in part, to the "memorial" component of waste prior to its amalgamation. I will speak more on this below.

Our daily experience offers many instances of this attitude toward waste. Indeed, waste is bothersome, and we often are preoccupied with hiding and collecting it, getting rid of it from our rooms, kitchens, apartments, and so on. In contemporary society, the care of regularly ridding our homes of waste is entrusted to efficient specialized services, which remove it from sight. For some time now, as a home owner, I have had to pay an "environmental sanitation tax" to defray the cost of precisely such a service. The waste is then hauled out of the city and dumped in landfills, often attaining gigantic proportions. In this way, cities have been literally ringed by a garbage belt which, in the absence of fortifying walls, delimits the urban space—that is, until we had recourse to incineration as an alternative means of disposal.[7]

We have already reached the point of national, even continental, expulsion of waste: "First World" countries export their toxic waste to the "Third World" in order to protect themselves from its dangers. Such scandalous trade, which perfectly obeys the logic described by Douglas, wound up rousing such popular indignation that it has been checked, if not halted altogether. But in the future, what shall we do with waste? For in the age of globalization, the village extends globally, while the face of the earth seems destined to take the shape of a monstrous megalopolis. There is no other exterior space into which waste can be cast out, unless, of course, we "export" it to an outer space, already polluted with countless space litter.[8]

In such circumstances the issue of waste disposal, or maintaining civic order and purity, takes on an almost existential dimension. How can we keep from being buried and thus endangered by our own waste? In this context, the German word *Entsorgung* finds its full appositeness: someone—a moral agent, a government authority, or a technical service—must assume the "care" *(die Sorge)* of removing waste. The word itself is child of the ill-ease introduced by the threat of nuclear waste, when it was realized that no method of disposal (submersion beneath the ocean, burial deep within the earth's crust, the construction of cement containers) could sufficiently protect us from the dangers of toxic nuclear waste. Generalized from this particular context, the term has come to express—and not without echoing the existential thrust of the Heideggerian "care," discussed by Hans Ulrich Gumbrecht in Chapter 7—the collective desire to disburden ourselves of the worries *(Sorge* in German, as well) of waste disposal by entrusting it to the care of specialized bodies.

Returning to Douglas, Jonathan Culler took issue with the static aspect of her treatment of the question.[9] In actual fact, though it is indeed rigorously synchronal, her approach is not static for all that. She postulates the existence of a liminal zone, between interior and exterior, where waste eventually terminates. This permits her to emphasize the ambivalence, in any system, that attends the categories of "waste" and, by extension, "disorder" and "impurity":

> Granted that disorder spoils pattern; it also provides the materials of pattern. Order implies restriction; from all possible materials, a limited selection has been made and from all possible relations a limited set has been used. So disorder by implication is unlimited, no pattern has been realized in it, but its potential for patterning is indefinite. This is why, though we seek to create order, we do not simply condemn disorder. We recognize that it is destructive to existing pattern; also that it has potentiality. It symbolizes both danger and power.[10]

Because of this fringe zone, the system remains open and retains contact with its other: waste and impurity. And while crossing this zone, the notion of waste can revert. A dynamic specific to the system can then unfold: the positive values of purity and order can prove bearers of sterility and death, while waste will turn out to provide energy and resource. Waste thus represents, in terms of the system, a potential source of revitalization.[11]

We might ask ourselves if we are not witnessing, in the cultural domain, a phenomenon that answers to the same logic. Following Douglas, the acculturation of waste could in fact be conceived of as an instance of the system taking an interest in its alterity and, after the stages of rejection and exclusion, establishing a new relation with its refuse. What once could only be regarded as waste, and treated accordingly, can henceforth be reintegrated in the system, recycled in a secondary process of production. Impurity thus suddenly finds itself newly valued.[12]

VALUE

During its 1992–1993 season, the *Théâtre des deux mondes*, in collaboration with Turin's *Teatro dell'Angelo*, staged the play *"Terre promise / Terra promessa"* (Promised Land) in Montreal. With nothing but pure gesture, no words, the production cast a stone slab in the lead role, if we can put it that way. A sequence of mimed scenes "told" the story of this object, which we might interpret as an allegory of an abridged history of civilization: after a variety of practical uses, the slab loses all usefulness and is discarded, only to be salvaged and to wind up placed in a museum as the centerpiece in a Zen garden.

This reenacted biography of an inert object illustrates nicely Michael Thompson's theory of waste.[13] The anthropologist provides us with a dynamic approach to the category of "rubbish," an approach that, as the subtitle to his book indicates, is centered around the notion of value. Not only does "rubbish" unfailingly summon the question of value, Thompson goes so far as to claim that "rubbish" is the category best suited to considerations of the processes of value-change in society. He hypothesizes that these processes necessarily involve the category of "rubbish," and he concludes: "The delightful consequence of this hypothesis is that, in order to study the social control of value, we have to study rubbish."[14]

In his often provocative argument, Thompson affirms, then, that the dynamic potential of every system (in terms of value-change) resides in rubbish itself. According to Thompson, and contrary to what seems to be the case with Douglas, the system, as a rule, has a history. For heuristic reasons, he prefers to reduce this history to the biography of concrete objects. In our theatrical example, it turns upon the life story of a "natural" object, subjected to various human usages. With Thompson, on the other hand, it is always a matter of artifacts, of objects produced by humans, more often than not by industrial means.[15] Yet his focus on the object whose biography he chronicles represents, in itself, an important shift with respect to histories of an anthropocentric kind—those that inevitably regard the human as subject and the object as "thing," fabricated, manipulated, and eventually destroyed. From Thompson's perspective, the object becomes the subject of its own history, with its own biographical course.[16] This approach effectively decenters the human subject, making it just one agent among many: that is, it reduces the human subject to just one of the contextual factors in the history of the object.

According to Thompson, the biography of every artifact is articulated in three stages, characterized by the different attitudes of users-consumers toward the artifact and, above all, by changes in what value the objects possess. As for the evolution of its value, every object, in principle, goes through two "catastrophes,"[17] yielding the following biographical sequence:

First stage: "transient value," which corresponds, *grosso modo*, to the use-value of the object and decreases over time and with use.

Second stage: "zero value," or the moment the object loses all use-value, at which point it falls within the category of "rubbish."

Third stage: "permanent value," where the artifact enters a new phase and category by acquiring an aesthetic, a museological, or a historical value. This value, moreover, can amount financially to rather significant sums, sums that in the end exceed, and often by far, the use-value of the object.

A more or less strict rule applies to this axiological progression of objects, according to Thompson: there is no direct transition from "transient value" to "permanent value," no way to bypass the category of "waste." In fact, this attributes great importance to a category of objects that we normally tend to remove or eliminate altogether, whether because of their worthlessness or threat of impurity and disorder (cf. Douglas' theory).[18]

Though very different, the theorizations of Douglas and Thompson are complementary, being that one is centered on the purity of the system and the other on the value of objects. After the rigorously synchronal approach of *Purity and Danger*, *Rubbish Theory* has the advantage of conceding a historical dimension to the systems under consideration and biographical histories to the objects examined. His approach articulates an intrasystemic dynamic. Once having become "waste," in the economic sense of the term, artifacts are not necessarily expelled from the system. Granted, these worthless objects often are cumbersome, and we generally prefer to stash them away—we all have our castoffs, old (almost) worthless objects we keep in the attic, the basement, at the back of the closet, or in the bottom drawer—but they remain, in some sense, on hand for possible progression to the last stage of their lives, a stage, however, that not all will reach.

To his credit, Thompson forces us to reflect on the status of these objects in limbo, awaiting a categorical change. In their own biographies, they are sort of *in transit*, in that "non-place," as yet uninformed of their new destination.[19] It is on the basis of this particular condition, which for Thompson represents the lowest axiological moment, that we can raise a number of objections in regard to his theory and thus reveal a few of its limitations. Three reservations in particular need addressing:

In the first place, "zero value" is an unwarranted simplification, for the value of an object is never economic alone. This, moreover, is one of the reasons that account for our scarcely rational behavior, from the perspective of daily economy, toward objects said to be worthless. Well after losing all use-value, an object can retain our interest for the memorial or affective value invested in it, which is why a worthless object is not necessarily without value to us.[20] Besides, the "zero value" that Thompson posits as the lowest axiological level can be reduced further still. An object that has become rubbish can take on a negative value, whether because of the threat it poses, following Douglas' theory, or because of the costs involved in its disposal.

Secondly, even "permanent value" is not as fixed as Thompson suggests. A change in aesthetic tastes, political regimes, or simply museum directors—or a combination of all three—can cause an object that has already reached the stage of permanent value to fall in our estimation. Unforeseen by Thompson, such vicissitudes may come about from mere forgetting, from an aesthetic or an ideological revaluation, from a desanctifying gesture, and so on. In this way, the tripartite schema of the theory does not take in the many turns that an object can suffer in its biography.

Finally, while Thompson's theory has the advantage of making us consider the wealth of objects making up our environment since the Industrial Age, one must recognize that it really only concerns a fraction of these objects. Most are hindered from completing the biographical course the theorist delineates for them in principle, whether due to material changes (this being the case for all objects of an organic nature) or their massive elimination by all of those services that rid us of worthless objects. Material persistence is a *conditio sine qua non*, but it is no guarantee that an object will reach the last step of its biography. A positive act of selection by a junk dealer, an artist, the curator of a museum, or a collector is still necessary.

Let us take some literary examples, for literary texts stage, by narrative fictions, the moment of selection whereby rubbish-objects complete the full cycle of destruction and creation of value. Hanta, the main character in Czech novelist Bohumil Hrabal's *Too Loud a Solitude*, is a professional book compactor.[21] Each day he transforms wasted books by the ton into old paper; each day, however, he saves a few books from the voracious hydraulic press and takes them home where, little by little, he builds a true bibliophile's library.

In *Gemini*, Michel Tournier invents—besides Alexandre Surin, "dandy of the dumps"—a character who specializes in salvaging from among the rubbish heaps worthless old objects destined for destruction:

> For my part, what I recognize in Briffaut is the all-round salvage man, able to be mechanic, old clothes man, dealer in junk, in paper, even in antiques. . . . He believes he has a mission which requires him to rescue things that have been thrown away, restore them to their lost dignity—more than that—to confer upon them an even

greater dignity: since, on being salvaged, they are promoted to the rank of *antique*. I have watched him at work on a rubbish heap. I have seen him extract a cracked porcelain coffee pot from the pile. With what priestly slowness he caressed the old utensil, turning it between his hands, running his finger over its scars and peering into its interior! That was the crucial moment! The coffee pot had been thrown away, it was no longer worth anything. Yet by an edict that depended on him alone, he could raise it to a value far above that of a similar brand-new object by sanctifying it as an antique.[22]

The story of this coffee pot, salvaged from the dump and sanctified an antique, illustrates marvelously Thompson's theory of the creation of value, which intercedes following the "zero value" stage in an object's life. Discarded, already buried in the shapeless mass of household garbage, it is "no longer worth anything," but this transition to the category of antique raises its value "far above that of a similar brand-new object."

But what of the rest, of all the objects mired in what Tournier calls "the soft white mass of refuse," in which this particular object was engulfed, intact, save for a few chips?[23] Undifferentiated, they are doomed in whole to the process of "pulverization, dissolution and rotting" that, according to Douglas, effects the transition of the impure object (for it is still perceived as an object) to the status of rubbish.

There is no need here to go into the multiple technical discourses of waste management, nor need we undertake to distinguish their methods of treatment. Nevertheless, we should bear in mind that the treatment of vast amounts of waste (which ever presupposes the destruction of discarded and worthless objects) poses today more than ever the question of value. The question is provocatively formulated in the title of Norbert Thomas' book, *Luxusware Müll*, which we might translate as *Trash, A Luxury Commodity*, or better still, *Luxuryware Rubbish*.[24] The title suggests, in fact, that not only can discarded objects, transformed into *Müll*—the singular collective of the German normally corresponds to "trash" or "rubbish"—once again become merchandise, they can even become luxury merchandise! Now this last aspect of the title is open to several interpretations: that our society enjoys the luxury of producing lots of waste; that the luxurious degree of our material well-being produces too much garbage; or even that a whole sector of the economy has come to be based on "waste" products, which cost some as dearly as any luxury, while others reap great profits.[25]

This book picks up the lively German debate, with its clear political overtones, that has arisen wherever economics and ecology converge. It underscores the economic value that waste can hold in such a debate—even when it does not wind up at an antique dealer, in a private collection, or in a museum—and, by that very fact, it suggests an additional aspect of Thompson's thesis. But a considerably broader issue lies behind the formulation of this economic value, one that we could qualify as societal or cultural, in the fullest sense of the word: the question of what kind of society we want to live in.

Thomas depicts two alternatives. On the one hand would be an advanced consumer society, in which the subject is defined by his or her capacity to acquire and expend consumer goods.[26] As we know, the production of enormous amounts of waste and the problem of their elimination are corollaries of this type of society. On the other hand, Thomas imagines a society that would otherwise distribute goods and riches and abandon the reckless pursuit of consumption. The problem of waste would be solved from the start by a decrease in production. But this "solution" presupposes a fairly radical change in values, or even mentality. Thomas reproaches German politicians for lacking the courage to commit themselves resolutely to this second type of society and for having de facto ratified the production-elimination scenario for vast quantities of waste.

It is in the context of this scenario that waste can become an important economic factor, indeed, a luxury commodity, but a commodity, as Gerard Bertolini suggests, with the status of resource.[27] Refuse would preserve a certain potential—much as Douglas suggested but according to an entirely different logic. On an economic level, this potential could take concrete form in the category of "resource," at which point, we could speak of a *socioeconomics of waste*, as the subtitle of Bertolini's book proposes.

Having once again become resource, waste would thus be reinserted within the economy out of which it had fallen, or from which it had been discarded during a first cycle of production-consumption. Meanwhile, this reintegration is possible only on the condition that things undergo a moment of negation as useful objects, a negation that can assume various concrete forms: an act of rejection, total devaluation, or material destruction. The economic revaluation of waste therefore occurs less in the form of recovered or salvaged objects than as a formless mass that must undergo a process of recycling in order to once again become material. It is only as salvaged material that waste can proceed to a second production cycle, at which time it occupies a place equivalent to the raw material in the first cycle. Seeing that it is a question of recycled raw material, we would be inclined to call it "secondary raw material"—at least that is the literal translation of the German technical term *Sekundärrohstoff*.

As potential resource, waste therefore reacquires value and becomes a commodity. It then can be treated as any other product, even traded on the stock exchange, on the condition, however, that it undergo a process of transformation, which sees it from a heterogeneous and degraded object back to the status of basic material (glass, metal, paper, etc.). In this way, it illustrates a kind of "creation of value" overlooked in Thompson's theory of waste. As a resource for a second cycle of production-consumption, waste represents a not-so-negligible economic factor in our society, one that is mobilizing numerous ventures and considerable capital at this moment.[28]

MEMORY

Without suggesting any simple or direct causal links, it is certainly within this twofold context of the problems created by the exponential increase in waste and its economic revaluation that a new way of dealing with the phenomenon of waste has arisen. The latter throws into relief a third semantic component of "waste": memory, and it occasions initiatives that explore the temporal dimension of the cultural phenomenon designated by "memory." Historiography has taken up waste as an object of knowledge. In fact, these days we see a scientific curiosity in the fate of that which humans discard, as well as what refuse can tell us about ourselves—in the attentions of both cultural history and anthropological archaeology.

Before taking up some recent studies in these fields, I will begin by formulating two paradoxes of sorts, which allow us to link the question of knowledge of the waste-object to memory. We will then have the opportunity to return to Douglas and Thompson, and to establish some connections between their otherwise rather dissimilar approaches. Rubbish, for Douglas, is an "in-between" state, both spatially and temporally: it describes an object bereft of its systemic functionality, though as yet not removed, a decayed object that finds itself "out of place," an object, then, that endangers order. In temporal terms, it concerns an object that has already lost its function in the system, that is no longer in use, but has not yet been discarded and cast outside of the system, where it will find its place henceforth. Here in this "in between," it retains an identity as a result of its ties to a former state of the system. Douglas recovers the memory of waste through the notion of identity. During this transitional moment, the waste-object still conserves all memorial capacities with regard to the system to which it once belonged. Debilitation of this memory goes hand in hand with removal of the waste-object and the material transformations that it endures. Though already out of place, the waste-object's memory-identity can be revived as long as it remains in between. This fleeting moment of subsisting memory also is the moment when waste represents the most virulent danger to the "purity" of the system.

It is, by definition, already doomed to oblivion, that is, to be rejected and put aside. But at this constitutive stage of the category of "waste," the object can still be recognized, removed though it may be, as having been part of the system. This moment of subsistence-intrusion thus confers upon it the dangerous power to enjoin: "remember!" In this sense, it is just as accurate to say that the waste-object is itself memorial as it is to say that it induces remembrance. In neither case, however, can memory be disassociated from its material presence.

Thompson describes a structurally and logically analogous characteristic of waste, but along epistemic lines: he begins with the very possibility of making waste an object of knowledge. Can waste be known?

> If rubbish resides in the gap between any cognitive framework of the universe and the universe, how, since we must always operate within a cognitive framework, can we ever see it? Alternatively, if we can see it, it must be within our cognitive framework, in which case it cannot be outside it which is where it is supposed to be if it is rubbish.[29]

From a strictly logical point of view, waste is either nonexistent or unknowable. Now it exists well enough, but it only holds the status of cultural category for the fleeting moment already described by Douglas—a point of view that Thompson winds up adopting in practically the same terms:

> That which we discard, shun, abhor, wash our hands of, or flush away, we are consigning to the rubbish category. Yet this is not quite correct. We only notice rubbish when it is in the wrong place. Something which has been discarded, but never threatens to intrude, does not worry us at all. . . . The discarded but still visible, because it still intrudes, forms a genuine cultural category of a special type—a rubbish category. That which is discarded but not visible, because it does not intrude, is not a cultural category at all, it is simply *residual* to the entire category system.[30]

From this we may conclude that what accounts for the memorial virulence attending the category of waste is equally what grounds the possibility of knowing those objects that are subsumable under this category. In any event, the two categorical determinations of waste are articulated according to the same quasi-paradoxical logic, making them concomitant. Consequently, knowledge is conditional upon the waste-object's negative, menacing, but transitory presence. This is equally what constitutes its memorial content and gives it the power to animate memory.

Knowledge and memory thus prove to be intimately linked when we undertake to include waste within a cognitive approach. Researchers who inquire into waste therefore have two scientific strategies available to them, both of which are in evidence today. On the one hand, one can go the route of an anthropology of waste, and on the other hand, of a cultural history of waste. In the space between, bridging the gap between anthropology and history is the archaeology of waste. Both the anthropological and historical approaches set out to understand a given human collectivity, its customs, behavior, and mind-set, by closely examining the waste it produces and casts aside.

Today the most widely known anthropological and archaeological study of waste is the project initiated by William Rathje toward the beginning of the 1970s at the University of Arizona.[31] The subtitle of his recent book, *What Our Garbage Tells Us About Ourselves*, sums up his anthropological concern. The project involves locating the observation point in that transitional moment that is the category of waste and understanding societies on the basis of what leaves through their back door. The ethnographic variant of this anthropology then physically proceeds with the daily gathering of the refuse produced by a collectivity, delivering at least part of this production to the table of the researcher, who then proceeds to count, classify, and register it. But above all, researchers make refuse speak! Indeed, the researchers set to work on the rubbishy materiality of their object; the latter interests them, however, only insofar as they can approach it as a sign and develop a method to systematically revive its memory. The material object is probed merely as a trace or as a memorial capsule. What interests the researchers is to seize its memorial potential, to disclose everything it "knows" about the society from which it came, specifically its structures, its behavior, and its material culture. Rathje and Murphy propose, moreover, to call this type of research "modern material-culture studies."[32]

Waste thus becomes the synecdoche for a whole complex sociocultural situation. It falls to the researcher to develop the necessary rhetoric to make it speak, to make it tell all it knows. It is then a matter of articulating not so much a discourse *on* waste but rather the discourse *of* waste itself: a discourse which, far from being content to base itself on an isolated object, receives its syntax from complex relations, from established proportions, from percentages calculated scientifically from the contents of trash cans. One emphatic assertion is meant to be retained: waste does not lie; it is the most truthful language a society holds with respect to itself.[33]

The archaeological variant of the anthropology of waste consists in reactivating "historical" waste: waste that has become "residue" by already being deposited in its proper place. The case related by Rathje and Murphy concerns a massive landfill in the state of New York, where industrial quantities of waste have been dumped since the beginning of the 1950s.[34] The researchers' method reminds one of the drilling done in geological exploration: a vertical probe takes samples of all the strata of deposited waste. These samples are subsequently analyzed, studied, and interpreted in order to awaken the by-now antiquated memory locked away in the objects drawn from the depths. To the anthropologist's work, which aims to understand the cultural practices of a society, is henceforth added the labor of the historian, whose task is to historically reconstruct a memory deposited in objects of an archaeological nature.

The authors draw on an anecdote, furthermore, in order to remind us of the proximity—in both the literal and figurative sense—between waste and ruins in the work of the archaeologist:

> To an archaeologist, ancient garbage pits or garbage mounds, which can usually be located within a short distance from any ruin, are always among the happiest of finds, for they contain in concentrated form the artifacts and comestibles and remnants of behavior of the people who used them. While every archaeologist dreams of discovering spectacular objects, the bread-and-butter work of archaeology involves the most common and routine kinds of discards. . . . When the British archaeologist Sir Leonard Woolley, in 1916, first climbed to the top of the ancient city of Carchemish, on the Euphrates River near the modern-day Turkish-Syrian border, he moistened his index finger and held it in the air. Satisfied, he scanned the region due south of the city—that is, downwind—pausing to draw on his map the location of any mounds he saw. A trench dug through the largest of these mounds revealed it to be the garbage dump. Woolley was certain it was, and the exposed strata helped establish the chronological sequence for the Carchemish site as a whole.[35]

Of course, no archaeologist would confuse ruins with waste; the latter could never claim the monumental status of the former. Their common function as documents, however, can lead them to be conflated in the work of reconstructing a historical reality from its attestative remains. In this sense, waste is just the flip side of the very monumentality that has its official aspect in the ruin. Since one cannot, in most cases, differentiate on the basis of the material composition of the objects that the archaeologist handles, the categorical classification between ruin and waste depends largely then on the researcher's point of view and his or her system of values.

Within a span of ten years, three major cities of the world—Paris, New York, and Berlin—mounted their own public exhibitions on waste.[36] For the time being, I will only consider Berlin, whose exhibition was held in 1995 and straddled ecology and history. Though organized under the auspices of the German Department of the Environment *(Bundesumweltamt)*, the exhibition dealt with a historical subject. The titular play on words, "*Geschichte(n) aus dem Müll*," effectively asserted the possibility of making *history* from waste, of activating the memory contained therein. But it also proposed to cull *stories* from waste—to take rubbish as the material basis with which to generate manifold narrative production—or even, to pluralize "history," to the extent that the same historical material could afford a historiography *from* waste or a historiography *of* waste. In fact, organizers of the exhibition, subtitled "*Abfall aus der Zeit Friedrichs des Großen*" (*Waste from the Time of Frederick the Great*), exploited both possibilities. The exhibition poster suggested some such thing. Its graphic design consisted of a montage of an eighteenth-century map of Berlin, superimposed on a color photograph of garbage unearthed in the course of digs carried out on the site of historic dumps in Berlin itself. The exhibition thus had as much to do with the history of Berlin as with the history of waste in the eighteenth century.

The latter type of historiography, which rehabilitates waste as a historical object, has caught on lately. This could be due to the vogue for certain new para-
digms of historiography, such as the *Histoire des mentalités*, the history of everyday
life, cultural history, and "New Historicism." To take just one example of a cultural history of waste, in her book *La Saga des ordures du Moyen Age à nos jours*
Catherine de Silguy retraces various stages in this history. Each chapter addresses
a specific aspect of the phenomenon as a whole: the battle against garbage, waste
sites in the urban landscape, recovery and recycling, and so on.[37]

Indeed, de Silguy's approach makes waste a "respectable" historical object
and contributes thereby to its interest in a cultural sense. But she does not partake, in any decisive way, in the task of conceptualizing waste. Whereas she only
employs the term "waste" in a figurative sense, the work of another historian accomplishes more in this regard by contributing a number of insights into the memorial dimension of "waste." That would be Greil Marcus, who takes up the
historiographer's task with one of Trotsky's metaphors: "the dustbin of history."[38]
Now, contrary to Trotsky, who fancied the dustbin of history for getting rid of
whatever had become "historical waste"—that is, those elements that had become residual in the course of history, historical agents divested of their role—
Marcus enjoys rummaging through dustbins. He takes a keen interest in the
rubbish of history, in everything that has occurred historically but has not been
retained by historiography or at least not by *official* historiography.

With this concern for what history has forgotten, rejected even, Marcus succeeds in revealing the gaps and fissures that throw official history into relief. In
seemingly insignificant chapters, he has written an alternative history, the flip side
of history. Above all, however, at least for our purposes, he reactivates the memory of historical waste by wresting it from a suspect oblivion, leaving room
thereby for the possibility of writing further historical narratives. As a system,
then, history is equally constituted by the ambivalent gesture of inclusion and exclusion, a gesture mirrored by the no-less-ambivalent one of valuation and devaluation. Yet what winds up in the dustbin of history, what is rejected and, in this
way, devalued, acquiring ipso facto the status of waste, can be reactivated to serve
as a support for counter-memory, a springboard for untold narratives. Thus even
when used as a figure of speech, the refuse found in the dustbin of history de-
ploys the memorial potential peculiar to the category of waste, while articulating
it with the two other semantic components of waste.

CONCLUSION

I am well aware of having privileged certain conceptual stakes of the category
"waste" over others, but I venture to think that the canvas of interrelations sketched
in this manner is detailed enough to warrant a conclusion.[39] A provisional

conclusion, granted; a conclusion open to subsequent research, which will come to correct and complete it. But a certain conceptual configuration already emerges, a configuration that I would begin by characterizing as paradoxical: waste is a category at once permanent and unstable, unavoidable and evanescent.

Waste is permanent and unavoidable, for there is no system—whether biological, technical, social, or historical—that does not produce remnants, remains, scraps, leftovers, that does not leave certain parts to decay, that does not secrete or reject. Anything in a system can become waste.

And it is unstable and evanescent, because waste is not meant to remain or perdure. It is but a category of transition, a limit-category. I have tried to apprehend this category in a dynamic between purity and pollution, between value and devaluation, between memory and forgetting. In a way, waste is the vector that points from the first to the second element in all three terminological pairings. It leads from the one without ever fully reaching the other, for as it tends toward the second term, the category of waste must decay and be nullified. It is that unstable position in which purity seesaws with impurity, value with nonvalue, memory with forgetting. The movement it describes, however, is never entirely accomplished. Were it to reach this limit-point, it would cease to be conceivable and, therefore, knowable.

From another perspective, waste itself appears as a limit, as a limit-object that indicates the transition within a given system from interior to exterior. Or, to put it in temporal terms, it marks the intrusion of the past into the present. From this vantage, what matters is the very ambivalence of the category "waste." For waste then appears in both the guise of systemic menace and regenerator. Waste lends itself as much to the operation of disposal, which presupposes material transformation if not destruction, as it does to the operation of recovery that presupposes the neutralization of its negativity.

Translated from the French by Brian Neville.[40]

NOTES

1. See my "Esthétiques du déchet," in *La mémoire des déchets: Essais sur la culture et la valeur du passé*, edited by Johanne Villeneuve, Brian Neville, and Claude Dionne (Québec: Nota Bene, 1999). My inquiry into the processes by which waste—as word, concept, or thing—enters the cultural sphere, and the ways in which it is articulated in aesthetics, stems from a preliminary reflection upon the reappropriation of cultural materials under the rubric of "recycling." See my "Le Recyclage culturel," in *Recyclages: Économies de l'appropriation culturelle*, edited by Claude Dionne, Silvestra Mariniello, and Walter Moser (Montréal: Les Éditions de Balzac, 1996).

2. Peter Sloterdijk, *Critique of Cynical Reason*, translated by Michael Eldred (Minneapolis: University of Minnesota Press, 1987), 151. The last line of inquiry also has been explored by Arthur Kroker and David Croo in their *The Postmodern Scene: Excremental Culture and Hyper-Aesthetics* (New York: St. Martin's Press, 1986).

3. Mary Douglas, *Purity and Danger: An Analysis of Concepts of Pollution and Taboo* (New York: Pelican, 1970).

4. The word corresponds to the German *Schmutz*, a term one finds in the title of Christian Enzensberger's literary essay, also inspired by Douglas' work: *Größerer Versuch über den Schmutz*, translated as *Smut; an Anatomy of Dirt*, translated by Sandra Morris (New York: Seabury Press, 1974). The French *souillure* properly translates the term, though *Schmutz* falls within the general province of *déchets*.

5. Douglas, op. cit., 7.

6. Ibid., 189.

7. As I approached the Argentinean city of Rosario one particularly gusty day, the plastic debris blowing in the wind and suspended in the trees around the city dump made this garbage belt clearly visible.

8. Today, experts estimate that there are 8,000 pieces of debris in space circling the planet.

9. See his *Framing the Sign: Criticism and Its Institutions* (Norman and London: University of Oklahoma Press, 1988), 168–82.

10. Douglas, op. cit., 114.

11. "Revitalization" is the term used by Virgil Nemoianu, who uses an analogous logic of inversion in theorizing the notion of "the secondary" (that which is not central to a system). See Virgil Nemoianu, *A Theory of the Secondary: Literature, Progress and Reaction* (Baltimore: Johns Hopkins University Press, 1989).

12. In the realm of aesthetics, Guy Scarpetta champions the cause of revaluation in his aptly titled book *L'impureté* (Paris: Grasset et Fasquelle, 1985).

13. Michael Thompson, *Rubbish Theory: The Creation and Destruction of Value* (Oxford: Oxford University Press, 1979).

14. Ibid., 10.

15. The example he treats in greatest detail is silk prints, kitsch objects fabricated in England from around 1879. Very fashionable at the outset, then disdained as being in poor taste, these prints have been coveted as collectibles and museum pieces ever since the 1960s.

16. This idea is further developed in the collection of essays edited by Arjun Appadurai, *The Social Life of Things: Commodities in Cultural Perspective* (Cambridge: Cambridge University Press, 1986); see esp. Igor Kopytoff, "The Cultural Biography of Things."

17. Thompson indeed draws upon René Thom's Catastrophe Theory.

18. This momentary absence of value is confirmed, moreover, on lexical grounds, particularly in English, where the predicates "useless" and "worthless" arise most frequently to qualify words such as rubbish and trash.

19. Marc Augé has attempted to theorize this "non-place." See Marc Augé, *Non-Places: Introduction to an Anthropology of Supermodernity*, translated by John Howe (London and New York: Verso, 1995).

20. Take the literary example of the stuffed, tattered parrot in Flaubert's "A Simple Heart," which Félicité worships to the point of confusing it with the Holy Ghost. Strictly speaking, the bird is worthless; still, it acquires for her the value of a sacred fetish.

21. Bohumil Hrabal, *Too Loud a Solitude*, translated by Michael Henry Heim (San Diego: Harcourt Brace Jovanovich, 1990).

22. Michel Tournier, *Gemini*, translated by Anne Carter (Garden City: Doubleday, 1981), 151–52.

23. Ibid., 101.

24. Norbert Thomas, *Luxusware Müll* (Düsseldorf: Zebulon, 1994).

25. Thomas argues the latter point, criticizing the "Grüner Punkt" system introduced by the German government as a way to bill producers of waste for the cost of its disposal.

26. On this topic, see Jean Baudrillard's *The Consumer Society: Myths and Structures* (London: Sage, 1998).

27. Gerard Bertolini, *Rebuts ou Ressources? La socio-économie du déchet* (Paris: Éditions Entente, 1978).

28. To take just one example among many, a recent article in the French magazine *L'Actualité* uses the term *alchemists* to describe researchers hired by the Canadian aluminum producer Alcan to produce metal from garbage. The article is subtitled, "At Alcan's Laboratories, Researchers Perfect the Materials of Tomorrow: Recycling Is the Watchword" (April 1, 1996): 50.

29. Thompson, op. cit., 79.

30. Ibid., 91–92.

31. William Rathje and Cullen Murphy, *Rubbish! The Archaeology of Garbage: What Our Garbage Tells Us about Ourselves* (New York: HarperCollins, 1992). The book recounts twenty years of research conducted by "garbologists" at the University of Arizona.

32. Ibid., 55.

33. "What people have owned—and thrown away—can speak more eloquently, informatively, and truthfully about the lives they lead than they themselves ever may" (ibid., 54). Rathje and Murphy base this claim on comparative studies that contrast a community's discourse on its consumption habits (established through interviews) with the "discourse of garbage," which irrefutably contradicts the former, revealing thereby the shortcomings of self-representation.

34. "The site was the Fresh Kills landfill, on Staten Island, in New York City, a repository of garbage that, when shut down, in the year 2005, will have reached a height of 505 feet above sea level" (ibid., 3).

35. Ibid., 10.

36. In Paris: *Déchets: L'Art d'accommoder les restes*, Centre Georges Pompidou, 1984. A catalogue was edited by Ariane Dellilez under the same title (Paris: Centre Georges Pompidou, 1984). In New York: *Garbage! The History and Politics of Trash in New York City*, at the New York Public Library, 1995. In Berlin: *Geschichte(n) aus dem Müll. Ein Austellung des Heimatmuseums Mitte im Umweltbundesamt*, 1995. The last title could be translated as *Histor(y)ies from the Trash*.

37. Catherine de Silguy, *La Saga des ordures du Moyen Age à nos jours* (Paris: Editions de l'Instant, 1989).

38. Greil Marcus, *The Dustbin of History* (Cambridge, Mass.: Harvard University Press, 1996).

39. To mention two further conceptual approaches, there is the psychoanalytic, based on the Freudian notion of anality, and the hermeneutic, which starts from the problem of the negation of meaning (whether in the form of the nonsignifying, of nonsense, or even the absurd).

40. The translator gratefully acknowledges the assistance of Jean Klucinskas.

6

Agencies

of Cultural

Feedback

The Infrastructure of Memory

WOLFGANG ERNST

These fragments I have shored against my ruins.
—T. S. Eliot, *The Waste Land*

RECYCLING INSTEAD OF FINALITY: the linearity of production—accumulation—consumption—devaluation—waste is being replaced by closed circuits, forcing memory-based culture to decode itself anew.

We have to get used to the fact that the possibility of recycling now applies to everything—no longer annihilation, but recycling. All historical relics—empires, the Church, communism, democracy, ethnic identities, conflicts, ideologies—can be endlessly recycled. History has not only materially stepped out of cyclical time to enter the economic order of recycling (as in the recycling of industrial and nuclear waste), but the form of history itself—with its narratives implying linear development—has lost its compulsory evidence. Art is aesthetic recycling; postmodernism provided the complementary cultural theory. The infrastructure of recycling, though, is less discursive, less apparent, and less symbolic; its nonimaginary memory is the archive.[1]

ARCHIVES

The practice of history provides a given society with the tools and institutions for processing its documentary relics (books, texts, narratives, registers, records, techniques, architectures, rituals, etc.) in organized *forms of remanence*,

monumentalizing them by law and with structures that transform the experience of time in protest against its passing.[2]

The idea of accumulating everything in a kind of general archive is a product of Modernity. Nevertheless, the archive is born of disorder;[3] the disorder of
images that once characterized the sales rooms, artists' studios, and *dépôts* of old
galleries makes sense once again from the perspective of chaos theory (the concept of entropy, as the second law of thermodynamics, has found its way into
cultural analysis). Under the roof of a then-deserted (now burned down) ware-
house on the Quai de la Seine, the studio of Parisian artist Pascal Kern represented such an interim step in the transition from art to archive: "A disorder of
sorts reigns in the images Pascal Kern shows us, a disorder of objects, materials,
allusions, in the image of the surroundings in which he lives and works upon
memories of wandering and drifting in derelict places, like waste sites, abandoned houses, and factories."[4]

At the beginning of the nineteenth century, after the ruptures of tradition
brought on by political and economic revolutions, a sense of loss created the discursive need for history in its emphatic sense. As a result of Napoleon's secular-
ization of church property, vast archives were opened to the European public,
which—like the delayed opening of the Vatican State Secret Archives around
1880—led to a sudden mass output of past data. Much of this data, decontextu-
alized from its former surroundings, was immediately turned into waste paper; in
fact, parchments were occasionally used as food packaging. As late as 1855, the
Berlin newspaper *Vossische Zeitung* (no. 124, May 25) announced, under the
rubric of "Miscellanea," the trial of an archivist at Nuremberg who had sold historic documents as waste paper and kept valuable *parergonal*, or supplementary,
materials such as seals, copper, and wax. Attached to the immateriality of philological information is a material margin, which we tend to consider in the monumental terms of value, rather than in a documentary way. By concentrating
hermeneutic attention on the meaning of the texts and channeling their semantics historiographically, that is, by mediating it in typography, the materiality of
manuscripts, as writing supports, became, in a sense, redundant.[5]

To counter-balance the loss of contextualized meaning, a philosophical construct of an emphatic idea of history was needed, together with pragmatic institutions, such as the post–Napoleonic source-editing enterprise *Monumenta
Germaniae Historica* in Berlin, sites for the storage of material artifacts, such as the
Germanisches Nationalmuseum at Nuremberg, and magazines for all kinds of
printed matter, such as the German Library at Leipzig (*Deutschen Bücherei*, from
1916). These institutions subjected desemioticized artifacts to a process of re-
semiosis,[6] transforming the archaeological status of both texts and objects as
monuments into documents of a history prefigured mainly in the narrative of the
nation. At the same time, this symbolic registration and transformation made

originals, in a sense, superfluous, once more condemning them to waste, since they would be symbolically preserved in other forms of writing. What transforms waste (monuments) into evidence (documents) is a hermeneutic operation, an archaeological act of historicization that turns, following Hegel's distinction between *Erinnerung* and *Gedächtnis*, exterior memory into meaningful remembrance. At work here are non-narrative, non-discursive *parerga* and regimes of description, such as signatures, inventories, and catalogues.

Prussian historian Leopold von Ranke put the confusing mass of Venetian diplomatic reports (*relazioni*, once the *feedback* medium of the republic's politics) in order by synecdochically recounting them as histories. What occurs in the guise of historical representation, that is, in temporalizing narrative, is in fact an effect of synchronization, of *cultural recycling*. The archival structures of information on the past converge in a radical presence of data; seen from an archival perspective, this kind of memory loses its association with a deep temporal dimension in favor of a cybernetic equation of past and present. Thus, we might say, *there is no memory*, unless inscribed metaphorically, that is, in spatial terms (as Ranke had done in describing the Venetian state archives).[7]

In the age of the Weimar Republic, the task of German archives, as defined by archivist Ernst Zipfel in 1926,[8] was the processing and storing of administrative documents in *real time*, in order to serve the needs of a democratic society. Between *memory* and the *real time analysis* of events, the archaeology of the present replaced history with an immediate archival *feedback*. The then director of the *Reichsarchiv*, Ernst Müsebeck, formulated the archival recycling of documents as a political task; he saw archives as a means to make governmental activity transparent. He actually asked that traditional archivists (usually medievalists) be replaced by professional "generalists."[9]

Today, electronic data processing provides storage and retrieval capacities that make it possible to actually *simulate the archive*. Instructions such as "memory" in the text-saving menus of computer software are a semantic archaism. In a way, these are not memories at all but data banks; the computer maintains the illusion of memory by translating its operations back into a language with which we are culturally familiar. The difference between presence and storage of data, though, is just a function of directing codes. In information technology, which governs the real, this difference has already been done away with; during the Gulf War, both missiles and news (about missiles) were in principle transmitted by similar (or the same) electronic rays. What we call memory is nothing but information scattered on hard or floppy disks, waiting to be activated and recollected into the system of data processing. *Monitoring*, as data representation, is nothing but a recursive move in respect to the human reader, the terminal being a *museal* display space against a background of archaeological silence (the silence of algorithmically computing numbers).

ARCHAEOLOGY

In 1869, architect and engineer J. T. Wood identified the temple of Artemis, one of the ancient wonders of the world, in the once Greek, now Turkish city of Ephesos. Wood managed to excavate parts of the ruins to secure fragments for the British Museum—*columnae caelatae*, figurative bases of columns from the period prior to and after the burning of the temple: "But the effort of raising these huge pieces of sculpture from such a depth led to an utter disregard of the plan of the temple as a whole, a problem which was never correctly solved."[10] Waste is not only the subject of the archaeological inquiry into the architecture of the past but also the result of a de(con)struction inherent to archaeological practice itself. The hunt for trophies is blind to structures, leaving possible evidence of (immaterial) relations in disorder: "Since then this site . . . has remained a desolate waste. A recent visitor expressed himself thus: '. . . Better to have left it covered than create such damage.'"[11]

Archaeological artifacts are immediately subjected to a semiotic gaze that turns them into decipherable historic documents,

> a database which, for the most part, has undergone a change of state by virtue of its very entry into the domain of the discipline. From *in situ* and unknown, to removed and researched, before it has any impact on knowledge, the evidence has largely lost its original integrity. Its meaning rests only in the information attached to it in the form of associated records.[12]

The act of registration, of inscription and contextualization, relates to the object in a *parergonal* way, transforming it from waste into a semiophor.[13] David Crowther differentiates between two kinds of artifact attributes: intrinsic (material, decoration) and relative (context, history, function). It is at this point that the material defect of semiotics, with respect to the materiality of the support, becomes apparent. In a way, their status as waste preserves artifacts, but this *memory of waste* is being destroyed in the very act of recalling it to hermeneutic attention by excavation:

> This change of state is more than just conceptual, it is physical. Material once in a state of equilibrium with its burial environment, be it waterlogged wood or copper alloy from a dry site, will begin to deteriorate unless elaborate steps are taken to secure its welfare. Such a resource is therefore in constant jeopardy and requires long-term care and management to minimize its inevitable devaluation and decay. It is a measure of the direct social relevance of archaeology that the repositories for its raw material, semi-digested or otherwise, should be public institutions whose principle functions are the provision of a cultural service.[14]

Up to now, archaeology has snatched cultural-historical values from the soil to supply museum storerooms; today, industrial and rubbish archaeology analyzes the present in *real time*. Memory is not immediately linked to the past but rather becomes radically present—present not in a historical but in an archaeological sense. Only by interpretative supplements, such as discursive texts, is evidence being transformed into the memory of a cognitive past.

The increase in archaeological disorder is the law of history as physics of time (Bolzmann). Close to the Mediterranean harbor of Alexandria, maritime archaeologists appear recently to have traced the fragments of another ancient wonder of the world; seven meters beneath the surface of the water, they have discovered a landscape littered with blocks of stone, which could be reread as the relics of its lighthouse (the *Pharos*). But it requires historical discourse, that is, narrative, to make sense of a heap of blocks. In Palestine, such stones are charged with multiple meanings; the fragments are not inherently gifted with any memory whatsoever but are linked to memories in conflicting perceptions.[15]

The aggregation of waste in archaeology is the deposit. What is required is a hypertextual rather than a narrative processing of such data, the return of the transparency of the palimpsest and the consequent relinquishing of the paradigm of hi/story in favor of archaeology proper—"the configuration of a space-as-information-model, within a historical context."[16] R. Boast and D. Chapman apply such a hypertextual model to excavation reports, visualizing the interrelationships between recorded and interpretative information entities:

> Archaeological interpretation has always referred ultimately to deposition. . . . Deposit is the basic constituent of all archaeological constructions by the nature of the record. Archaeologists do not have access to events, but to the depositional consequences of events. This creates a primacy of deposition and stratigraphy to which all other data must ultimately relate.[17]

Archimagination turns data clusters into decipherable patterns. The excavation of the prehistoric urban dwelling of Catalhöyük, on the Anatolean plateau, overseen by Cambridge University (and recently concluded under Ian Hodder), led to the discovery of all sorts of ornamental figures on artifacts, which raised the open question of whether these were evidence of pure aesthetic play or encoded messages requiring pattern recognition. The electronic video documentation of the excavation was provided by the Academy of Design and the Center for Art and Media Technology at Karlsruhe. This kind of digital memory serves purposes of both documentation and virtual reconstruction through computer animation; as such, it effaces the traditionally substantial difference between registration (the archive) and imagination (virtual reality), with the wire-frame model in archaeological sampling serving as mediator.[18]

Archaeology is a science which, in order to gain knowledge, has to simultaneously destroy its own body of evidence; the cost of cultural historical memory is the production of waste. Being exposed to all kinds of light and weather by excavation, the excavated structures are exposed to further ruination. Archaeology is, then, the science of waste; sampling is its method and basic operation, since its findings are always already latent, waiting to be recycled.[19] Historical imagination is dependent on figuration; the archaeological *waste land* does not provide (in terms of rhetorical figures) t(r)opological landmarks for such imagination. The perception of archaeological data clusters is being seduced by and to historical imagination—first in the medium of narrative and its institutional setup (the museum) and recently by *virtual reality*—as though the past, as history, had not always already been just that.

From the years 205 to 208, Emperor Septimius Severus provided for the public display of a marble ground plan of the city of Rome. Only since 1562 has the memory of the fragmented *pianta marmorea* been restored, step by step; Bellori edited some fragments in 1673, under the title *Fragmenta vestigii veteris Romae*. Archaeology has made countless efforts to reconstruct the whole plan, but perhaps its fragmentary state is a more adequate representation of reality than any imaginary totality: "The city of today is no longer characterized by hierarchies and differences: it appears as a set of disconnected fragments. At the same time, architects can no longer make use of those instruments of urban control that originated with the modern era."[20]

The modern desire for planning and ordering the ancient map of Rome is constantly undermined by archaeological *monumenti non localizzati* and *frammenti con topografia non identificata*; in the epigraphical index to the publication of the remaining fragments, even the first letters of inscribed words are occasionally missing, thereby thwarting the possibility of ordering knowledge alphabetically. What the visitor gets is an attempted reconstruction, a kind of *rhizome* on the interior court walls of the present *Museo Capitolino*; only the taxonomic museum medium can try to make memory out of relics. "Rome, as it now exists, has grown up under the Popes, and seems like nothing but a heap of broken rubbish, thrown into the great chasm between our own days and the Empire, merely to fill it up," as one American put it.[21]

Alternatively, archaeology practices *cluster analysis*—a non-discursive statistical technique and the true *memory of waste*. The *Monte Testaccio* in Rome is exclusively composed of fragments of ancient vessels (amphorae); its archaeological *cluster analysis* does not strive for aesthetic values, such as specimens of ancient art, but rather it provides a data bank on ancient economy. German archaeologist Heinrich Dressel discovered this informational value in a first dig in January 1872, subsequently registering and publishing the ancient trademark stamps from the vessel fragments on forty-five pages of the venerable *Corpus Inscriptionum*

Latinarum—Roman past means mass data, whether as town or as empire: a veritable *Read Only Memory*. Those digs have resumed: "With all the fiscal information it contains, painted on fragments of the oil amphorae, it constitutes the only economic archive of the Roman Empire."[22] Information is what counts: "the documentary value is the chief result." The computer transforms the materiality of broken, inscribed pieces into the immateriality of information: "While stamps and inscriptions, imprinted and painted on the pottery fragments, are turning into information 'bits', the decipherings of their meaning, the features associating them, the people and activities they hint at, remain the most intriguing theme of the research."[23]

"There is a pile of sand, but no history":[24] The entropy of traces is a case for archaeology, which outstrips the capacities of historical imagination. Here the computer disposes of a better memory of waste on which to *count*; only its calculating operations are able to make sense out of the apparent chaos. Waste is the sublime catastrophe of imagination, which only the sublime mathematics of a difference machine can restore to visualization by a computing called *imagineering*, that is, the metonymic transformation of non-intuitive data into graphics. Thomas Quarry proclaimed it from Casablanca in an advertisement for IBM:

> A sliver of bone revealed a chunk of history when Dr. Jean-Jacques Hublin unearthed a few fossilized skull fragments. Then Dr. Hublin and a team of IBM scientists fed this shattered jigsaw puzzle into a unique program called Visualization Data Explorer. The tiny pieces helped form an electronic reconstruction of our early ancestor, the first *homo sapiens*. This new IBM technology has turned time back 400,000 years, uncovering clues to the origins of mankind.[25]

Calculation beyond human cognition is capable of solving the riddles of the past. The computer has restored the Sphinx in front of the pyramid of Cheops in detail; Mark Lehner of the Oriental Studies Institute at the University of Chicago, Illinois, has superimposed photographs of the Sphinx with portraits from the statues of pharaohs; through photogrammetric composite pictures, he has reconstructed the most probable archetype of the Sphinx, which might bear the features of Pharaoh Chefren (fourth dynasty). Over centuries, the figure had been buried by the blowing sands; around 1400 B.C.E., the Sphinx was unearthed and restored by Pharaoh Thutmosis IV (according to an ancient text, the Sphinx had spoken to the sovereign, then a prince, promising him the throne of Egypt if only he would remove the sand).

Do archaeological ruins still speak? In 1896, A. S. Murray visited the ancient site of Ephesos and reported on its entropic state: "The entire area was overgrown with vegetation, and the few visible remains were lying about in such confusion that no definite plan could be distinguished."[26] This is a kind of disorder that human capacities of *pattern recognition* can no longer decipher; only as data arrays, and only in a different architecture, can these traces once more become legible—the *architexture* of chips and information systems. The ruin of the former *Frauenkirche* cathedral, one of the casualties of the Second World War bombardment of the city of Dresden, is currently being transformed into a serial magazine of shelves, storing the array of individual stones currently being registered digitally by computer programs, in order to reconstruct the building from its scattered elements. The virtual reality of the *Frauenkirche* is *interval* memory, memory *in the meantime*.[27] The same is true of a project undertaken by the Parisian *École française d'Extrême Orient*, envisaging the reconstruction of the 900-year-old ancient Baphuon temple of Angkor in Kambodia. For that purpose, around 500,000 stones, scattered about the ruin, have to be restored to their previous emplacement. An infographics company provides three-dimensional photographs for the computer modeling of the temple, which then provide a conceptual grid in which to insert the fragment.[28] Once again, the computer provides a better memory of waste than does historical, that is, human, imagination. Every religious service repeats the Judeo-Christian injunction to remember ("Do this in the name of my remembrance") at the moment of the transubstantiation of the Holy Spirit; this imperative can now be programmed. But however virtually objects can be saved from destruction, we may exclaim with Chandler: "We now seek the Temple in vain; the city is prostrate, and the goddess gone."[29]

While most classic industrial zones in Europe are presently being transformed into open-air museums of the Industrial Age, these areas are suffering severely from a very different kind of tangible heritage: the burden of waste disposal and soil contamination over the last 200 years, a kind of memory that is difficult to deal with in aesthetic ways. In fact, museums of industrial heritage function as a distraction from actual industrial legacies, that is, the contaminated soil as a chemical store. Soil, industrial fallow land, is the true tragic archive. For an example of storage as semiotic challenge, Thomas Sebeok has asked how a depository of nuclear waste can be made noticeable for future generations, ones that may no longer be acquainted with the current alphanumerical code.[30]

How to collect waste? The classical rhetorics of *recollection*, described by Frances Yates as an *Art of Memory*, corresponded to the order of the museum. The (public) museum's space for historically internalized cultural recollection is spatially separated from its (hidden) storage space. Whereas Hegel, in his *Phenomenology of Spirit*, made this correspondence an element of the philosophy of history, Walter Benjamin broke with such assumptions; and where Hegel considers the process of digestive remembrance to be the interiorization of the past *(Er-Innerung)*, Benjamin associates a contrary exteriorization of the self, which explodes the confines of its private interiority with involuntary memory:

The "disorder" of this anarchic *Bildraum* (which, if spatial, is anything but homogeneous) dislocates the orderly "gallery of images." The *Weltgeist* passes in review the procession of its "monuments," the *Geister*, which successively "relieve" one another after their respective turns of duty.[31]

MEMORY/INFORMATION/MEDI@RCHAEOLOGY

Owing to a semiosis that turns materialities and corporealities into immaterialities and pure information, the explosion of media has contributed to a radical transformation of the relation of objects to time and space. In the age where speed brings about the disintegration of the categories of space and time, and where dematerialized information is stocked in recording systems in real time, places such as the museum become nostalgic retro-effects.

If culture, according to Juri Lotman and B. A. Uspenski, is defined by its capacities to transform the inclination toward oblivion into memory,[32] then the growing predominance of intermediary storage *(Zwischenlager)* contributes to a radical transformation of the economy of history. The ideal of accumulation is part of the humanist legacy: to Renaissance readers, the letter of the text was latent energy waiting to be activated by the act of reading-as-interpretation; this notion is being replaced by circulation, to borrow a New Historicist term, by recycling "mnemonic energies" (Aby Warburg). The paradox is that the electronic *media* create (falsely, technically speaking) the illusion of an immediate access to the past. Around 1900, this treasure had become partially dead capital. UI Order No. 43, of January 9, 1905—issued by F. Althoff, of the Prussian Ministry of Education, to the Director General of the Royal Library in Berlin and to the directors of Prussian university libraries—requested that "dead books" be stored apart from contemporary collections, or that out-of-use books even be destroyed.[33]

In fact, capital strives to minimize the temporal extent of storage (which is, thus, "dead capital"); by a supply-demand relationship aiming at real time, the electronic supply system of the Benetton company virtually programs its storage time to zero. Electronic random access to the stores turns memory into the omnipresence of commodities. What looks like a by-product of this recycling is in fact the establishment of a new *epistemé*, the standardization of knowledge, which is technically concealed, while producing a cult of cultural difference on the surface.

What will happen to the "memory of waste" under conditions of electronic storage, when the hermeneutic instrument for differentiating between value and rubbish in things to be stored is abolished in order to make place for a cybernetic register of non-hierarchical hypertexts? The electronic age succeeds in erasing the opposition between monumental inscription and discursive flow.

Precision and fast variability exist side by side; digital codes are able to register and undo those registers in virtual real time.[34] The analysis of the restructuring of our relationship to the past has to be as fast as its object; to achieve this, negotiation with what we perceive as past has to be freed from the supremacy of historical discourse, which has controlled such negotiations for the last 200 years. What is needed under postmodern conditions is the free accessibility to storage spaces.

The computer is not interested in the analytical laws of identity and difference but rather in algorithms to master data. Thinking must assume the form of computing: combining and devaluating the semiotic status of representation. The stable relation between sign and reference will be undone in favor of juxtaposing signs—which has already been the spatial principle of museums, archives, and libraries. Argumentation is being replaced by notation.[35] But, against the hypertextual euphoria of free navigation through data landscapes, and the liberation of the text from Gutenberg-era bulwarks against the seemingly arbitrary and endless shift of signifiers, our attention should be directed to the kind of barriers that arrest such flow in a nonarbitrary way, restrictions such as passwords. Engineering of memory involves hierarchical modularization; each module strives at hiding as much information about its own processing as possible—*information hiding*.[36]

The restructuring of our relationship with the past (Hegel's *Aufräumarbeiten*) undoes the supremacy of historical discourse, which for such a long time has distracted attention from the recursive practice of information storage. Feedback, replacing linearity, declares a moratorium on narrative.

> An "information sickness"—caused by the speed and quantity of what impinges on us, and abetted by machines we have invented, that generate endless arrays—threatens to overwhelm personal memory. The individual, we complain, cannot "process" all this information, this incoming flak. . . . Can public memory still be called memory, when it is increasingly alienated from personal and active recall?[37]

What will happen to the art of memory when mass media—with their accent on selecting current documentation—tend increasingly to privilege the present over the past? The digitization of images decouples them from their denotative reference in real archives; *memory* is being transformed cybernetically into synchronic information networks. This decontextualization has been put forward already by analogue techniques of reproduction (e.g., photocopy).

We have come to the point where the world no longer experiences itself in terms of life evolving in time but rather as a network interfering with itself; a Cartesian net of coordinates requires the transformation of aesthetics into computable discourse analysis. Storage replaces expansion; the placement of items is being defined by its relations and described formally in terms of arrays, trees, and grids. The ordering of coded elements, their distribution in structures, or at ran- dom, becomes a function of memorial capacities. Demography makes this challenge transparent: we have arrived at an epoch where space is represented in terms of storage relations.[38]

The Internet has turned the notion of the archive into a metaphor for *data retrieval*:

> It was soon realized that each site providing its own anonymous *ftp* area with its own material would make it difficult to find and catalogue the available information. The answer to this problem was to provide archives; machines dedicated to the task of serving files via anonymous *ftp*. These archives collect together material from other anonymous *ftp* areas scattered through the Internet and present it in a single location.
>
> The job of the archive maintainers is to keep the archives up-to-date and to try and organise them in an orderly fashion.[39]

Registers of symbolic memory (museums, archives, libraries) are about to lose touch with the digital cybernetics of information storage, consequently turning cultural memory itself into a museum space.

The electronic archive no longer emphatically differentiates between memory and waste. There is no technical distinction between sense and nonsense, syntax and semantics; the spacing of *différance*, of delay of perception, is being annihilated. Opening spaces of reflection, of suspense, of *epoché*, may turn out to be the function of the museum, as opposed to the accelerated processing of data today. Now that the real space of the museum has lost its pride of place as the most advanced storage medium, in matters of cultural and image memory (i.e., in its function as the "mass medium" of the nineteenth century) it must reconsider its role. Having become an institution and, as such, reached its genealogical end, the museum—the classical terminal for parcel post from the history of art and culture—must now redefine itself anew with respect to aging storage techniques. In such a way, it is becoming the place of reflection on its own successor technologies. The demand upon the museum is thus pointing the way to mobilizing the accumulation of the depot, making it publicly accessible, as well as recycling stored stocks in the exhibition area. The memory, the basis (store), of the museum is liquefying, therefore, its depot increasingly reflects the switching technique of its successor media.

Memory can no longer be grasped in spatial metaphors (which, to date, has been the rationale of museological inventories and catalogues[40]); aesthetic stores turn into cybernetic units and administrative monitoring. The *Dépôt légal* in Paris, where a copy of every publication is obligatorily kept, is no longer serving library purposes but its non-discursive double. In the galleries of defunct mines, the military archives of Freiburg have set up a microfilm store; here copies exist of all sorts of relevant administrative and cultural-historical documents of the Federal Republic of Germany, in the event of a nuclear attack on the original: the origin of memory is here the anticipation of war. Stores also mean delaying death. *Réserves*: under that very title, artist Christian Boltanski once installed and stacked metal boxes, filled with photos of victims of the Holocaust, with loudspeakers murmuring the names of the dead—counting numbers instead of telling narratives. Memory is passing from narrative space to digital computation, escaping from the figurative deception on which historical imagination is dependent.

Still, electronic data banks are not the death of imaginary memory. Though basing the representation of storage on the flawless use of stored information, they do not exclude play. The digital archive may merely aim at storing information; the energetic texture of memory, though, is based on counter- and disinformation, which amounts to a memory of waste.[41]

NOTES

1. This chapter is based in part on my article "Arsenale der Erinnerung," in the exhibition catalogue *SPEICHER: Ein Versuch über die Darstellbarkeit von Geschichte/n* (Linz: Offenes Kulturhaus Linz, 1993), 63–72—for a Dutch and an English adaptation, see "Arsenalen van de Herinnering"/"Arsenals of Memory," in *Mediamatic* 8:1 (1994): 1913–1920—and on my paper "Zwischenlager: Feedback Museum," read at the symposium *Feedback: Das Phänomen der Rückkopplung in Kunst und Wissenschaft*, organized by Giannozzo Kunstverein (Berlin) in the old monastery of Plasy (Czech Republic), September 2–4, 1994.

2. Hannes Böhringer, program text for the conference *Feedback*, op. cit.

3. See Arlette Farge, *Le goût de l'archive* (Paris: Seuil, 1987).

4. Bernard Marcadé, in the exhibition catalogue *Fictions colorées* (Paris: Zabriskie Art Gallery, 1985), n.p. (my translation).

5. See Wolfgang Struck, "Geschichte als Bild und als Text: Historiographische Spurensicherung und Sinnerfahrung im 19. Jahrhundert," in *Zeichen zwischen Klartext und Arabeske*, edited by Susi Kotzinger and Gabriele Rippl (Amsterdam and Atlanta: G. Rodopi, 1994), 349–61. The twentieth annual report of the *Germanisches Nationalmuseum*, January 1, 1874, reports on the acquisition of ancient parchments in order to prevent them from being sold as waste paper.

6. See Uwe Jochum, "Das tote Gedächtnis der Bibliothek," in *Verband der Bibliotheken des Landes Nordrhein-Westfalen: Mitteilungsblatt* 45: 4 (1995): 64, 66.

7. Leopold von Ranke, *Studien und Portraits zur italienischen Geschichte*, edited by Willy Andreas (Wiesbaden and Berlin: Vollmer, 1957), ch. 2, "Die Verschwörung gegen Venedig im Jahre 1618"; see esp. pp. 86–90, "Neue Quellen—Das Venezianische Archiv."

8. Angelika Menne-Haritz, "Das Provenienzprinzip—ein Bewertungssurrogat? Neue Fragen zu einer alten Diskussion," in *Der Archivar* 47:2 (1994): 231.

9. Ibid., 232ff., referring to, Ernst Müsebeck, "Der Einfluß des Weltkrieges auf die archivalische Methode," lecture on the 20th *Deutscher Archivtag*, Danzig, 1928, in *Archivalische Zeitschrift* 38 (1929): 144.

10. Adolf Michaelis, *A Century of Archaeological Discoveries* (London: John Murray, 1908), 103.

11. Ibid.

12. David Crowther, "Archaeology, Material Culture, and Museums," in *Museum Studies in Material Culture*, edited by Susan M. Pearce (London: Leicester University Press, 1989), 42.

13. For a discussion of the semiophor as an artifact, understood in an allegorical as opposed to a pragmatic sense, see Krzysztof Pomian, *Collectors and Curiosities: Paris and Venice, 1500–1800*, translated by Elizabeth Wiles-Portier (Cambridge: Polity Press, 1990).

14. Crowther, op cit., 42.

15. See the documentary film by Bernard Mangiante, *Galilée—au nom des pierres* (France, 1995).

16. Lily Díaz, "A Simultaneous View of History: The Creation of a Hypermedia Database," in *Leonardo* 28: 4 (1995): 257.

17. R. Boast and D. Chapman, *Archeologia e calcolatori* 2 (1991): 221–22.

18. Heinrich Klotz, "Zivilisation der Steinzeit," in *Frankfurter Allgemeine Zeitung*, October 28, 1995.

19. See Roger S. Schofield, "Sampling in Historical Research," in *Nineteenth-Century Society: Essays in the Use of Quantitative Methods for the Study of Social Data*, edited by E. A. Wrigley (London: Cambridge University Press, 1972), 146–90.

20. Anna di Noto et al., *Metamorfosi* 1–2, thematic issue "Città archeologica/città contemporanea" (April–August 1985): 92.

21. Nathaniel Hawthorne, quoted in Henry Sussman, "*The Marble Faun* and the Space of American Letters," in *Glyph Textual Studies* 1 (1986): 131. Free from Eurocentric ballast, the American knows how to see things; Sussman writes: "Hawthorne repeatedly described Rome as a heap of concentrated and somewhat excremental junk, anticipating a fundamental concern with garbage on the part of such twentieth-century writers as T. S. Eliot, Ezra Pound, and Wallace Stevens."

22. José Blazquez Martinez, cited in Stelio Martini, "Un archivio ignorato nel Monte delle Anfore," in *Roma* 39, anno V (1992): 22 (my translation).

23. Ibid., 26ff.

24. Theodor Mommsen, *Römische Kaisergeschichte: Nach den Vorlesungsmitschriften von Sebastian und Paul Hensel 1882/86*, edited by B. u. A. Demandt (Munich: Beck, 1992).

25. *Wired* 3:03 (March 1995), n.p.

26. Quoted in David George Hogarth, Preface, *Excavations at Ephesus: The Archaic Artemisia* (London: British Museum, 1908), n.p.

27. See Edmund Hug's article, "Letztlich eine Frage der Architektur," on the CeBIT '94 fair at Hannover, in *Frankfurter Allgemeine Zeitung*, May 15, 1994.

28. "Steine mit dem Computer sortieren," in *Frankfurter Allgemeine Zeitung*, April 12, 1995.

29. Quoted in Edward Falkener, *Ephesus, and the Temple of Diana* (London: Day and Son, 1862), 346.

30. Thomas Sebeok, "Pandora's Box: How and Why to Communicate 10,000 Years into the Future," in *On Signs: A Semiotics Reader*, edited by Marshall Blonsky (Oxford: Basil Blackwell, 1985), 448–66.

31. Irving Wohlfarth, "Walter Benajmin's Last Reflections," in *Glyph* 3 (1978): 189.

32. Jurij M. Lotman und B. A. Uspenskij, "Zum semiotischen Mechanismus der Kultur," in *Semiotica Sovietica* 2 (1986): 859.

33. See Hartwig Lohse, "Tote und 'scheintote' Literatur," in *Bücher für die Wissenschaft: Bibliotheken zwischen Tradition und Fortschritt*, edited by Gert Kaiser (Munich: K. G. Saur, 1994), 143–58.

34. See Aleida Assmann, "Fest und flüssig: Anmerkungen zu einer Denkfigur," in *Kultur als Lebenswelt und Monument*, edited by Aleida Assmann and Dietrich Harth (Frankfurt: Suhrkamp Verlag, 1991), 181–98, n. 18.

35. Martin Groß, "Ein neuer Buchtyp: das bibliographische Bulletin," in *Ästhetik und Kommunikation* 18:67–68 (1987):4–6, n. 5.

36. Entry "Software-Engineering," in *Schüler Duden: Die Informatik*, edited by Meyers Lexikonredaktion, scientific editing by Volker Claus and Andreas Schwill, 2d ed. (Mannheim: Dudenverlag, 1991), 473.

37. Geoffrey Hartman, "Public Memory and Its Discontents," in *RARITAN* 24 (1994): 24.

38. See Michel Foucault, "Other Rooms," in *Essential Works*, vol. 2, edited by James Faubion, translated by Robert Hurley et al. (London: Penguin Books, 2000), 175–85.

39. "Information and archives on the Internet," http://www.hensa.ac.uk/www94/internet.html.

40. See Thomas Ketelsen, *Künstlerviten, Inventare, Kataloge: Drei Studien zur Geschichte der kunsthistorischen Praxis* (Ammersbek: Lottbek Jensen, 1988), part II and III.

41. Henri-Pierre Jeudy, "Die Musealisierung der Welt oder Die Erinnerung des Gegenwärtigen," in *Ästhetik und Kommunikation* 18:67–68 (1987): 23–30, esp. 35.

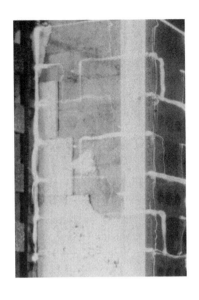

7

Being

Authentic

The Ambition to Recycle

Hans Ulrich Gumbrecht

WHAT WE CALL "AUTHENTIC" PRESENTS ITSELF as something primordial and elemental. "Primordial" in the sense of the German *Ursprung*,[1] that is, as something that participates in (or is at least in touch with) an absolute beginning, "elemental" because what appears as belonging to an absolute beginning is expected to possess the powerful beauty of neatness and transparency, without lacking complexity. Due to this double implication of being primordial and elemental, the authentic has the authority of what is pertinent.[2] Hardly ever do we attribute authenticity to an experience without wanting to suggest that its content or object of reference substitute what the mere belief in the presence of the authentic has always already defined as inauthentic. This is exactly how the specific value and function of the authentic become manifest, in that it has the authority of something that imposes itself as immediately pertinent.

The perception of the authentic as being primordial (and, with it, its specific value and potential function) results from the impression that it has been superseded by cultural materials that are less primordial (whatever this may precisely mean in each individual case) and that therefore do not carry an authority-claim. The most appropriate (if not the only) way to make appear as primordial, elemental, and authoritative whatever we call authentic is to stage its discovery as a cultural

A translation appears in the French companion volume to this book, *La mémoire des déchets: Essais sur la culture et la valeur du passé*, edited by Johanne Villeneuve, Brian Neville, and Claude Dionne (Québec: Nota Bene, 1999).

recycling. Thus the experience of the authentic becomes one that seems to impose itself against things that look more recent, more superficial, and less neat. So close indeed is the relationship between authenticity and cultural recycling that we are tempted to describe cultural recycling not only as leading to the authentic but as the very production of authenticity. At the same time, it is true that, in the present intellectual climate, we have become skeptical about the status of phenomena that claim to be part of an absolute beginning—even if we do not subscribe to the repertoire of concepts staging our contemporary moment as "postmodern" (and hence as *ursprungs-los*). Our present is, to say the least, a bad moment for the acceptance of the authentic as pertinent. It also is a bad moment for the belief that what the truly authentic needs in order to impose itself is recycling, that is, a being rediscovered under layers of posterior materials and debris that had caused its oblivion. The more skeptical approach to cultural recycling as the production of authenticity is the theory that by merely pretending for something to be old, to have been forgotten, and to need rediscovery, one produces effects of authenticity. Seen from this second perspective, authenticity would no longer be the result of a recycling but rather the result of a gesture that produces effects of primordiality, that is, a reality-illusion for something that cannot exist in reality. It is difficult for us to avoid the conclusion that the production of authenticity is fake recycling.[3]

Before the end of the nineteenth century, the use of the words "authenticity" and "authentic" was remarkably (not to say dramatically) different from what we have so far tried to analyze.[4] They then referred to situations of authorship and ownership, to particularly close relations between human subjects and (mostly) material objects. Today this meaning has only survived on the art market and within the legal system. Here the word "authentic" still points to the status of an artwork or a text whose attribution to a certain artist/author has been confirmed. In a similar sense, "authentic reading" can be a synonymous expression for "literal reading," that is, for a reading that tries to stay close to the author's intention and marks a distance vis-à-vis all kinds of interpretation conceding large amounts of freedom to the interpreter.

The profound change in the meaning of "authentic" and "authenticity" took place in the context of the so-called "Conservative Revolution."[5] As the Conservative Revolution was the reaction to a crisis of those (often broadly institutionalized) thought-patterns that had shaped early Modernity, in particular the age of Enlightenment, its impact makes plausible the specific transformations that the concept of "authenticity" underwent.[6] The point of convergence for a number of changes is an immanentization, more precisely an immanentization of those structures that had been characteristic for the classically modern subject/object-paradigm. If it is true, firstly, that the Conservative Revolution coped with a collapse of the subject/object-paradigm, this helps us understand why the new notion of authenticity no longer thematized relations of authorship and propriety (which would have presupposed a strict separation between subject and object). Instead of belonging to a subject or an agent (and instead of being thus identified), whatever is deemed authentic has ever since been expected to carry its own value and to impose its own immanent authority. With the vanishing of the subject-position, secondly, the Conservative Revolution no longer disposed of a role that guaranteed the production of truth in the sense of an "objective or adequate rendering of the world." The authentic neither reveals a truth nor justifies itself through the reference to a truth—rather, its immanent authority-claim is an effect of the immanentization of a mimetic truth-concept. The authentic, so to speak, wants to be the convergence of a thing with its truth. Finally, the Conservative Revolution marked the first moment in European culture when (after centuries of philosophical critique) the broad belief in the existence of transcendental worlds had disappeared. There were no "other worlds" left from which to justify, to condemn, or only to judge the sphere of the everyday.[7] Before the background of this double vanishing, the vanishing of the subject-position and the vanishing of transcendence, it becomes obvious that the new concept of authenticity pinpointed a historically specific paradox. It was the paradox of a claim for "higher" values in a world that had been doubly confined to its own immanence. As a consequence, authenticity took over functions of the transcendental in a world that no longer allowed for transcendence.[8] We may speculate that the self-staging of the authentic as historically remote substitutes a hierarchical (i.e., transcendental) remoteness that is no longer available. If, in addition, we denounce as "fake" any recycling that produces (or pretends to produce) authenticity, this means that we refuse to live with the paradox of a quality-leveling within a world of sheer immanence.

During the 1920s, those self-staging techniques of the authentic that we have now described as the production of hierarchical superiority within a sphere of immanence reached an unheard-of variety and sophistication.[9] The worldwide success during these years of the music, lyrics, and choreography of Argentinean tango, for example, was facilitated by an affinity between the specific historical environment and a dancing ritual that presented itself as the trace of an earlier, somehow more real, and vaguely foundational world (perhaps the performance of the tango is indeed nothing more than the production of such an evocation).[10] But if, for the Argentinean public, the authenticity of the tango came from its perception as part of a remote mythical past (a past, that is, bare of any concrete historical reference), geographical remoteness was an equally important condition for the enthusiasm that the tango generated in Europe and North America.

There is a surprisingly coherent logic of cultural zones to which the aura of authenticity was projected. Authenticity was expected to dwell and flourish in all of those regions of the globe that appeared "marginal" compared to the industrial, economic, and urban centers of "modern life." This is true for the southern part of South America as well as for Spain, whose seemingly archaic cultural rituals, in particular bullfighting,[11] attracted intellectuals and artists from all over the world, but the rule applies to all types of African American music and performance (they were almost obsessively associated with—mostly uncertain—African origins), to the idealization of rural life forms from Scandinavia, and even to Martin Heidegger's personal claim that he could only efficiently think and work in his Black Forest cabin.[12] Wherever the possibility of establishing such (often imaginary) temporal and spatial distances was not easily available, for example, in the presentation of Fascist ideology and Fascist art as innovative, a vague claim of profoundness emerged as the standard recourse that allowed for a quasi-transcendence in a purely immanent world.[13] This profundity-claim connected perfectly with the presentation of the authentic as recycled cultural material (as material that had been previously superseded by less worthy cultural objects). At the same time, the profundity-claim was complementary with a long-standing topology that had staged any act of reading and understanding as the penetration of a surface toward a sphere of depth.[14] There is, however, one important difference between the hermeneutic surface/profundity-pattern and the depth-claim of authenticity. Hermeneutics stages the surface level (which is the level of the signifiers) as "purely material," whereas it imagines the level of depth (the level of the signified meaning) as having no materiality at all. The authentic, in contrast, does not allow for such a leveling of a material surface and a deep meaning (of a signifier and a signified). As a consequence of the general immanentization, the authentic is both material and meaningful. It does not leave a space for objects without meaning.[15]

One cannot help calling Martin Heidegger's *Sein und Zeit [Being and Time]* "epoch-making"—and this is true even for the specific topic with which we are dealing here. Written in 1926 and first published in the spring of 1927,[16] *Being and Time* not only contains the most complex unfolding of the new concept of "authenticity,"[17] it also is regarded as the decisive event and turning point in the history of this notion.[18] Beside his thorough thematization of "authenticity," Heidegger produces an authenticity-effect through the specific ways in which he stages the philosophical core problem, that is, "*the question of the meaning of Being.*"[19] Starting with a quote in which Plato points to this question as an unresolved issue, Heidegger introduces his own book with a gesture of cultural recycling. He claims to be the first to reintroduce a topic of which Plato was still aware but which has hence been superseded by lesser philosophical concerns:

> Do we in our time have an answer to the question of what we really mean by the word "being"? Not at all. So it is fitting that we should raise anew *the question of the meaning of Being.* But are we nowadays even perplexed at our inability to understand the expression "Being"? Not at all. So first of all we must reawaken an understanding for the

meaning of this question. Our aim in the following treatise is to work out the question of the meaning of *Being* and to do so concretely.[20]

Having thus set the stakes for his project, Heidegger emphasizes that his exclusive level of reference will be the "average everydayness"[21] of human existence (according to Heidegger, once again, a sector largely forgotten by the tradition of occidental philosophy). What will only become explicit later on, in the chapters referring to the existential challenge of death,[22] is already the reason for this self-imposed limitation. Heidegger's philosophy rejects any dimension that could be compatible with traditional dimensions of transcendence. He therefore participates in the movement of immanentization that we have identified as characteristic of the Conservative Revolution. At the same time (and taking up the second structural element that constitutes this intellectual context), Heidegger has no space for a human subject that would be eccentric to the world of objects.[23] Human existence can only and exclusively happen as "being-in-the-world."[24] What the world, on the other hand, offers to human existence is its "aroundness."[25] A subject (or, rather, a form of human existence), however, for whom a position of eccentricity vis-à-vis the world is no longer available cannot occupy the traditional human role in the production of knowledge and truth. In short, without eccentricity, human existence is unable to become an agent of knowledge and truth production. Truth, therefore, must now be reshaped as a form of experience that produces and imposes itself (instead of being produced and propagated). It is parallel in that to the authentic, which always appears as the inseparable union of an object and its truth (of something material and its meaning). Parallel also to the authentic as carrying its own evidence and authority, the concept of truth in *Being and Time* is defined as "Being unconcealed." This implies that Being (if one could say so) becomes the agent of its own "unconcealment." In order to explain such a conception of truth, whose origins and external motivation we could easily trace in Heidegger's contemporary intellectual environment, he ends up recurring, once again, to the primordial horizon of Greek philosophy. He recycles the Aristotelian notion of *aletheia [αληθεια]* as a precursor for his own conception of truth and, going back one step further, he even claims that there is a pre-Socratic origin for the meaning of *aletheia*:

> The *αληθεια* . . . signifies the "things themselves;" it signifies what shows itself—*entities in the "how" of their uncoveredness*. And is it accidental that in one of the fragments of Heraclitus—the oldest fragments of philosophical doctrine in which the *logos* is *explicitly* handled—the phenomenon of truth in the sense of uncoveredness (unhiddenness), as we have set it forth, shows through?[26]

Under such historical and systematic premises, it becomes highly expectable that Heidegger introduces—indeed, must introduce—a concept of authenticity as soon as he tries to establish a hierarchy of values. In this sense, whatever he alludes to as the "authentic" form of existence represents a higher value—but also a form of existence whose superiority Heidegger cannot seriously argue, because he lacks a transcendental or an eccentric perspective from which to justify such a hierarchy. Heidegger seems to be aware of this difficulty,[27] and he also seems to fear the intellectual (and even stylistic) embarrassment that inevitably results from any positive description of what is held to be authentic.[28] *Being and Time*, therefore, unfolds the value of authenticity *e negativo*, above all in a long section that illustrates different modalities of the inauthentic, such as "idle talk," "curiosity," "ambiguity," and "falling."[29] Even in those infrequent passages where it becomes grammatically impossible for Heidegger to bypass the word "authenticity," it remains unspecific and pale:

> This downward plunge into and within the groundlessness of the inauthentic Being of the "they", has a kind of motion which constantly tears the understanding away from the projecting of authentic possibilities, and into the tranquilized supposition that it possesses everything, or that everything is within its reach. Since the understanding is thus constantly torn away from authenticity and into the "they" (though always with a sham of authenticity), the movement of falling is characterized by turbulence.[30]

What ends up imposing itself in the reading of *Being and Time* (and what Heidegger's readers indeed remember) are different aspects of inauthenticity—with unmistakably negative values attributed to them. It remains quite unclear, in contrast, what attitudes and life-forms shall be regarded as authentic. This is probably the case because, refraining from fully developing both sides of the distinction between the authentic and the inauthentic, Heiddeger avoids, as best he can, the obligation to make that value judgment for which he has no adequate position.

More than in any explicit thematization, the positive aspects that shape Heidegger's understanding of authenticity come to bear in the forms with which he presents his thought. Following the passage in which he introduces the Greek notion of *aletheia*, Heidegger enters into a brief reflection about the systematic value, within his philosophy, of these forms, more specifically about the systematic value of what he defines as "elemental words." This reflection accounts for his recourse to (and, sometimes, his invention of) archaic-looking German words as well as for his more general fascination with the most chronologically remote traditions of European philosophy:

> In citing such evidence (sc. the Aristotelian notion of αληθεια) we must avoid uninhibited word-mysticism. Nevertheless, the ultimate business of philosophy is to preserve the *force of the most elemental words* in which *Dasein* expresses itself, and to keep the common understanding from leveling them off to that unintelligibility which functions in turn as a source of pseudo-problems.[31]

The oldest words, those words, we may supplement, whose origin seems to be close to the very origin of Western thought, are supposed to have a systematic value and authority. Heidegger suggests that they also come with a particular clarity, preserving which constitutes an obligation for modern philosophers. It is difficult to imagine a more compact, complete circumscription of the authentic than this very paragraph from *Being and Time*.[32] Probably the most famous (and certainly the most extensive) example of Heidegger's habit of conceptual and cultural recycling, however, is the chapter in which he develops the notion of "care" *(Sorge)* on the basis of a Latin fable whose earliest version comes to us from the Augustan age.[33] Heidegger calls this fable a "pre-ontological document,"[34] and the outcome of its narrative, according to which "Earth" and "Jupiter" will possess the body and the spirit of *homo* after "its" death, whereas "care" will possess it during its lifetime, indeed functions as the strongest argument provided by *Being and Time* for the central position assigned to the concept of "care" within the analysis of human existence. Here and otherwise the authority of authenticity has replaced the authority of a systematic argument.

Can there be any authenticity (or, more precisely, can there be any authenticity-claim) without such a staging as product of a cultural recycling? The answer is that there might be modalities and rituals other than cultural recycling that achieve the staging of authenticity—but that, on the other hand, it is difficult to imagine authenticity without any kind of staging. For the claim that authenticity may exist without any staging would have to presuppose the problematic conviction that authenticity become evident in and by itself, that it jump "straightforwardly out of the phenomena."[35] The complementary question is whether there can be any cultural recycling that is not fake. This second question takes us to the limits of the metaphorical use of the concept of "recycling." Applied to processes happening in nature and analyzed by science, our question (then based on the nonmetaphorical meaning of "recycling") is absurd—for what should it mean to attribute "fake" to nature? However, as far as "cultural" recycling goes, there is no recycled object from the past that is not, first of all, an object of desire and an invention of the present. Heidegger would not have "recycled" the *Cura*-fable without a preceding systematic interest in the concept of "care," and he only etymologizes those German words whose contemporary meanings are important for his thought.

To say that the authentic is the product of cultural recycling and that there is no cultural recycling without fake sounds like accusing those who use the concept of "authenticity" of "bad faith." This is certainly not my intention. On the contrary, I think that only because Heidegger believed in the possibility of experiencing the authentic, the authenticity-effects produced by his discourse turn out to be (at least intrinsically) convincing. More importantly, we have to admit that, until the present day, Western philosophy has not overcome the specific problems that motivated the

Conservative Revolution and the turning in the meaning of "authenticity." We are more than ever aware that the eccentric observer-positions that we sometimes attribute to ourselves are precarious, epistemological illusions. We continue to reject dimensions of transcendence. Consequently, we are still struggling to find (or to produce) a kind of knowledge that could be authoritative and pertinent. There are just two—diametrically opposed—gestures that try to achieve this in our epistemological situation, which is yet shaped by the collapse of the subject/object-paradigm and in which, therefore, the structure of a confrontation and a distance between an observer-subject and a world of objects are not available. We can either privilege (individual or collective) subjecthood and then minimize the pertinence (or maximize the "plasticity") of the world. This option leads to the discourse of constructivism in which "worlds" and "realities" are constantly "invented," "constructed," and "negotiated." The alternative option is ontology—which endows the side of "reality" with authority and pertinence and must therefore reduce (or even completely eliminate) the functions traditionally attributed to subjecthood. There is probably no ontology—at least no ontology under contemporary epistemological conditions (i.e., no ontology without transcendence)—that does not bring forth a concept at least similar to "authenticity," and no constructivism can, on the other hand, easily tolerate such authenticity-concepts. To say (as I did earlier) that there is hardly any authenticity without a staging as cultural recycling and that in addition there is no cultural recycling that is not fake means to be extremely skeptical about authenticity and the authentic. It also means that, for this skepticism, one has to pay the price of embracing subjecthood and the intellectual style of constructivism. As we are getting increasingly tired of strong subjectivity-claims and of the seemingly infinite intellectual freedom granted by constructivism,[36] we may become, once again, more tolerant vis-à-vis ontological worldviews and their inherent authenticity-concepts (for what such tolerance may be worth).

NOTES

1. See Theodor W. Adorno, *Jargon der Eigentlichkeit: Zur deutschen Ideologie* (Frankfurt: Suhrkamp Verlag, 1964). Quotations are from the English translation: *The Jargon of Authenticity*, translated by Knut Tarnowski and Frederic Will (Evanston, Ill.: Northwestern University Press, 1973), 45–46, 99. Throughout my notes, I will try to engage in a dialogue with this outstanding (and outstandingly witty) book.

2. See Adorno, op. cit., 144. Adorno describes the (according to him) "false transcendence" of the authentic *(des Eigentlichen)* in the following words: "For this transcendence is really none at all; it does not, in the Kantian way, go beyond the possibility of experience, but rather behaves as though experience is itself unmediated, incontrovertible, aware of itself as if it were face to face with itself."

3. Reading Adorno's almost obsessive critique of "authencity" written between 1962 and 1964, one begins to wonder how historically specific (i.e., how specifically "postmodern") such doubts regarding the status of anything "primordial" may actually be. See p. 122: "What is essential, and what is accidental, hardly ever springs straightforwardly out of the phenomena."

4. See the entries *"Authentisch"* and *"Authentizität"* in *Historisches Wörterbuch der Philosophie*, vol. 1, edited by Joachim Ritter (Basel: Schwabe, 1971), 691–93.

5. See, among many other publications on this topic, Ferdinand Fellmann, *Die Gelebte Philosophie in Deutschland: Denkformen der Lebensweltphänomenologie und der kritischen Theorie* (Freiburg: K. Alber, 1983), 98–109. Adorno (pp. 3–4, 92–93) proposes the same historical contextualization for the change in the meaning of "authenticity." The invention of the German concept *Eigentlichkeit* (whose popular use during the 1950s offers the main point of reference for Adorno's book) is one of the rare cases that indeed go back to a single author and a single publication, that is, Heidegger's *Sein und Zeit*, which came out in 1927 (see below). Also see "Being-in-the-Worlds of 1926: Martin Heidegger, Friedrich Blunck, Carl Van Vechten," the final chapter of my book *In 1926: Living on the Edge of Time* (Cambridge, Mass.: Harvard University Press, 1997).

6. See Adorno, op. cit., 45: "The Jargon, a waste product of the modern that it attacks."

7. See my "'Everyday-World' and 'Life-World' As Philosophical Concepts: A Genealogical Approach," in *New Literary History* 24 (1993–1995): 745–61.

8. Adorno, op cit., 11: "Expressions and situations, drawn from a no longer existent daily life, are forever being blown up as if they were empowered and guaranteed by some absolute which is kept silent out of reverence." Also see p. 16: "This content is referred to the immediacy of life. Theology is tied to the determinations of immanence, which in turn want to claim a larger meaning, by means of their suggestion of theology: they are already virtually like the words of the jargon."

9. I am drawing, in this section, on the entries "Authenticity vs. Artificiality" and "Authenticity = Artificiality [Life]" from my book *In 1926*, op. cit.

10. See my "Die Stimmen von Argentiniens Leichen," in *Merkur* 499 (1990): 715–28.

11. Not surprisingly, the thoroughly archaic-looking structure of the *corrida* is, to a large extent, a product of the nineteenth century.

12. Regarding Heidegger's work on an individual aura of authenticity, see Pierre Bourdieu, *The Political Ontology of Martin Heidegger*, translated by Peter Collier (Stanford: Stanford University Press, 1991), 40–54.

13. See Adorno, op. cit., 14–15: "A loudspeaker becomes necessary. 'Statement' wants to announce that something which was said has come from the depth of the speaking subject; that it is removed from the course of surface communication."

14. See my "Das Nicht-Hermeneutische: Skizze einer Genealogie," in *Interventionen* 5 (1996): 17–36.

15. See Adorno, op. cit., 44: "With the assertion of meaning at all costs, the old antisophistic emotion seeps into the so-called mass society."

16. According to Theodore Kisiel, *The Genesis of Heidegger's Being and Time* (Berkeley: University of California Press, 1993).

17. Heidegger's German equivalent is *Eigentlichkeit*. If he is not the inventor of this substantivation, it at least marks one of those cases in which Heidegger relaunches and popularizes a highly eccentric word within the academic vocabulary.

18. See Ritter, op. cit., 692: "Within Philosophy of Existence *[Existentialphiloso-phie]*, the German word *'authentisch'* and its equivalents become the standard translation and the standard substitution of Heidegger's term *'eigentlich.'* These words are not only applied to human attitudes but also to human products" (my translation).

19. I am quoting from the English translation by John Macquarrie and Edward Robinson, in Martin Heidegger, *Being and Time* (New York: Harper & Row, 1962), 19.

20. Ibid.

21. Ibid., 69.

22. Ibid., 279–311.

23. This eccentricity was constitutive for the classic notion of subjectivity. Its absence may have motivated Heidegger to replace the concept of "subjectivity" through "(human) existence."

24. See Heidegger, op. cit., 78ff.

25. Ibid., 134ff.

26. Ibid., 262.

27. This is why, on the one hand, he insists that "idle talk," "curiosity," and so on are not inferior forms of existence (he has no argument at hand to prove his point) whereas, on the other hand, he cannot avoid describing them in a very negative light (of course he is "in favor" of authenticity). See Adorno, op. cit., 96: "As an impartial contemplative of essence, Heidegger allows for the fact that inauthenticity 'can define existence in its fullest concretion.' Yet the accompanying words, which he attributes to this mode of being, are essentially vituperative."

28. See Adorno, op. cit., 96–97: "In the end, however, Heidegger's philosophy does not want to have anything to do with the cultural philosophy in which such questions [questions regarding a positive determination of the authentic] appear."

29. Heidegger, op. cit., 210–24.

30. Ibid., 223.

31. Ibid., 262.

32. Regarding the "archaic in language" in Heidegger, see Adorno, op. cit., 42.

33. Hans Blumenberg dedicated one of his last books to the central motif of this fable: *Die Sorge geht über den Fluss* (Frankfurt: Suhrkamp Verlag, 1987).

34. Heidegger, op. cit., 243.

35. Adorno, op. cit., 122.

36. See my "Form without Matter vs. Form As Event," in *Modern Language Notes* 111 (1996): 578–92.

Part II
Site

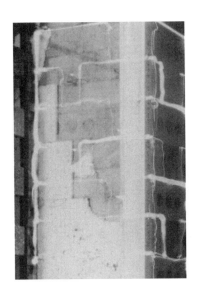

8

Mould, Rubble, and the Validation of the Fragment in the Discourse of the Past

Stephen Bann

THIS CHAPTER IS GOING TO BE, INITIALLY AT ANY RATE, a tale of two stones. The first is a stone that looks like nothing in particular, which would hardly produce any reaction in you at all, if you saw it on a country road, unless you just happened to trip over it.

All of you will know of the remarkable feat of engineering which, completed in the recent past, has succeeded in depriving Great Britain of its status as an island. I refer of course to the Channel Tunnel. Imagine the situation down there under the Channel when the two vast subterranean holes, one commenced from the French side and the other from a valley beneath the Downs, behind Folkestone, edged ever more closely toward each other through the limestone rock, until finally there was just a thin membrane separating the two workings: on one side, you could say, there was France, and on the other side, England. This screen of rock, facing like the god Janus in two directions, for a brief time epitomized the radical heterogeneity of two cultural systems brought into abrupt collision. It was to keep this status only for that instant, but as it happened, the official photographer of the Tunnel project gathered up the fragments as soon as the breakthrough had taken place. This is one of them (see Figure 8.1). Turning it over, we can still imagine one face as being England, the other France.

My purpose here is to discuss the particular discursive regimes to which this and a few other such objects and images belong. In this particular case, I shall have no hesitation in suggesting that it belongs to the discursive and indeed epistemological regime known in the sixteenth and seventeenth centuries as

FIGURE 8.1   "Janus Stone," photo by Stephen Bann.

"curiosity," a regime whose governing principles have been brilliantly described in the writings of Krzysztof Pomian and rehearsed more recently in my own, more particularized study of the Cabinet of John Bargrave, *Under the Sign: John Bargrave As Collector, Traveler, and Witness.*[1] The Anglo-French Janus Stone, if so we can call it, fits within the parameters of that practice of collecting that was relentlessly directed toward the singular object. This was indeed the primary reason the scientific spirits of the age, such as Bacon and Descartes, so strongly attacked curiosity: in attaching itself to the special and singular case, it militated against the inductive approach, which drew logical conclusions from the obser-vation of whole classes of objects.

In the case of this stone, an opposite mechanism is put into operation. Out of the almost indefinitely large number of pieces of rubble that remained from that large partition, this particular one has been chosen not for its representative or gen-eralizing properties but because I choose to see it as a symbol. I choose to store it in the top drawer of my dressing table just as John Bargrave chose to store in his Cab-inet of Curiosities, "several pieces of cinders, pummystone, and ashes of the Mount Vesuvius, near Naples."[2] I should add that Bargrave chose to memorialize Mount Vesuvius in this way for a precise reason: Mount Vesuvius was, on each of the four journeys he undertook throughout Europe in the 1640s and 1650s, the "poynt of my reflection," in other words, the precise spot at which he "[faced] about" to commence his return journey. Just as the twin signatures of England and France are inscribed on my odd little stone, so the cinder from Vesuvius is a marker for a jour-ney, an indication that it has been undertaken and completed successfully.

What needs to be done to consolidate the status of my object, which I am endowing with a mild level of apotheosis by talking about? Bargrave's "cinders, pummystone, and ashes" are lying around in his cabinets. For want of clear label-ing, I at any rate cannot tell one from another. Bargrave did, however, perform upon certain of the objects he bought or filched in Rome a secondary process of symbolization. A chip of an obelisk lying in a Roman circus, or a piece of Roman glass known as *paste antiche*, was cut and polished to form the shape of a heart; in my reading, this secondary signification implies that the exiled church-man from a vigorously Royalist family was using the objects casually collected in his wanderings to constitute a discourse of loyalty to the Stuart monarchy. By the same token, I might arrange for this hunk of stone to be artfully cut into a heart shape and inscribed in such a way as to signify my own lifelong dedication to the cause of Anglo-French cultural understanding.

This is about as far as this stone will go, in my argument in this chapter. But my strategy in using it as an example has, I hope, been clear. The object of cu-riosity enters history in two ways: one is by the overdetermination introduced by the individual collector who decides to give it a narrative, which will be, to a greater or lesser extent, historically significant. In this respect, the object functions as a souvenir, in Susan Stewart's sense of the term.[3] The other entry into history is more problematic. I could say that the object of curiosity enters into history by being already historicized, as part of a cognitive domain proper to the early mod-ern period, and perhaps to Foucault's Renaissance *episteme*. This would not, how-ever, account for the persistence of such remarkable phenomena as "*La Collection de Mama W.*," recuperated by Daniel Spoerri and put on show by Jean-Hubert Martin at the Château d'Oiron in Poitou. Here we can see, amid a host of other similarly classified and identified objects from a collection assembled by a German noblewoman in the late nineteenth century, "a little stone" brought back in 1880 from the prison on the Ile Sainte Marguerite, where the "man in the iron mask" was confined, a "ball from the Battle of Waterloo," or a "tiny fragment of the first German flag to fly over the Cathedral of Strasbourg" on June 21, 1871, torn off by an officer in the 9th regiment of Bavarian infantry.[4]

What I will do, therefore, is keep this model of historicity—the mode of valuing the object from the past—in suspension as I introduce another, more powerful discourse of the fragment. It may well be that the very convergence of attention on curiosity—of which writings such as my own and Pomian's and displays such as the Château d'Oiron are evidence—indicates that Postmodernity demands, very precisely, a relativization of the master narrative that I am going to rehearse, but this does not remove the necessity of seeing it clearly. Indeed, it renders that objective all the more possible, and desirable.

To begin on this track is to follow the furrow already traced out by many writers who have insisted on the entirely new character of historicity given to the object by the new "historical-mindedness" ushered in by the Romantic movement in the early part of the nineteenth century. An exemplary text in this respect would be Alois Riegl's "The Modern Cult of Monuments: Its Character and Its Origin," written in 1903 as a preface to the legislative proposal for the protection of historic monuments in the Austro-Hungarian Empire.[5] This is, as you will know, the text in which for the first time the concept of "age-value" is formulated in such a way as to distinguish it clearly from "art-value" and "historical value." "Art-value" is something that can be assessed by connoisseurs; "historical value" requires the estimate of art historians. But "age-value," as Riegl explains, requires neither aesthetic training nor knowledge to be securely communicated: "The most simple-minded farmhand is able to distinguish an old belfry from a new one." Yet Riegl does not try to gloss this apparently extraordinary claim. What I need to do is construct a summary genealogy of the historical fragment in order to make it more comprehensible.

First of all, the precondition of "age-value," for Riegl, is, nonetheless, a visible degree of cultural formation. "A shapeless pile of rubble is no longer able to convey age-value; there must be at least a recognizable trace of the original form, that is, of man's handiwork, whereas rubble alone reveals no trace of the original creation."[6] Does a flint wall have age-value? It is a debatable point, not only in terms of Riegl's statement but also in terms of my own experience. Take for instance the remaining wall from the Roman town of Rutupiae, or Richborough, on the Kentish coast near Sandwich, site of the original Roman invasion of Britain. It seems to have regressed arguably to an almost mineral state, resembling a cliff or quarry and not a man-made artifact.

On the other hand, this stone fragment is imprinted with the signs not only of "man's handiwork" but of a particularly self-conscious, systematic dressing (see

Figure 8.2). It is not accidental, and it clearly comes from a structure of some degree of refinement. In fact, it comes from the Belvedere, at Waldershare near
Dover, built (among other reasons) to look down along the Kentish coast at the
site where the Romans and St. Augustine, in their turn, first landed. If I were to
take a flint from the ruins of Richborough, it would remain a flint. If I take a
piece of rubble from the workings of the Channel Tunnel and tell a story about
it, its new status as an object depends radically on the conditions for preserving
and repeating that story. But in this case, I would argue, the supplementation is
not so necessary. A flake of stone shaved off this early eighteenth-century building, designed by the Earl of Burlington, preserves a dynamic relationship to its
original location. It seems to want to leap back, like an arrowhead, into its niche.

Now I should insist that, in making this judgment along the lines of Riegl's
argument, I am not claiming to reproduce the kind of estimate that such a fragment might have provoked in the early eighteenth century. Quite the opposite,
it is precisely the fact that this fragment represents a "classical" architecture,
whose procedures go back as far as the fluting of the columns of Greek temples,
that gives it its pathos at a time when the "classical" has become a vehicle for nostalgia and retrospection. In other words, to look at this object in the way that
Riegl intimates implies that we are already historically distant from it. In terms of
its architect, the Earl of Burlington, we can only imagine that such a fragment—
let us say, accidentally chipped off by a clumsy stone mason—would have been
mere rubbish and the occasion for the carving of a new stone to take the place of
the botched one. But to look at it with the eyes of the subsequent period is to
perceive it as a fragment animated by its very relationship of lack or imcomple-
tion vis-à-vis the whole object, which we way or may not be able to identify.

I have to trace this argument summarily, but I hope that the point will be clear.
In the latter part of the eighteenth century (and not before), the discourse of the
historical fragment is initiated as a discourse of part and whole, animated by a strong
affective and even libidinal impetus. When the Kentish Rector Bryan Faussett installed a mutilated figure in his Pavilion in 1769, he took care to supplement it (as
he did indeed in the case of all of the objects placed there) with an inscribed text
lamenting the earlier fate of this "truncam"—truncated figure—to which he has,
after many years of it being dragged from place to place, given an "asylum."[7] But
in this respect, I would argue, he was not simply acting in the tradition of the great
age of curiosity and lending a personal dimension to the siting of a rare and curious object. He was subscribing already, one might say, to the great myth of the rebirth of the past, to which the Romantic period would later give full expression.

What I need to emphasize in relation to the development of this myth of rebirth, or resurrection, is the profoundly dialectical character of the process that
gave rise to it. There is perhaps no need for me to quote yet again the fundamental passage from Foucault's *Les Mots et les choses* on nineteenth-century society's

FIGURE 8.2   "The Belvedere at Waldershare," photo by Bob Chaplin.

sense of being dispossessed of the past, which I have discussed several times before. As this chapter is concerned with images, I shall invoke one or two that convey this process graphically. French artist and architect Jacques-Pascal Virebent shows in his wash drawing from around 1800 the agents of Father Time "veiling" antiquity: "*Les Temps voilent l'Antiquité.*"[8] But of course the effect of such veiling is to render the imperfectly glimpsed but enticing forms even more fascinating. If only a fragment of the Sphinx-like sculpture remains in view, it is nonetheless redeemed as a fragment from the discreet masking about to take place.

In this respect, it can be seen to reflect a direct parallel to Thomas Stothard's image, engraved perhaps a little later as the frontispiece to his *Monumental Effigies*, which illustrates the caption: "The Monumental Effigies rescued from time."[9] Virebent renders the fragment appealing in the very process of veiling it. Stothard, however, takes the already constituted fragments from the medieval period and propels them into a kind of apotheosis. They will live again in the plates of his repertoire, provided with its own backdrop of historical information and biographical narrative with which to reanimate the effigies of the sleeping warriors.

These two prints by Virebent and Stothard represent, I would suggest, two sides of the same coin. Their logic could be expressed by the idea that only what is veiled, and fragmented by that process, can become sufficiently particularized and sufficiently invested with desire for the process of dynamic recuperation to be activated. This is, of course, a different way of saying, as Foucault did about the transition from the classic to the modern *episteme*, that humanity's dispossession of history caused a countervailing need to reinvent a history centered upon itself. Where I add a nuance of difference is on drawing attention to the peculiar concreteness of this process that implied, very precisely, giving a narrative to the fragmented object.

Linda Nochlin has written recently on the "fragmented body" as the characteristic sign of our artistic culture in the modern period. In this respect, she parallels the argument developed by Adrian Stokes in *Reflections on the Nude*, that the representation of the body in our century can only be at the price of fragmentation, and that collage is the characteristic sign of this.[10] I wish to add to this diagnosis the point that what is lost is not simply the metaphor of wholeness implicit in the classic treatment of the nude figure, but the persistent identification between the notion of bodily wholeness and the access to an unmediated past, which is dramatized *a contrario* by the rise in the prestige of the historical fragment. John Leech's wonderful plates for *The Comic History of England* (1847) offer a glimpse of the power invested in this development. In his "Terrific Combat between Richard Coeur de Lion and Saladin," the "monumental effigy" is indeed rescued from time, as the historical "other" is relativized by an exotic oriental otherness. The price of Coeur de Lion's "terrific" vitality is the armageddon of doll-like body parts that litter the battleground.[11]

Take the story up to our own period and you have a similar economy, touching the body but also involving the notion of access to the past in Giulio Paolini's fine collage work, *Wounded Niobid*. Here lies one of the sons of Niobe, whose sad story is told in Ovid's *Metamorphoses*. As a result of the pride of their mother, Niobe, they were killed off one by one by the arrows of the offended god Apollo. The angular elements of collage that hover above the lifeless body—itself a prototype for so many post–Renaissance painters—serve both as the arrows of Apollo, bringing death and decay to the flawless body, and as a kind of negative image espousing it, as when the lowest fragment follows the form of the upraised arm. Everything here is a fragment—even, and perhaps especially, the photocollage of the Niobid. It is only through the collision of fragments and the metonymy operated on the signifying chain by our own desire for wholeness that the scenario perhaps coheres.

I have been telling my tale of two stones, and perhaps I have found an alibi for the second of them: the slice of the stone facing from the façade of the Waldershare

Belvedere. Apollo is only by metonymic connection the God of the Belvedere. But perhaps this is his stone arrowhead, shot from a great height and fallen to earth, so that we can dream on the impossibility of ever restoring it to its origin. But I have a further, supplementary tale to tell, which begins once again with "curiosity" and comes up to date. You will have noticed that, in my account, the fragment has been characteristically the *stone* fragment, rescued from the condition of amorphous rubble, and its avatar, the neatly sliced fragment of collage. Yet if, as I have suggested, the intensified sense of the past that develops in the latter part of the eighteenth century is routed by way of the body in its different states, then surely a place must be found not simply for the descent into meaninglessness, whereby the fragment becomes rubble, but also for the condition of decay or deliquescence, whereby the fragment loses its boundaries and becomes part of a mass not merely amorphous but liquid. The first word in my title is "mould," and the quotation that lies behind that is Nietzsche's famous remark, from *The Use and Abuse of History for Life*: "The antiquarian breathes a mouldy air."[12] It remains for me to look briefly at how the discourse of the fragment is inflected by the sense of bodily decay and to point to a transitional image in which its association with the development of historical-mindedness is emphasized.

When John Bargrave—the collector of curiosities with whom my account began—visited the Franciscan friars of Toulouse in their great church around 1650, he was shown a great subterranean chamber stocked entirely with desiccated bodies. It appears that the burial ground of the church had the rare property of preserving rather than allowing the buried corpses to decay. Perhaps in consequence the friars were only too anxious to take their visitors down to see the array, and if possible, to get them to accept a specimen or two. Bargrave was offered the whole body of a little child which, as he puts it, "out of curiosity" he ought to have accepted. But he was traveling light, on his way to Italy, and so he took only a broken-off fragment, "the finger of a Frenchman."[13]

It is indeed striking that no special awe is attached to this, as Bargrave tells the story and enters it in his catalogue. The regime of curiosity finds room for this, as for other rarities, and its status as a former part of a living body appears irrelevant. That particular route of access from the part to the whole appears foreclosed. On the other hand, when contemporary artist Andres Serrano represents the crossed hands of a corpse in the morgue, with the laconic title *The Morgue (AIDS Related Death)*, we surely pay attention. It is quite true that, as Daniel Arasse has argued, the strategy of Serrano's large Cibachrome images is precisely to provoke comparisons with the post–Renaissance tradition of bodily representation, in particular, the sumptuous tints of the Venetian painters with their concern to show the blood circulating beneath the skin. But the Serrano image is even more vivid in that, after a certain point, it exceeds the representational regime insofar as we know that this is the pallor not of beauty but of decay. The fragment refuses to be a fragment, despite the relentless framing effect, precisely because its boundaries remain fluid: they are those of a metamorphosis not yet completed.

My purpose is not, however, to linger on this comparison but to ask how the change implicit in it can be related to the broad history of the fragment traced here. It is necessary to abandon then the model of visual clarity represented by the Belvedere fragment and to delve underground—not into the Channel Tunnel but into the crypt of a Roman church.

This is the passage in which the French painter, François-Marius Granet—a resident of Rome throughout most of the Empire and Restoration period—describes the special attraction that led him to paint in the crypt of the Roman church of San Martino in Monte, despite strong advice to the contrary:

> The walls [of the crypt of San Martino in Monte] are covered in a greenish down that is brought on by humidity and lends this interior an almost unimaginable color. The spot was well suited to my tastes; my mind was made up there and then, even though my monk assured me that I could not possibly work in such a place as this . . . none of these arguments had any effect. My picture was already there in my mind's eye. It was settled, next day there I was among the dead, who alone resided in this vast tomb.[14]

Granet's account is full of the sense of transgression with which he approached the task of recording the greenish atmosphere of this subterranean home of the dead. Here it is not a question of the stone as an object of curiosity, or of the stone as Apollo's arrow, or a fragment of collage. In fact, the stone is all around, though Granet's special objective is to clothe it with the patina of decay, in such a fashion that the qualities attached to the gleaming white body laid out in the crypt become invested in the entire space, even when the body itself is not included. It would take too long for me to explain how Granet, no doubt in consequence of this voluntary self-immersion in the subterranean sphere, finds the motivation to paint what is arguably the first true historical painting, that is, a work in which the dialectic of loss and recovery is projected upon a scene defined essentially as past and irrecoverable. But that is how, in my view, the discourse of the past intensifies in such a way as to become very much more than the tale of two stones.

NOTES

1. See Krzysztof Pomian, *Collectors and Curiosities: Paris and Venice, 1500–1800*, translated by Elizabeth Wiles-Portier (Oxford: Polity Press, 1990); Stephen Bann, *Under the Sign: John Bargrave As Collector, Traveler, and Witness* (Ann Arbor: University of Michigan Press, 1994).

2. Bann, op. cit., 71.

3. See Susan Stewart, *On Longing: Narratives of the Miniature, the Gigantic, the Souvenir, the Collection* (Baltimore: Johns Hopkins University Press, 1984).

4. See Daniel Spoerri, *La Collection de Mama W.*, published for the Château d'Oiron, 1993.

5. See Alois Riegl, "The Modern Cult of Monuments: Its Character and Its Origin," in *Oppositions* 25 (fall 1982), translated by Kurt W. Forster and Diane Ghirardo.

6. Ibid., 33.

7. See Stephen Bann, *The Inventions of History: Essays on the Representation of the Past* (Manchester: Manchester University Press, 1990), 111 ff.; *Romanticism and the Rise of History* (New York: Twayne, 1995), 91–94.

8. Reproduced in the catalogue *Corps de la Mémoire*, vol. 2 (Toulouse: Espace d'Art Moderne et Contemporain de Toulouse, 1995), 4.

9. Reproduced in Stephen Bann, *The Clothing of Clio* (Cambridge: Cambridge University Press, 1984), 66.

10. See Adrian Stokes, *Reflections on the Nude: Critical Writings*, vol. 3, edited by Lawrence Gowing (London: Thames and Hudson, 1978), 301–42; Linda Nochlin, *The Body in Pieces: The Fragment As a Metaphor of Modernity* (London: Thames and Hudson, 1994).

11. See Gilbert Abbott A'Beckett, *The Comic History of England* (London: Bradbury, 1851–1852), 95.

12. Friedrich Nietzsche, *The Use and Abuse of History*, translated by Adrian Collins (Indianapolis: Bobbs-Merrill, 1978), 20.

13. Bann, *Under the Sign*, op. cit., 6–7, 14, plate 3.

14. Quoted in Isabelle Néto-Daguerrre and Denis Coutagne, *Granet Peintre de Rome* (Aix-en-Provence: Musée Granet, 1992), 84–86 (my translation).

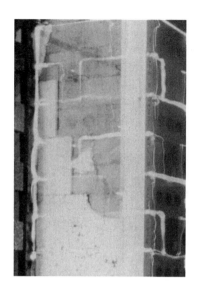

9

Parthenon, Nashville

From the Site of History to the Sight of Memory

Éric Méchoulan

America, you have it better
Than this, our old continent,
With no castles fettered
And no stone monuments.

In times of great life
Your spirit untroubled be
By idle strife
And vain memory.
          —Goethe, "Den Vereinigten Staaten"

WHAT DOES IT MEAN TO POSSESS A PARTHENON AT HOME, when one is not an Athenian? Not a small reproduction, mind you, but the *re-creation* of a full-scale Parthenon. Such is the experience of any Nashville citizen. But what kind of experience is it to behold a modern Parthenon amidst the green spaces of Nashville Centennial Park—a nice place, indeed, for a Sunday stroll?

The story begins in 1895, America is experiencing an economic depression, showing signs of mounting anxiety in the face of an exacerbated industrialization and mass immigration, more and more menacing to the agrarian ideal.[1] In commemorating the 100th anniversary of its accession to the Union, the State of Tennessee finds an effective way to divert public concern and recycle a fantasized past. A Centennial Exposition Company is founded, the "cornerstone" of which is the building of a replica of the Parthenon—a seemingly appropriate project for Nashville, already known by this time as the "Athens of the South."[2]

Thus, within a year, it was done. Set between the Pyramid of Cheops and the Memphis Building, adjacent to a Chinese Village and a Giant See-Saw, was a Parthenon for all citizens to behold, whether one were boating across an artificial lake in a romantic Venetian gondola (with native gondolier) or jaunting about astride an Egyptian camel. In the wake of the exposition, "Nashvillians expressed [the] hope that its site would become a public park and that the Parthenon replica would be preserved."[3] Or so the official record of the events has it. And just as the Centennial Project enjoyed popular favor, so too was there public demand for maintaining this symbol of community itself. Public indeed, for such initiatives must originate with the people, rather than an elite, since the latter must always appear to obey the former, at least as far as the sense of collective identity is concerned!

By 1907, however, the Parthenon's plaster ornamentation had deteriorated; it was repaired, "complying with public demand" and "at great expense." But by 1920 it was in such disrepair that a decision was made to close it down in order to rebuild the structure, "again at public demand."[4] Once again, even if the plan was conceived by an elite few, the story attributes the idea to popular demand and to a collective sense of identity, for history founds the collective self, just as people ground history: Nashvillians, and Americans by extension (for it was the Centennial of the entrance of Tennessee into the Union), engaged their self-presentation as the modern Athenians, as the true democrats.

Between 1920 and 1931, a new replica was built, a Parthenon meant to endure, to withstand the vicissitudes of time, like its Grecian namesake. As the author of record puts it, in an elegant yet innocuous oxymoron, "an original replica."[5] Original concept indeed, one that erases the temporal disjunction and gives to the reproduction the status of what it reproduces! Such use is authorized by two previous occurrences of the concept of replica. In the Foreword by Charles Moss, a local personality of the .1950s, we read: "It is a replica, yes. But defying all the laws of grammar, we will call it 'an exact' replica, so true to detail has been its reproduction and so renowned its presence."[6] It is, thus, an "exact replica" not only because of the quality of the re-creation but also because of its impact on the public and the effect of presence that it produces. Detail and fame make it an "exact replica": a replica of a building *and* a replica of its proper effect.

In his Preface, which follows Moss' Foreword, Charles Creighton concludes with pride that "children of every civilized nation are taught the history of this ancient temple. Those in Middle Tennessee can study an exact replica"—this time without quotation marks or any sort of modalization.[7] By this explicit opposition, we are encouraged to admire how the passivity of all other nations (who "are taught") is supplanted by the activity of Tennesseans (who are able to study it by themselves). In this manner, tradition and inheritance are replaced by autonomy and study.

But returning to the "original" edition of 1968, of which this revised edition is a "replica," we discover that, in actuality, Creighton's Preface *preceded* Moss' Foreword, and that the phrase "exact replica," in quotation marks, was functioning both as quotation and justification of Creighton's innovation. If the revised edition inverted the expository order of the story of the Centennial Exposition and its subsequent developments, it is no doubt because, from a contemporary point of view, a foreword must come before the author's preface. In this case, however, it provides a legitimating order as well: quotation marks and modalization to begin with, followed by direct use, as though the immediate use of the original edition had to be coerced into the legality of discourse.

Of course, since the matter is of some civic importance, it must follow the correct steps. At the same time, since the "original replica" must produce a feeling of immediacy, it has to mobilize opposite instances; this way, the Nashville Parthenon can become "our Parthenon" (as one Nashvillian wrote): "[I]t became a symbol of the civic aspirations of the 'Athens of the South.'"[8] Building the scene of civic aspiration is indeed what matters here or, more to the point, building the scene of civilization. In the words of Anne Roos (who was responsible, in the 1970s, for the recreation of the statue of Athena, once found in the Greek Parthenon): "Since the late nineteenth century, we have had this beautiful building as a mirror in which to see ourselves in the surroundings that represent another great era in Western Civilization."[9] The implicit claim that modern America is *equally* a great era in Western Civilization, one that mirrors itself and contemplates itself in another great era of creation, is telling. We understand now why it can be an "original replica": the reproduction of the ancient Parthenon is not a trivial re-creation, but proof of America's greatness.

The Greek Parthenon is to the one in Nashville what Athenian democracy is to the American—a reference and a mirror in which the latter is allowed to contemplate and enjoy itself. Civic harmony is the locus of civilization: "This, then, may be said of the Parthenon: As in the earlier days, even so now, young and old, rich and poor, are alike made happy by its sheer beauty, and inspired by its history to reach up for a higher and better life."[10] It is not by chance that people insist so much on children as the very *legato* of civic life. Charles Creighton, the architect of the reconstruction in the 1920s, was inspired to write his story of the Nashville Parthenon by the sight of children visiting the monument. And Anne Roos underlines that the statue of Athena was made possible by "the anonymous contributions of hundreds of children and other Parthenon visitors."[11] It is striking that this sort of claim still underlies many visitors' comments. In the Visitor's Book, one can find comments along similar lines: "I remember when I was a kid, I enjoyed walking everyday along the Parthenon, and now my children and grandchildren are able to get the same feeling." The transmission of experience built into tradition still exists, but only in the form of an aesthetic experience that endures across generations, in which old and new mix together like Old and New World in the Parthenon itself.

But here, in contradistinction to the building or, moreover, the dwelling of tradition, novelty is of greater value than age. In the first place, it is *more complete*. What we have in Nashville is the Parthenon as it would have appeared to Pericles' eyes. (I must admit that my greatest surprise, on first seeing the Nashville Parthenon, came from the fact that I beheld a Parthenon with a roof!) When Benjamin Wilson, director of the Parthenon in the 1950s, considered the restoration of the Greek Parthenon, he could not help reversing privileges of time: "The people of the entire world, especially those of America, look on with good wishes for the restoration in the Old World of that which has *already been given* to the New."[12] The Nashville Parthenon short-circuits time: it is at once ancient and modern.

The strongest evidence for this is to be found in the way Wilson describes the very material of the American Parthenon. Considering the cost, it is understandable that it would not be built of marble. It had to be constructed of reinforced concrete, but a special concrete that, through the effects of artificial illumination, "very closely resembles marble."[13] The concern, though, is not economic alone; it also is a matter of time: "Reinforced concrete is the most durable of all building materials and at the same time the most economical." Moreover, it permits a representation of time itself, since, "by a careful selection of materials, the color of the Parthenon at Nashville in daylight is brownish yellow, the same as the ruin at Athens. . . . Under the influence of the floodlights the concrete is rendered the color of the marble and the visitor sees the Parthenon at Nashville as Pericles saw it at Athens."[14] How superior the Nashville Parthenon must be then: it resembles the contemporary ruined temple by day and the intact ancient temple by night, thus summing up old and new, past and present, foreign and native.[15]

This accounts for the monument's curious emplacement between past and future, between the finished and the just beginning. In this way it resumes the artistic discourse of Modernity. Where Bouguereau, for instance, one of the great academic painters, or *pompier*, of the end of the nineteenth century, greatly valued "finished paintings," the Impressionists (and Modernity itself) preferred "unfinished" works that made visible the process itself and the impossibility of definitive achievement. Degas is reported to have ironically answered Bouguereau's motto with words to the effect that, "Bouguereau's paintings are finished, but not begun." Indeed, what Modernity seeks is a beginning, not an ending, hence the ambiguous status of the Parthenon at Nashville, which has to be both old and new, a replica and an original, a re-creation and a true beginning.

It is not only a matter of external appearance though. Inside the temple there are both treasures of the Old World (copies of the Elgin Marbles and, since 1989, a copy of the Phidias statue of Athena) and "treasures" of the New World (in the basement—an innovation of the American "replica"—people can admire the Cowan Collection, which consists of sixty-three original oil paintings by American artists). In this way, Nashvillians testify to their own eternity: history itself is their identity. They are able to resist loss and temporal damage, because they unite the very ancient and the very new without any obvious break. No surprise, then, that Anne Roos unfavorably compares the postmodern recycling of classical antiquity to the Nashvillian experience: "[C]itizens [of Nashville] did not need architect Michael Graves and the 1983 installation of the allegorical "Portlandia". . . to reawaken their enthusiasm for the classical tradition. *They had never lost it.*"[16] The Parthenon at Nashville is a testimony to the identity of history, the authentic *translatio studii* by which America has inherited the Greek legacy. It dissolves time in the immediacy or synchronicity of its presentation.

This is how Nashvillians, with the "original replica" of Phidias' Athena, can be in perfect synchronization with the very *momentum* of history: "At this time when great social movements toward open societies are occurring around the world," writes Anne Roos, "we are fortunate to be able to mark such a moment in history in this way."[17] There is more at stake here than simply shaping America's past; what matters is establishing the universal validity of America's timing and its fitness as a model: "The people of America are realizing more and more the value of the beautiful and demanding its recognition. The Parthenon is playing a large part in this, let us say, new birth. It has become the mecca [*sic*] of thousands of people whose enthusiasm causes other thousands to follow."[18] (Note once more that everything derives immediately from the people, and that America is *the* locus of modern civilization, just as Athens was the origin of Western culture.) This brings to mind the words of one of Saul Bellow's characters: "Everybody needs his memories. They keep the wolf of insignificance from the door."[19] It is the same with people and communities. Collective memory is a way to carve out a place in indifferent time, but this place has to be immediately at hand: one has to be *on the spot*, at the very scene of history. That is the story of modern history.

As David Lowenthal remarks: "So 'authentic' is their replica, Tennesseans brag, that the Greeks would have to study the correct details in Nashville in order to rebuild the original. But authenticity ends outside the portico." And he adds: "Whether or not they improve on the originals, however, replicas lack their history of felt relationships."[20] True enough, but things are still more complex, since the replica *creates* a new history of relationships, beginning, as Walter Benjamin observed, with the relation to the past involved in the reproduction. Benjamin posited that "[to] write history thus means to *cite* history. It belongs to the concept of citation, however, that the historical object in each case is torn from its context."[21] Likewise, the re-creation of the ancient Parthenon operates like a citation in a new context.

Now, experience *of* ruins and experience *in* ruins are two different things. Historical experience is an experience of a caesura, of a rupture between past and present; it is structured by the loss of the past as present. History is an experience of mediation; it is an experience *of* ruins. At Parthenon, Nashville, history seems to offer the experience of immediacy, but—paradoxically enough—an immediacy of duration: history as tradition, not as scientific discourse; history as something present, not as an object of study. A "short-sighted" history, so to speak. But the Nashville Parthenon also is "short-sited," since its site is not atop a temple-crowned hill but rather in the middle of a level park in front of a Holiday Inn, where one enjoys the added convenience of waking to see the Parthenon at eye level—no need so much as to look *up*. As we well know, history is what flattens myths and divinities. The "citation" of the Athenian Parthenon in the parentheses of the Centennial Park shortens the work of historical mediation; it makes the past present and gives a feeling of immediacy, something "short-cited," then.[22]

These remarks were prompted not only by the sight of the Parthenon in Nashville but also by a paper given by Mark Wigley (at a conference held at Vanderbilt University), in which he brilliantly showed how Le Corbusier's insistence that the site generates the architectural design is belied by his practice of recycling the same projects, once they had been rejected, for different sites. But it is a contradiction only if we conceive of an architectural site as a geographical spot. As far as the Parthenon is concerned, it seems that its site is nothing but history. Literally, the Parthenon was built in the middle of what has been called the *Centennial* Park, as a commemoration of a renaissance (the accession to the Union). Self-legitimation, as is always the case with commemorations, uses history as a way of producing an identity that can be recognized universally, because it shares the universal history of the struggle between culture and nature, and because it testifies to its own mark in universal history. If Le Corbusier can recycle his own creations in different places, without contradicting his principle of homogeneity between site and building, it is because geographical spaces most assuredly can be heterogeneous while sharing nonetheless the same fundamental history—modern history, that is, which has been constructed as our *scene* of intelligibility. The Parthenon at Nashville contributes to the building of the modern space of America.

The story could end here, but history alone is no longer all that is at stake. Memory becomes far more crucial. It is striking, for instance, that, in the Visitor's Book, people are not asked to provide comments or note their appreciation; instead, it is literally requested: "Please, share your memories." And people respond accordingly in not proffering any comments but by recalling previous occasions and sharing personal memories incited by the Parthenon. The feeling of historical accuracy is indeed important, but more as a proof of national strength than as a way of experiencing the past. At this point, it is no longer history but collective memory that matters, as we can see in one visitor's legacy: "What beautiful place! And what testament to the South (the TRUE SOUTH!) I was impressed by the historical accuracy and effort put into the Parthenon. SAVE THIS PLACE!" Historical expertise does not operate for the sake of historical experience or for the sharing of universal values of culture but as an *effort* of the South, and as a *legacy* to the South. The Parthenon in Nashville was less a geographical site than a historical place—today, it is a memorial mirror.

It would seem that the Parthenon "authorities" understood as much, since they did not "situate" this Visitor's Book at the exit, near the shop where one buys *souvenirs*, as is customary, but, on the contrary, in the middle of the circuit, in what the Ancient Greeks (so one is informed in the pamphlet provided at the entrance) called "the Treasury." Marvelous insight indeed, since today the true treasury is nothing else than memory. Even more than history, memory is the locus of consensual identification. As John Gillis puts it: "Commemorative activity is by definition social and political, for it involves the coordination of individual and group memories, whose results may appear consensual when they are in fact the product of processes of intense contest, struggle, and, in some instances, annihilation."[23] If the marvelous story of the Parthenon, Nashville, delivers a moral, it must be one of civic aspiration and consensus, one that exalts grandeur and permits one to forget about contests.

No more than individual memory, collective memory is not a place of harmony. When Freud arrived for the first time in Athens, he had this surprising thought: "So all this really *does* exist, just as we learnt at school!"[24] For Freud, it was as though he had been *consciously* convinced, at school, of the historical reality of Athens, while nevertheless remaining *unconsciously* skeptical. But for the psychoanalyst, such an explanation would be far too simple. After self-analysis, Freud realized that:

> It must be that a sense of guilt was attached to the satisfaction in having gone such a long way: there was something about it that was wrong, that from earliest times had been forbidden. It was something to do with a child's criticism of his father, with the undervaluation which took the place of the overvaluation of earlier childhood. It seems that the essence of success was to have got further than one's father, and as though to excel one's father was still something forbidden. . . . Our father had been in business, he had had no secondary education, and Athens could not have meant much to him. Thus what interfered with our enjoyment of the journey to Athens was a feeling of *filial piety*.[25]

Such is exactly what the experience of the Parthenon at Nashville *does not* give. Modern America has to prove both the value of the legacy and its expunction in forgetting. Nowadays people experience it not only as a locus of history but as a place of memory. Collective memory must operate according to filial piety in order to communicate a common feeling of identity and, even more, of immediacy. But such a collective memory, we must beware, is not the same as traditional memory: it rests on the bedrock of history and its inscription on monuments. The Parthenon is not a temple where rites of filial piety are reenacted; it is a monument where rights of consensual immediacy are made visible, then felt. The story of the Parthenon leaves behind the expert dimension of history to enter the authoritative realm of gossip.

Translated from the French by Brian Neville.

NOTES

1. I would like to thank Ann O'Byrne (Vanderbilt University) for helping me find documentation on the Nashville Parthenon.

2. It must be said that it is precisely at this time that the Acropolis and the Parthenon in particular were "properly" restored, when all foreign elements, every sedimentation of time (like the Moslem cupolas, the Frankish tower, the Italian belvedere, etc.) were demolished and forgotten. See Lya et Raimond Matton, *Athènes et ses monuments du XIIe siècle à nos jours* (Athens: Institut français d'Athènes, 1963). As Christine Boyer notes, even modern Athens had to conform to the idea of the ancient city: "Two cities arose side by side: a new Athens that borrowed from everywhere and came to resemble nowhere, and the scenographic illusions of ancient Athens, ephemeral as a dream." See *The City of Collective Memory: Its Historical Imagery and Architectural Entertainments* (Cambridge, Mass.: MIT Press, 1994), 170.

3. Wilbur F. Creighton, *The Parthenon in Nashville, From a Personal Viewpoint* (Brentwood: J M, 1968, rev. ed., 1991), 17.

4. Ibid., 19.

5. Ibid.

6. Charles Moss, Foreword, in Creighton, op. cit., n.p.

7. Ibid., Preface, n.p.

8. Ibid., 57.

9. Quoted in Creighton's rev. ed., op. cit., 54.

10. Benjamin Franklin Wilson III, *The Parthenon of Pericles and Its Reproduction in America* (Nashville: Parthenon, 1955), 139.

11. Anne F. Roos, "The Story of the Nashville Athena," in *The Nashville Athena: A Symposium* (Nashville: private publication, 1990), 3.

12. Wilson, op. cit., 31 (emphasis added).

13. A biography devoted to the inventor of this concrete is titled: "The Man Who Made Cement Beautiful"!

14. Wilson, op. cit., 39.

15. That is exactly what one visitor wrote in the Visitor's Book: "Gives a better understanding of how beautiful the original parthenon [*sic*] in Grece [*sic*] was. It's better than the original!"

16. Roos, op. cit., 4 (emphasis added).

17. Ibid.

18. Wilson, op. cit., 138.

19. Saul Bellow, *Mr. Sammler's Planet* (New York: Viking Press, 1970), 190.

20. David Lowenthal, *The Past Is a Foreign Country* (Cambridge: Cambridge University Press, 1995), 292–93.

21. Walter Benjamin, *The Arcades Project*, translated by Howard Eiland and Kevin McLaughlin (Cambridge, Mass. and London: Belknap Press/Harvard University Press, 1999), 476.

22. As I was reading the Visitor's Book, I could not help transcribing one superb comment from a student at Columbia: "An amazing achievement. As a student of Greek Archaeology this is as complete an experience as one can get, without travelling to Greece (and even there, their Parthenon is in ruins!)." Of what use then to travel to Athens if *their* Parthenon is in ruins? Short-sighted history indeed!

23. John Gillis, "Memory and Identity: The History of a Relationship," in *Commemorations: The Politics of National Identity*, edited by J. Gillis (Princeton: Princeton University Press, 1994), 5.

24. See Sigmund Freud, "A Disturbance of Memory on the Acropolis," in *Standard Edition*, vol. 22, translated and edited by James Strachey (London: Hogarth, 1986), 241.

25. Ibid., 247–48.

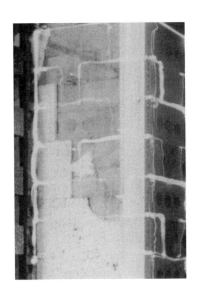

IO

Taking Lanterns
for Bladders

Symbolic and Material
Appropriation in the Postmodern

Wlad Godzich

A FEW YEARS AGO, I WAS IN MONTREAL, where I had been invited to present a version of this chapter as a keynote address for a conference originally entitled *Mémoires des déchets/Memories of Waste*.[1] As I said then, I must admit that I found it very difficult to understand the conference title. In its French version, it seemed to incite me to remember waste matter *[les déchets]*, which could have been in keeping with some vague ecological awareness. Or perhaps the title was a genitive, and we at the conference were requested to ponder the somewhat ridiculous problem of the memorial capacities of waste matter and their eventual contents. Or, seeing that we were to meet within a university institution, that we had been called upon to present theses *[mémoires]* on waste matter. Finally, since I was acquainted with the organizers of the conference, and was aware of their penchant for irony, perhaps it was a matter of declaring *ab initio* the worth of theses, as, here and there, duty requires of us, not only as academics but as citizens, as "members of a cultural community."

However, these speculations were interrupted, in the nick of time, by the English version of the title, which appreciably reduced the semantic field of the word "memory" and added a Proustian note to the positivism of the French title. But here another problem arose: how to understand that I was invited to reflect on *les déchets* and on waste, at one and the same time. The former are not only plural but constitute the very idea of quantity, since waste matter is the quantity lost in the use of a product, whereas "waste" is related to the German *Wüste*, deserted, and designates absence, much like the Latin *vastus*—devastated.

This juxtaposition of the abundant, if not the over-full, and the deserted or de-sertification was far too peculiar to be fortuitous. In its own way it stated one of the most significant themes of contemporary ecological movements, though the theme goes back as far as Malthus, and further still to the Provençal poets: to wit, that it is the over-full that brings about death and disappearance. As Bernard de Ventadorn reminds us, the tree that goes unpruned will produce too much fruit. It will bend under its burden and break, or the overabundance of branches will prevent it from producing and reproducing and, as the expression goes, the desert will reclaim its rights. The theme of quantity, and the need to reduce it in order to stop a gap, will occupy my attention in this chapter, pro-viding I succeed in articulating it with the theme of memory.

Before moving on to this, and seeing that I am elucidating titles, permit me to say a few words about my own title, since it too is rather unclear and further-more highlights its own lack of clarity where it seems to invite one to take lanterns for bladders. In the title one may recognize the inversion of the French saying *"prendre des vessies pour des lanternes"* [to take bladders for lanterns],[2] which has always struck me as rather obscure and suggestive that this obscurity was not altogether fortuitous either. According to the dictionaries, the French expression, which dates from the nineteenth century, signifies "to grossly fall for some trumpery," which would then give us the following inversion in English: "to gross out by means of a trump"—something that is not entirely extraneous to my concerns. But before I get to this, I must further engage in a little bit of lexicog-raphy. "*Prendre des vessies pour des lanternes*" is a corruption of a much older ex-pression, "*vendre vessies pour lanternes*" [to hawk bladders as lanterns], and before that, "*faire vessies lanternes*" [to pass off bladders as lanterns], which means that originally the expression did not mean to grossly fall for some trumpery, but to grossly trump another, and that the benighted Self appears only with the advent of Enlightenment reflexivity.

But how can one trick others into taking bladders for lanterns? No doubt there is a formal similitude, and perhaps a like translucence between the two objects, but it is great leap from there to mistaking one for the other.

Vessie, the French word for bladder and cognate of vesicle, "little bladder," allows us perhaps to understand how this leap was made. This word designates, in man and in woman, just as in certain animals, the musculo-membranous reser-voir in which accumulates the urine produced by a body during the digestion of food. Hence, it is an organ in charge of gathering what, in poetic fashion, is known in English as "waste matter" and in French as "*les déchets.*" But this word also designates the very same organ when taken from the body of an animal, dried, and filled with air; it then takes on the meaning of some useless matter, or trumpery. In other words, a bladder full of waste matter is important, whereas one filled with air is not. This at least has the merit of shedding some light on the respective value of urine and air. All the same, it hardly illumines our lantern, rather, it leaves us further in the dark. Waste matter, it would seem, is more important than air, no doubt because of its prior occupation of the bladder: an original *noblesse oblige*.

Meanwhile, the relentless *Grand Robert Dictionnaire historique de la langue française* adds that, like bladder, *vessie* designates, and since 1690 at that, a membrane of whatever material, inflated with air, placed inside the membrane of a ball; furthermore: "as in Latin, the word was used (c. fourteenth century) in reference to a blister *[ampoule]* on the skin." Here is the clue we were looking for: this ampullaceous vesicle on the skin, this common blister *[cloque]*, filled with air or water, it matters little which, is pregnant with the future (*en cloque de l'avenir*, as the French say). For although it could not know that, someday, the word *ampoule* also would come to mean the little glass bulb enclosing an incandescent filament that enables any one of us to take up the injunction "*fiat lux*," in all efficacy and with just the flick of a switch, it remains, nonetheless, that this "*vessie-ampoule*" is pregnant with that future.

Captious individuals will object that I am playing with words, and that in no way does the *Grand Robert Historique* authorize me to see in the use of the word *vessie* for *ampoule* during the fourteenth century the forerunning sign for the use of the word *ampoule* in the context of electric light. This, despite the fact that it was indeed during the fourteenth century that the expression "*vendre vessies pour lanternes*" saw the light of day—an expression that to me seems entirely clear, if not luminous, since one day a lantern will indeed need a bulb.

To these peevish few, I would simply retort that they do not know what memory is. Those of us who bothered to read and reread Derrida's moving *Mémoires: For Paul de Man*[3] know that memory is not recollection but is in fact a time machine, and that words, no less than human beings, can carry within them—be pregnant with, possess the Holy Ampulla, be equipped with a bladder that contains—the future as well as the past. And we know that if we want there to be a present, that is, that liminal zone between past and future, it is in our full interest that such be the case. Otherwise, we will find ourselves ever pursued by an all consuming past or about to be engulfed in a no less voracious future which, in either scenario, holds out little to us except the prospect of an unappetizing trip through an intestinal tract that threatens to transform us into waste matter.

I, for one, prefer to follow *Maître* Jacques' lesson and to find that *vessie* already contained *ampoule*, well before that little rascal Edison had the idea in 1878 to evacuate a small crystal globe and place carbon paper inside it to turn it into an electric lightbulb. The *vessie* carried the memory of the electric lantern to come, and it played its trump by expelling the vulgar urine, replacing it with light.

So much for "hawking" or "taking bladders for lanterns." Let us now turn to the inversion of my title, "taking lanterns for bladders." Does it not in turn denote the age-old activity of memory, which calls upon us to remember the bladder in the lantern? Can the lantern claim autonomy simply because it fulfilled the ideal of light? Are we not blinded by this lantern light to the bladder that carried it within? Must the lantern dispose of the bladder like some waste matter? Must Modernity cut itself off from its past, treating it as though it were only good for the dustbin of history? The object of my inversion is what Walter Benjamin called the *Jetztzeit*, the "time of the now" that is ever pregnant with both the past and the future.

Accustomed to an environment that does not always provide them with enough to eat, peasants of the Peruvian Andes have a saying that goes: "*Quién caga por la mañana es goloso*" (He who craps in the morning is a glutton). Indeed, he lacks foresight and risks feeling the pangs of hunger in his gut, now empty for the rest of the day. The wary peasant prefers to hold onto a full paunch, even if it is only waste matter, rather than to feel gaping hunger inside, to feel consumed by the hunger gap, for the cordilleran peasant knows that the *Jetztzeit persists* on the crest created by the forward thrust and conjuncture of past and future.

Taking lanterns for bladders is therefore a practice of the *Jetztzeit*, in which past and future are not remote zones, one for ever completed, the other ever in abeyance, but a practice of their circulation, of their setting in motion, of their cycling and recycling.

Allow me to submit for our contemplation the curiosity whose image is re-produced in Figure 10.1. This thing was made in a Ghanaian village around the beginning of the 1980s. According to a five-year plan worked out in the capi-tal, this village figured as the future site of a power station. The plan was con-ceived as yet within the vision of an African-styled socialism dear to Kwame N'krumah, who had postulated that one did not have to await the coming of communism to electrify, and who had foreseen in the megaproject damming of the Volta—a programmatically named river indeed—the means with which to modernize the country and bring light to the people of Ghana, that is, modern Enlightenment. Ultimately the plan had to be shelved, a casualty not only of the deposition of N'krumah and successive coups d'état but, above all, of the policy of structural adjustment advocated by the International Monetary Fund (IMF) following the first Mexican debt crisis in the early 1980s. For quite some time the inhabitants of the village had to resign themselves to wait for the coming of Mazda among them, and as a crowning irony, the government of one northern country had just delivered to them a large quantity of lightbulbs, in anticipation of their imminent electrification. We would never be so ill willed as to suspect an all too common act of commercial dumping, with concomitant tax breaks for the supplier of the bulbs. The fact remains that the inhabitants of our village found themselves with a large quantity of bulbs on their hands, in an area with-out any electricity and condemned by the IMF to remain an electrical desert for some time to come.

FIGURE 10.1   "Oil lamp made from an electric bulb and tin
can. Kumase, Ghana," Eduardo Paolozzi, in *Lost Magic Kingdoms and Six Paper Moons from Nahuatl* (London: British
Museum Publications, 1985), 37.

Since they had to see their way clear to a solution, the inhabitants of the village fabricated objects like those we see in Figure 10.1. They took lightbulbs, withdrew the metal base that enables electrical conduction, removed the incandescent filament, let the inert gas therein escape (a certain krypton, which did not scare them, seeing that the IMF had just apprised them that they were no supermen, only poor African villagers), and filled the cavity either with kerosene or oil. They then took tin canisters and Coke or beer cans, discarded by the swarms of experts, inspectors, and military men who, from time to time, had beleaguered their village, cut them up, and made supports for the bulbs filled now with inflammable liquid. This is how lanterns once again became bladders, confirming thereby the arduous two-way trip on which they could be sent.

And as circulation cannot be reduced to a simple come and go, this object found its way out of the village in which it saw the light of day. It set off for Accra, the capital of the country, where it found the favoring regard of Scottish sculptor, Sir Eduardo Paolozzi, whose name testifies as well to a certain circulation. Paolozzi gave it pride of place at the Museum of Mankind in London, where he was invited to create an exhibition. It was photographed and included in the exhibition catalogue, which I was given as a present in 1994, in Philadelphia. I brought it back to Geneva to make a slide for my opening address at the Montreal conference. It is of no small importance to learn that London galleries now lay in stores of these things in Ghana, only to sell them at such a high price that a modestly salaried academic cannot afford to purchase one.

I would like to recommend this object as the starting point for our meditations on memory and waste matter, in the hope that it may illuminate our reflections by its own *sui generis* (but not bilious) light.

Meanwhile, permit me to recount another little incident, this time concerning memory. Some time ago, I was in Bern for the meeting of a university planning commission, a body whose tasks are not without bearing on our reflections here. Upon this body devolves the responsibility of making suggestions about the best way to prune the dead wood in the university institution and of determining, in these times of hegemonic market economy, the place that one can still allot to what the Germanic Swiss call *"Orchideenfächer,"* those specializations, such as literature, that are beautiful like orchids and just as parasitic. Exceptionally, our work finished ahead of time, and some two hours remained before my next appointment. To my great satisfaction, I discovered that the local theater was showing the current Jean-Luc Godard film, which I had not yet had the chance to see, *Woe Is Me*—that is the title of the film, as well as an *a parte* reflection on the congestion of my schedule.[4]

As you are no doubt aware, in his film Godard casts one Gérard Depardieu in the role of God, no less, who returns to earth, in the area of Geneva, not to see if one can walk upon the Lake of Geneva with the same ease as one can upon

Lake Tiberias or the Sea of Galilee, but to spread the good word of love. In this respect, Godard's film puts us in mind of Pier Paolo Pasolini's *Teorema*, which we would be wrong to assume signifies "theorem," in the geometric sense of the term; rather, it means "things (said) of or by God." In the latter film, one will recall, a handsome young man, an angel, descends to earth and takes up residence among an upstanding family of the Roman bourgeoisie. In turn, he seduces each member of the family—the maid, the young woman, the son, the mother, and the father—only then to abandon them, leaving a gap that no one knows quite how to fill. Godard's film is not quite as ironic as the gospel according to Pier Paolo. What struck me, and this is all I will allow myself to evoke at this moment, is the very beginning of the film where Godard himself, in a voice-over, reads or recites the following text:

> When the Baal Shem had a difficult task before him, he would go to a certain place in the woods, light a fire and meditate in prayer—and what he had set out to perform was done. When a generation later the "Maggid" of Meseritz was faced with the same task, he would go to the same place in the woods and say: We can no longer light the fire, but we can still speak the prayers—and what he wanted done became reality. Again, a generation later, Rabbi Moshe Lieb of Sassov had to perform this task. And he too went to the woods and said: We can no longer light the fire, nor do we know the secret meditations belonging to the prayer, but we do know the place in the woods to which it all belongs—and that must be sufficient; and sufficient it was. But when another generation had passed and Rabbi Israel of Rishin was called upon to perform the task, he sat down on his golden chair in his castle and said: We cannot light the fire, we cannot speak the prayers, we do not know the place, but we can tell the story of how it was done. And, the storyteller adds, the story which he told had the same effect as the actions of the other three.[5]

This text, which Gershom Scholem relates as having been told to him by S.Y. Agnon, was very familiar to me, for I had cited it at the very beginning of my study of prose.[6] Back then, what had interested me was the power of signifying practices. This time, I am curious about what Agnon's little tale, taken up by Godard, has to say about memory. The succession of generations of rabbis stresses indeed a progressive loss of knowledge and memory, without—and therein lies the paradox—this hindering in any way whatsoever the rabbis' power. The contents of memory, its substance, are lost, whereas its efficacy remains. Godard's decision to evoke this story, at the outset of a film in which God, it seems, has lost all substantiality, serves as a warning: just because God is now emptied of substance, just because He is the waste matter from another culture, the culture of belief, does not mean that He is without efficacy. That is the theorem, Q.E.D. It can be understood, on an elementary level, by observing that God has little need for theologians, or men and women for that matter, in order to remain God. God only becomes that much more mysterious. Rephrasing this in the vocabulary of Walter Benjamin that I was just using, God forsakes the "*Jetzt der Erkenntniß*," the now of knowing, and the "*Jetzt der Erkenntnisse*," the now of things known, to take refuge fully in the pure "time of the now," the *Jetztzeit*.[7]

But is it only God who withdraws in this way? That is the question that should, it seems to me, concern us today. Is God the only waste matter to recover an efficacy? And what then would be the nature of that efficacy? I can only sketch something of an answer at this time, and to do so I cannot help but return to certain texts that are at the heart of my reflections, namely, the writings of Kant.

We will recall that in the section on the "Transcendental Aesthetic" from the *Critique of Pure Reason*, as much as in the first "Introduction" to the *Critique of Judgement*, Kant tells the story of what we might call the psychogenesis of the modern subject.[8] This subject, we should bear in mind, is destined to play the role of *hypokeimenon*, that is, the ground not only of knowledge and cognition, of action and judgment of the beautiful, but of the world itself, given that its activity consists in assuring the transformation of this world into a collection of objects for the subject it has become. I would like to slow down Kant's reasoning in order to draw attention to the stages of this constitution of the subject.

For starters, Kant observes that our relation to the world is mediated by the sensorial apparatus with which we are equipped. The latter is always more or less alert, and it determines the nature of our interface with the world. Of course, Kant wants to make judgment the prototypical activity of human beings, and he is eager to reach the moment when judgment is not only possible but actually rendered. But his intellectual probity obliges him to enumerate the intermediary steps. Consequently, he ascertains that there exist forms of cognition of the world that are available to me without my needing recourse to judgment or even consciousness. For instance, if I have got in the habit of taking hot baths, it could happen that, on a particularly humid day, my body—by my skin and respiratory tract—reminds me of, or rather remembers, the impression produced on it during its brief sojourn in the hot or warm bath water. It will indeed be my understanding *(Verstand)* that formulates the judgment that the air is moist, but it will reach this judgment on the basis of a sensorial intuition, doubled by a memory that we could say is entirely corporeal.

This corporeal memory is at once troubling and reassuring. Reassuring, because it confirms our continuity with the things of this world, but troubling insofar as it is beyond the control of consciousness and higher faculties such as understanding, or even lower faculties such as intuition. In the Kantian architectonics, this corporeal memory holds a place analogous to that held by imagination. The latter, one will remember, is called upon to compensate for the shortcomings of understanding by providing us with an Idea of reason, to prevent understanding from getting stuck in its powerlessness and upon discovering the falsity of its pretensions to substitute itself for reason.

When imagination intervenes to give us an Idea of reason, it gives not the substance of reason but the form of this Idea. With what then does this corporeal memory provide us? Certainly not a form, since control over the latter belongs to the higher faculties. Summarily, I would say that it gives us a materiality independent of all form. And a materiality without form, for Kant, is something without substance and, worse yet, something that is not locatable with respect to the all-important distinction between a priori and a posteriori. Indeed, insofar as this memory presupposes an experience, in the most empirical sense of the term, it belongs to the a posteriori. But the a posteriori is governed by the presence of a subject that knows how to locate things and differentiate between, among others, a priori and a posteriori. Now, in the case before us, there is nothing of the kind. There is no subject, but neither are we on the side of Pure Reason. In other words, we are not on the side of the *noumenon*. We are simply outside of the *"Jetzt der Erkenntniß"* (the now of knowing), that is, in the gap between a priori and a posteriori.

But let us follow the Kantian psychogenesis a bit further. Kant supposes the existence of a subsequent stage. Here there is still no subject constituted as such, and consequently no objects *(Gegenstände)* in the world, since the presence of the latter presupposes (and entails) the existence of a subject. No objects without subjects, and vice versa.

Kant resorts to two words to designate the formation of this dyad: *Vorstellung* and *Darstellung*. Normally, both are rendered as "representation," but they are not equivalent. *Darstellung* is composed of the word *Stellung* (standing, position, placement) and the prefix *da*, meaning simply that the placing is effected in an indefinite space, any space that, while no doubt susceptible to specification, remains indefinite. And this space is indefinite because there is as yet no subject to give it its orientations. I would translate it as "emplacement," capturing in the prefix "em" this notion of indefiniteness. In contrast, *Vorstellung* is located with respect to someone before whom *(vor)* the *Stellung* has been effected. Here looms the subject, and we enter completely into the well-known Kantian schema; the object is the *Gegenstand*, a *Vorstellung* of which is provided by the subject's understanding. The *"Jetzt der Erkenntniß,"* the now of knowing, has come to pass.

Kant's text quickly glosses over this distinction, and it was necessary that I draw it up in its hurry in order to isolate the moment which, in the Kantian psychogenesis, precedes the formation of the object and the constitution of the subject. This moment holds no interest for Kant, since it is followed inevitably by its modern realization. But to us, the masters of speed and celerity, who perform slow motions and fast forwards, and who know that such movements are never only one way, this almost accidental and anodyne stage in Kant's reflection may seem, on the contrary, of great interest. It would be the moment when there would not as yet, or no longer, be either subject or object. It would be the moment when the categories of space and time—which we know render experience possible—are not as yet, or no longer, wholly operational. Finally, it would be the moment when form—which we know is the contribution of the human spirit to the world—has not as yet been able, or known how, to deploy itself, or has already begun to resorb itself.

This moment is not the perfect analogue of the desubstantialization of God, which preserves and, who knows, increases in this way his or her efficacy. It is the moment when objects are, or once more become, things. But not things in the sense that they are opposed to objects as the *noumenon* is opposed to the *phenomenon*, but rather things in the sense that they are both one and the other, at one and the same time and without distinction. They can seesaw to one side or the other—to be or to exist—but they also can just as well be content to *persist* on the crest, not falling to one side or the other, things then, and not waste matter, since there is waste matter only from the perspective of a subject.

And somewhere among these things, there is this curious entity that is not yet, or no longer, the subject; an entity that does not as yet, or no longer, assume the weight of the world but that receives the impulses and intensities of the world, and itself tries to persist. Neither being nor existent, equally beyond the ontological as the ontic, this entity finds itself in a world of which it is a part, not as fallen angel nor nascent superman but as a *persistence*, which looks to preserve its energy and to gather more. Its emplacement in the gap does not immobilize it. On the contrary, it constrains it to movement, a movement in an uncharted space, without orientations, a movement for which speed and celerity are far more important than direction.

Waste matter exists, therefore, only with respect to the *"Jetzt der Erkenntniß."* It is the waste matter of such thinking. In the other temporalities, there is the indifferent persistence of things, a persistence that is not bereft of efficacy and that functions in the mode of bidirectional memory.

Translated from the French by Brian Neville.

NOTES

1. The conference was held on March 23–26, 1995. The original address appears in the French companion to this volume, *La mémoire des déchets: Essais sur la culture et la valeur du passé*, edited by Johanne Villeneuve, Brian Neville, and Claude Dionne (Québec: Nota Bene Éditeur, 1999). The talk was given before a backdrop of the projected image of a recycled object found in Ghana (see Fig. 10.1) and accompanied throughout by the music of Steve Reich's *Different Trains*, a composition for string quartet

and tape (Steve Reich, "Different Trains," perf. The Kronos Quartet, Elektra/Nonesuch, 1989). Over a sound track composed of the recorded reminiscences of his governess, and the voices of train porters and Holocaust survivors—along with European train sounds of the 1930s and 1940s—Reich's piece travels in memory between the experiences of his childhood and those of his Jewish contemporaries in Europe. Like the visual, the aural elements of Wlad Godzich's presentation helped substantiate his conclusion on the temporal heterogeneity of memory. [Eds.]

2. The expression presents certain difficulties in translation. An English equivalent for the French "*prendre des vessies pour des lanternes*" would be the expression "to believe that the moon is made of blue cheese," which clearly substitutes a different set of associations, evacuating the waste matter of the bladder for the more palatable gastronomic reference. Out of respect for the semantic integrity of this chapter, we have chosen to use the French expression as far as possible. [Tr.]

3. Jacques Derrida, *Mémoires: For Paul de Man*, translated by Cecile Lindsay, Jonathan Culler, Eduardo Cadava, and Peggy Kamuf (New York: Columbia University Press, 1989).

4. *Hélas pour moi [Woe Is Me]*, directed by Jean-Luc Godard, Les films Alain Sarde/Véga Films, 1993.

5. See Gershom Scholem, *Major Trends in Jewish Mysticism* (New York: Schocken, 1941), 349–50.

6. Wlad Godzich and Jeffrey Kittay, *The Emergence of Prose: An Essay in Prosaics* (Minneapolis: University of Minnesota Press, 1987), 10.

7. See Walter Benjamin, "Theses on the Philosophy of History," in *Illuminations*, edited by Hannah Arendt and translated by Harry Zohn (New York: Schocken, 1969), esp. pp. 261–63; *The Arcades Project*, translated by Howard Eiland and Kevin McLaughlin (Cambridge, Mass. and London: Belknap Press/Harvard University Press, 1999), esp. pp. 456–88.

8. See Immanuel Kant, *Critique of Pure Reason*, translated by Werner S. Pluhar (Indianapolis: Hackett, 1996); *The Critique of Judgement*, translated by James Creed Meredith (Oxford: Clarendon, 1952).

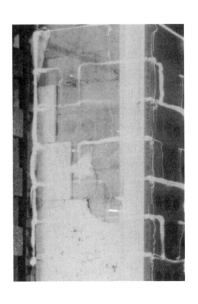

II

History's
Mortal
Remains

Valeria Wagner

¿Porqué es necesario que mueran los que murieron?
¿Porqué es necesario matar y morir?
—Subcomandamente Marcos, in the name of the EZLN

"WHY WAS IT NECESSARY FOR THOSE WHO HAVE DIED TO DIE? Why is it necessary to kill and to die?"[1] These questions were raised by the Subcomandamente Marcos at the outset of negotiations between the EZLN (Ejército Zapatista de Liberación Nacional) and the Mexican federal government, which officially started on February 21, 1994. Although Marcos is referring to the specific necessity of resorting to an armed struggle in order for claims to justice, equality, and democracy to be, simply, heard,[2] these two questions also can be raised with respect to the making of Western history in general—a long history of systematic oppression, revolt, wars, and countless anonymous, forgotten deaths, perpetrated in various names for the sake of controlling the course of events. Marcos' questions may sound naive, and could be given an easy answer: the oppressors kill the oppressed in various ways in order to have their way; the oppressed fight back to defend their lives and ways. But such an answer would only restate the facts—that people die and kill to further various ends—without responding to the point of Marcos' questions: that killing and dying need not be necessary, and that we should consider what it is that makes them the necessary means, as the EZLN puts it, "to walk history" *(caminar la historia)*. The suggestion is that the necessity in question is not situated in the realm of actual historical events (in the laws of "nature," or of the "real") but in the "laws" ordering our understanding of history today. In what follows, I address Marcos' questions from the perspective of this suggestion: Why does our concept of history impose the necessity of killing and dying? How are death and necessity articulated in our understanding of history?

A "fable" recounted by Jean-François Lyotard as a description of the "current historical situation"[3] can provide a sketch of the configuration of history, death, and necessity. The tale, which he purports to be "reasonably well accredited" in "very serious milieus," is in fact an account of the current situation of (our understanding of) history—or, in Lyotard's words, it is the "grand narrative that [the postmodern world] stubbornly tries to tell about itself."[4] What it tells itself, according to Lyotard, is a post–Darwinian version of history, in which life systems struggle against each other for energy. In this struggle, verticality and language give "the system called Man" advantage over other life systems. This system constitutes itself in different forms of aggregations, among which, in turn, the systems called liberal democracies prove to be the fittest for survival because of their greater ability to control events. The Sun's imminent death, however, threatens to extinguish even these fittest of life systems, and Man accordingly begins to envisage the possibility of emigrating from Earth and from the solar system.

This tale obviously represents the grand narrative of progress that still dominates historical understanding. It takes up, as if to illustrate them, the three basic features that Walter Benjamin, in his "Theses on the Philosophy of History," attributes to the notion of progress "as pictured in the minds of the Social Democrats":

> Progress . . . was, first of all, the progress of mankind itself (and not just advances in men's ability and knowledge). Secondly, it was something boundless, in keeping with the infinite perfectibility of mankind. Thirdly, progress was regarded as irresistible, something that automatically pursued a straight or spiral course.[5]

Pictured, this time, in the minds of postmoderns, Mankind (Man) continues its boundless and irresistible progress: indeed, in Lyotard's tale not even the death of the Sun constitutes a limit to such progression; nothing seems capable of stopping Man's skyward migration. Benjamin adds, moreover, that "the concept of the historical progress of mankind cannot be sundered from the concept of its progression through a homogeneous, empty time,"[6] a concept which itself depends, as we will see, on the possibility of sundering the present from the past. Accordingly, in Lyotard's tale, the definitive emptying of time and disposal of the past seems bound to take place as Man prepares to leave not only the earth behind but also his mortal remains: the system, we are told, is already devoting research "to the problem of adjusting or replacing human bodies so that human brains would still be able to work with the only forms of energy left available in the cosmos."[7]

Nightmarish as it sounds, this fable has the clear advantage of being, in Lyotard's words, as yet only "the dream that the postmodern world dreams about itself,"[8] and as such of foregrounding the conditions for the irresistibility and boundlessness of the advance of the metanarrative of progress—namely, the consumption and elimination of bodies. Indeed, not only is the metanarrative of progress literally propelled by mortal remains at the "end" of the tale, but these sustain throughout the narrative's forward drive—until the movement toward post-terrestrial life begins, human bodies are the necessary purveyors and processors of the energy feeding life systems. This fact, however, must be silenced lest Life, the entity that supposedly engenders necessity (Life must go on), collapse into the billions of mortals it consumes—in other words, lest the whole narrative artifact itself collapse. Indeed, mortal remains sustain, more crucially, the apparently self-sufficient and necessary relationship between progress and Life (the survival of the species or of the best life system), and the acknowledgment of their protagonism would invalidate the inexorability of the narrative logic—the irresistible and boundless narrative drive.

Lyotard's account thus suggests that, under the aegis of the metanarrative of progress, the concept of history requires deaths—and it needs them, more specifically, forgotten and out of sight, to set the conditions for an irresistible drive toward the future, unimpeded by the weight of the past. How deaths can be the means to impose the future and discard the past is not, however, self-evident. In order to investigate this, I now turn to Aeschylus' *The Oresteia*,[9] which at least three commentators have read as "a grand parable of progress."[10] By this the commentators meant that the trilogy stages the structural changes that made Greece, or at least Athens, "Western," and that consequently either civilized it or marked our entry into civilization (democracy). These stereotypes are too familiar to need refutation, but they indicate that the trilogy affords a reading in terms of progress, and more specifically in terms of the inaugural step into progress. What is interesting for our purposes is that in Aeschylus' trilogy the step into the modality and temporality of progress is preceded by a number of deaths, articulating a struggle for the recovery of mortal remains.

As is well known, *The Oresteia* recounts the cycle of revenge that decimates the House of Atreus. The basic plot can be told in a few words: in *Agamemnon*, Clytemnestra kills Agamemnon because he had previously killed Iphigeneia, their daughter; in *The Choephori*, Orestes, their son, kills Clytemnestra because she killed Agamemnon, his father; in *The Eumenides*, Orestes is pursued by the Furies for matricide but, protected by Apollo, seeks refuge in Athena's temple, is given a democratic trial, and is acquitted. It is this third play that nourishes the reading of the trilogy as a parable of progress: Orestes' acquittal, entailing the "taming" of the Furies, gods of revenge, would secure the establishment of a democratic judiciary system. More importantly, representing the overpowering of the law of revenge, the taming of the Furies inaugurates a new temporality, based on the possibility to decree the finality of the past. Indeed, the particularity of revenge is that it treats the past as an ongoing event and has no respect for linear temporality: on the contrary, it disrupts sequential order, as it denies that what is past is over. To pacify the Furies—who call themselves "the proud heart of the past"[11]—is thus tantamount to acquiring a certain guarantee that the future will flow smoothly, and it is with this argument that Athena wins the goodwill of the guardians of revenge:

> As time flows on, the honours flow through all
> my citizens, and you, throned in honour
> before the house of Erechtheus, will harvest
> more from men and women moving in solemn file
> than you can win throughout the mortal world.[12]

As the Furies accept the promised "flowing honours" and, instead of conjuring up the past, joyfully "sound [their] blessings forth,"[13] there seems to be no impediment to the continued, smooth, eternal flow of time.

Athena's "democratic trial," however, does not outlaw revenge altogether: it condemns Clytemnestra's, but sanctions Orestes'. Insofar as the two revenges are fairly straightforward—Clytemnestra avenges her daughter's death, and Orestes, his father's—the reasons for the different treatment they receive should be sought in the significance of Iphigeneia's death, which indirectly launches the cycle of revenge concluding with Athena's judgment.[14] This death has a particular status within the trilogy, because it is not itself perpetrated to revenge another death. It is, however, related to another revenge, appearing even as its enabling condition. In the Chorus' words, Iphigeneia is sacrificed "to bless the war that avenged a woman's loss."[15] Agamemnon gives her up for sacrifice, following the diviner Calchas' advice, in order to placate Artemis, who has sent an ill wind preventing the Hellene fleet from setting sail for Troy. From this perspective, her sacrifice takes on the significance of an exchange: Iphigeneia for Helen, a woman for a woman. More importantly, however, her death can be read as purchasing the future from the gods: her life, which she has still to live—she is young—for the future that Agamemnon and his troops want to secure; her issue—she is a virgin—for an issue for the troops. And it does purchase the immediate future of the troops by changing the wind, thus setting, very concretely, the conditions of possibility for the Greeks' participation in the war. Her death also confers a character of necessity on the "higher" order of events into which it is subsumed, for, as her life was, in a sense, "due" to her, so should be the future for which it was exchanged.

The kind of necessity produced by Iphigeneia's death is not, to be sure, of a natural order—the sacrifice does not predetermine a course of events that could then not otherwise unfold. The "necessity" her death produces is rather of the order of an *ought*, binding agents to their actions as though they could not do something else. This is apparent in the Chorus' account of how Agamemnon takes the "decision" to give his daughter up for sacrifice. Agamemnon finds himself in a typical tragic situation of having to "choose" between worse and worse: to put an end to the life he fathered or to "desert the fleets" and "fail the alliance"—"Pain both ways and what is worse?"[16] The first option, as Agamemnon realizes, will bring doom upon him, even though it has been legitimated by the god's will ("Law is law!").[17] The second option is not only dishonorable but implies blocking the course of a project that is already in the making. Sparing Iphigeneia's life, moreover, does not make up for this closure of the future: it offers no issue for itself, it does not present itself as capable of generating events, it has no hold on Agamemnon's future—it does not awaken his *ought*.[18] Thus Agamemnon complies with the god's demand, submitting to, rather than actively taking up, the future that Iphigeneia's death will open up: "Then he put on/The harness of necessity."[19]

The sacrifice of Iphigeneia, then, can be seen as enforcing, rather than responding to, necessity: instead of being the necessary condition for the Hellene fleet to sail, it appears as the condition creating the necessity—in the sense of the "drive" or the "ought"—for them to sail on and for events to pursue a given (although not fixed) course. Her death is necessary, in a sense, to create necessity, to harness the course of events. Before her death, it is still possible that the fleet will not sail—once it takes place, however, the ensuing events acquire a certain irreversibility and finality, by the status that Zeus himself, as Apollo tells us, has attributed to all deaths:

> . . . once the dust drinks down a man's blood,
> he is gone, once for all. No rising back,
> no spell sung over the grave can sing him back—
> not even Father can. Though all things else
> he can overturn and never strain for breath.[20]

Death is the one event that once a fact is absolutely beyond repair, beyond even the utmost god's power of healing. And, as there is no raising the dead, there is no going back on the sacrifice of Iphigeneia, and hence no altering the necessity it has conferred on the sailing of the troops. It is in this sense that ensuing events are "given": her death seals other possibilities and inaugurates a course from which there is no turning back. Thus if Agamemnon "puts on the harness of necessity" when he "decides" to comply with his daughter's sacrifice, her death puts the harness of necessity on events.

Clytemnestra's revenge, bringing Agamemnon the doom he expected, has far-reaching implications in light of the significance of the death to which it responds. It is, above all, an overt refusal of and revolt against the subsumption of Iphigeneia's death into the logic of a higher order of events. Thus in defense of her treacherous murder of Agamemnon, she tells the Chorus her own version of the events, in which the long-term consequences of Iphigeneia's death are flatly ignored: "he sacrificed his daughter . . . /to charm away the savage winds of Thrace."[21] Here the incongruity between reason (a charm to stop the wind) and act (killing) detaches Iphigeneia's death, as a bare fact—all the more bare and factual in that it is irreversible—from the sequence of events leading to the Trojan War. In a similar gesture, she mocks the Chorus for attempting to cover the fact of Iphigeneia's death by inscribing Agamemnon's act in the narrative sequel of Helen's elopement with Paris.[22] As she clings to the isolated fact of her sacrifice, Clytemnestra retrieves Iphigeneia's mortal remains from the future-bound fabric into which it was wrought—neither what followed her death, nor what it supposedly allowed to occur, can harness to the past the sheer event of her daughter's death. The event of her death prevails, as an event, in the present, regardless of its place in any given sequence of events, and is therefore accessible to action, subject to other sequels, and definitely not gone forever. Thus if death was capable of generating future events in the case of Agamemnon, in Clytemnestra's, it is capable of regenerating the past in the present.

What we have, then, is a double generative function of death: on the one hand, it propels events into the future, investing them with a certain character of necessity derived from its unique status of irreversibility; on the other hand, the event of death prevails through time regardless of its place in a given sequential order, opening the present to the past, and the past to action. Agamemnon's crime enforces the former, Clytemnestra's, the latter. It is thus comprehensible that Clytemnestra's death should be sanctioned with Orestes' trial, for her revenge destabilizes Athena's temporal regime. Iphigeneia's death instead enables this temporal regime, but in order for it to prevail, the fact of the death itself must be overlooked, lest further claims to Iphigeneia's mortal remains reawaken the disruptive forces of the past. Accordingly, Iphigeneia's death is forgotten in Orestes' trial, engulfed into the narrative of his vengeance for his father's death. As with all narratives of progress, or all gestures in accordance with this metanarrative, what is at stake is the avoidance of the double generative effects of deaths: their role in the making of history must be played offstage. But, as I now want to suggest with a discussion of what could be staged as a sequel to Aeschylus' trilogy—as the post–Athenian struggle to free the past from the harness of the metanarrative of progress—deaths can never be sufficiently out of sight and the past never sufficiently left behind.

The military dictatorship that took power in Argentina in March 1976 presented itself as the responsible head of the family (of Argentineans), forced to take drastic measures (the elimination of subversion) to reestablish order in the family house (the nation).[23] This order was enforced with the sacrifice of "siblings": between 20,000–30,000 people were tortured and assassinated during this period, as part of the "Process of National Organization." The military dictatorship covered up the bare facts of these deaths by "disappearing" people, a strategy that, as it is generally agreed upon, had the specific objective of spreading terror in the population, terror that would in turn enforce the "forgetfulness" of the events producing it. Accordingly, there was no attempt to hide the fact that there were disappearances, for its acknowledgment confronted people with the possibility of undergoing the same "fate." The official discourse could then appear as a shield against this possibility, because it provided the criteria determining the choice of the disappeared: only subversives were eliminated, and were subversive all those refusing to acknowledge the necessity of eliminating subversion.

Thus as Francine Masiello points out, the middle class was "surprisingly blind" to the reigning repression and was all too ready to endorse the discourse of the dictatorship: "the disappearances of acquaintances or of the young couple living around the block were often interpreted by ordinary citizens as an indication of the victim's guilt of attempting sedition."[24] Here the disappearances are acknowledged only to be waved away into the military regime's narrative logic, under which they suffer a second disappearance: indeed, while the discourse of the dictatorship legitimated the disappearances, it denied the government's responsibility for them and even put into question their advent.[25] The disappeared thus disappeared at once from life and history. As one survivor put it, "[I]f the sewer is the destiny of trash, military prisons were the sewer of our history."[26]

The method of disappearing people also worked to reinforce the prevalence of the military's version of history by producing unintelligibility beyond its narrative confines. Thus the mother of a seventeen-year-old says of her own state following his disappearance: "I could not have said 'I feel as if my heart had been taken away from me,' no: it was the intelligence."[27] As she insists throughout her testimony, his disappearance remained incomprehensible, not so much because it was unmotivated and arbitrary, but because the uncertainty it maintained about his being alive or dead tore the fabric of reality. Thus although reason claimed that the disappeared had been killed and were dead, the unreality of these deaths prevailed: "You saw them go out, and nobody ever brought him back dead, nobody ever gave sufficiently concrete details. And then your part of unconscious fantasy never encounters reality."[28] Here death cannot crystallize into fact, because the memory of the event of death is missing to the point that it cannot even be reconstituted by hearsay. There is thus no "bare," irreversible fact capable of configuring a narrative with its own criteria of intelligibility, and the disappearances remain beyond narrative grasp, engrossed in the atemporal *non-lieu* of the government's account of events.

On the one hand, then, terror imposed blindness and endorsement of the official narrative upon most citizens, while on the other hand those directly concerned by the disappearances were at pains to produce a narrative providing a grasp on events, because the status of the disappeared could not be stabilized in the fact of death. It is thus that, instead of a narrative, the Mothers of the Plaza de Mayo produced an impossible claim: "They were taken away alive, alive we want them back." In perfect keeping with the logic of the discourse of the dictatorship, this claim seized on the unstable status of the disappeared to affirm the persistence of the event of their disappearance: they are still disappeared, so they can still be found; what has disappeared can reappear. Like Clytemnestra's revenge, then, the claim voiced by the Mothers of the Plaza de Mayo countered the attempt by the military regime to enforce the finality of the past. But protected as it was by the logic of the military discourse, their claim could not, like Clytemnestra's revenge, be silenced with further disappearances or deaths. Indeed, although the Mothers were persecuted and many of them disappeared alongside their children, the claim itself could only be dispelled with the proof of the deaths of the disappeared. Such a proof, however, could not be given, for it would not only have exposed the perpetrators to trial, but it also would have offered up the dead to be publicly claimed. Thus the claim of the Mothers of the Plaza de Mayo to the mortal remains of the disappeared survived the military dictatorship, and continued to be voiced against subsequent efforts to ensure the finality of the past.

The democratic government that came to power in December 1983 attempted to open the past to public inspection and reconsideration: in 1984, the National Commission on Disappeared Persons (CONADEP) published a report (Nunca Más) listing the names of the known dead and the disappeared; from April to December 1985, it conducted trials against military personnel responsible for tortures and assassinations. But under pressure from the armed forces, and in accordance with its own historicist view of history, it eventually passed a law decreeing the end of all further trials (Ley de Punto Final, December 1986), followed by another law absolving all those who had "only" followed the orders of superiors (Ley de Obediencia Debida, June 1987). With these two laws the past was declared to be final and concluded, a declaration reinforced in December 1990 by the presidential pardon of all those who had been sentenced in 1985. But in March 1996, twenty years after the beginning of the military "reign of terror," as it has come to be called, an organization of children of the disappeared (HIJOS) filed a new habeas corpus for all of the disappeared, testifying to the continuing efficacy of the Mothers' claim, and to the inefficacy of formal closures against the persisting event of the disappearances. More significantly, as Argentinean historian Alejandro Moreira points out, the Mothers' claim has resurfaced mysteriously during the democracy in a series of unconnected events bearing no direct relationship to the past, but which have shown the past's continuous and concrete bearing on the present.[29] I conclude with a short account of three of these events, and with the suggestion that the Mothers' claim has, at least to some extent, successfully unharnessed the past and freed its events into the streets of the present.

The first example is of the Jewish community of Buenos Aires which, victim of two bloody terrorist attacks, took up the Mothers' weekly march around the Plaza de Mayo to demand government investigation of the affair. The Mothers' march, it should be stressed, epitomized their refusal to forget, to pretend that the past was "over": their feet traced a circle joining present and past, within which the government's advance into the future was suspended. When the Jewish community "borrowed" their emblem, however, there was no attempt to relate the use that they were making of it to the disappeared, for whom the march was first inaugurated. Such a disconnected use of the form of the Mothers' claim suggests that the refusal to close down the past that it represents has taken on an existence of its own.

This is confirmed by the second example: during the first years of the democratic government, a banker was kidnapped by one of the then "unemployed" paramilitary groups. The media followed his wife's efforts to have his disappearance investigated, disclosing the corrupt judiciary system inherited from the dictatorship. Thus the situation of the relatives of the disappeared people was reproduced and publicized under another guise: this time, indeed, the victim was not an evil subversive but a respectable banker.[30] This time, moreover, the disappearance had serious political repercussions: it was discovered that the Minister of the Interior had bribed the police in order to have the investigation opened, forcing him to resign. Eventually, the investigation led, many years later, to the discovery of the banker's body, showing that the disappeared can indeed reappear, albeit dead. In the meantime, the banker's wife founded a private institution called Citizen's Power (Poder Ciudadano) to promote human rights and democratic values. Here the connection between the banker's disappearance and the disappearances during the military dictatorship is again at once obvious and devious and cannot be resolved by appealing to causality—in this case, the paramilitaries' unemployment is, at best, a side effect of the "restructurations" of the "Process of National Organization." The combination of familiarity and lack of causal connection with the past suggests, again, that the past has broken loose and is somehow incarnated in present events.

Similarly, the demand for justice on the part of the relatives of a conscript assassinated by his superiors, a case that sadly recalls the practices and impunity of the military during the dictatorship, met with such mass support that eventually the system of compulsory military service was abolished. Although it is clear that economic reasons making such a step possible did exist—the costs of military service were too great, and the army was in the throes of a structural crisis—the role played by the reaction of the population cannot be dismissed. It also seems clear, although difficult to prove, that the single death the population was reacting against must have been charged with past injustices and with the frustration over the Argentinean defeat in the Malvinas/Falkland Islands War. Would the conscript's death have been the drop that filled the present with the past?

What is particularly striking in these three incidents is that none of them is the product of a concerted effort to revive the past:[31] they do not involve human design, although they involve humans in what appears to be designed to redress past wrongs. This semblance of "poetic justice" is all the more surprising given the lack as well of a concerted effort to articulate these incidents with past injustices. It would in fact be difficult to integrate them into current political discourses or to comprise them in a single narrative linking past to present. And yet they seem to be direct responses to past events, pursuing and amplifying them. But whatever is happening here, one thing seems certain: time in Argentina is neither empty nor homogenous—it overflows with the distant and immediate past. These, according to Benjamin, are not good conditions for Mankind's historical progress: let us hope he was right.

NOTES

1. "Informe de Marcos, 23 de febrero 1994," EZLN. *Documentos y comunicados* (México: Ediciones Era, 1994), 164. All translations from the Spanish are my own.

2. His report continues: "And we are addressing everyone: governors and governed; what is going on in this country, so that it is necessary to die and to kill in order to say a few small and truthful words, without them being lost in forgetfulness?"

3. Jean-François Lyotard, "The Wall, the Gulf, and the Sun: A Fable," in *Political Writings*, edited by Bill Readings and Kevin P. Geiman and translated by Bill Readings (Minneapolis: University of Minnesota Press, 1993), 120–23.

4. Ibid., 120.

5. Walter Benjamin, "Theses on the Philosophy of History," in *Illuminations*, edited by Hannah Arendt and translated by Harry Zohn (New York: Schocken, 1969), 260. It should be noted that progress can no longer be identified solely as "evolution" or change from the worse to the better. Thus for Benjamin, the "perfectibility of mankind" is only "in keeping" with its boundless and irresistible advance through time, but neither sustains it nor participates in it. The sense that the advance must be from the worse to the better is in fact dispensable for the notion of progress itself.

6. Ibid., 261.

7. Lyotard writes: "What Man and 'brain' or, better, the Brain and its man would look like in the days of this final terrestrial challenge, the story did not say." Lyotard, op. cit., 123.

8. Ibid., 120.

9. I will be referring to two rather different translations of Aeschylus' trilogy: Philip Vellacott's *The Oresteian Trilogy* (Middlesex: Penguin, 1959) and Robert Fagles' *The Oresteia* (Middlesex: Penguin, 1977). Fagles' translation is closer to the original, and unless otherwise stated, is the one from which I quote. I use Vellacott's more evocative translation only where it corresponds to Fagles'. References to Aeschylus in this chapter are to line numbers.

10. Thus in their introduction to *The Oresteia*, Robert Fagles and W. B. Stanford argue that, "What Aeschylus builds upon the house of Atreus is a grand parable of progress, as Richmond Lattimore has described it, which celebrates our emergence from the darkness to the light, from the tribe to the aristocracy to the democratic state." Fagles, op. cit., 16.

11. *The Eumenides*, op. cit., 848, 880.

12. Ibid., 862–66. In Vellacott's translation, Athena's promised future is even more smoothly progressive: "For the coming age/Shall see her [Athens'] glory growing yet more glorious," (in Vellacott, op. cit., 851–53).

13. Ibid., 997.

14. According to Apollo, Orestes should be acquitted because he has not committed a crime against his blood: "The woman you call the mother of the child/is not the parent, just a nurse to the seed . . . /The man is the source of life—the one who mounts" (ibid., 666–69). But in his introduction to his own translation, Vellacott argues that Apollo's defense of Orestes does not hold: his arguments are contradictory, and Aeschylus himself would question the reliability of Apollo as a witness. What is clear is that although Agamemnon's sacrifice of Iphigeneia is condemned in the play, it is not mentioned in defense of Clytemnestra.

15. *Agamemnon*, op. cit., 225.

16. Ibid., 212–13.

17. Ibid, 216.

18. The passage relating Agamemnon's decision is in fact a difficult one. In Fagles' translation, we have: "Pain both ways and what is worse?/Desert the fleets, fail the alliance?/No, but stop the winds with a virgin's blood/feed their lust, their fury?—feed their fury!/Law is law!—/Let all go well" (ibid., 212–17). Here the option of deserting the fleets seems to be simply unthinkable ("No"), and it is its unthinkability that makes feeding the wind's fury thinkable. Fagles' translation thus supports my argument. But a more literal translation of the passage, suggested by George Varsos, could run: "Which of these would bear no harm?/How could I become deserter of ships/by failing the alliance?/since, the wind-arresting/sacrifice of a maiden's blood wrathfully/and in wrath to desire/is right by custom. Let it be good." Here what would determine Agamemnon's choice is that "it is right by custom to desire in wrath the wind-arresting sacrifice of a maiden's blood wrathfully." This translation raises a number of questions: is the sacrifice right because it is ordained by custom or because it is wind-arresting? For whom is it right to desire it? For Agamemnon or for the gods? And what is this "right by custom *[Themis]*"? Does it simply legitimate Agamemnon's decision, or is it also the source of the necessity to which he harnesses himself? These questions, however, do not really rule out my reading of Agamemnon's endorsement of choice capable of generating events rather than that which only blocks their course.

19. *Agamemnon*, in Vellacott, op. cit., 217–18. Fagles' translation is: "And once he slipped his neck in the strap of Fate,/his spirit veering black, impure, unholy,/*once he turned he stopped at nothing*" (in Fagles, op. cit., 217–19, emphasis added).

20. *The Eumenides*, op. cit., 655–59.

21. *Agamemnon*, op. cit., 1442–44.

22. "Pray no more for death, broken/as you are. And never turn/your wrath on her, call her/the scourge of men, the one alone/who destroyed a myriad Greek lives/*Helen the grief that never heals*" (ibid., 1490–95, emphasis added). In Vellacott's translation, the lines run: "*Is fact so gross a burden?*/Put up no prayers for death;/Nor turn your spleen on

Helen,/As if her act had ordered/The fate of fighting thousands/And robbed their souls of breath" (in Vellacott, op. cit., 1463–68, emphasis added).

23. On the self-presentation of the military government, see Beatriz Sarlo, "Política, Ideología y Figuración Literaria," in *Ficción y política: La narrativa argentina durante el proceso militar* (Buenos Aires: Alianza Editorial/Institute for the Study of Ideologies and Literature, 1987), 39, 44. Needless to say, the military itself contributed to the social and political "chaos" from which it pretended it would save Argentina. For a discussion of the role of paramilitary organizations before 1976, see the analysis of the pre-dictatorship "system of terror" by Justo Escobar and Sebastián Velázquez in *Examen de la violencia argentina* (México: Fondo de Cultura Economica, 1975).

24. Francine Masiello, "La Argentina durante el Proceso: las múltiples resistencias de la cultura," in *Ficción y política*, op. cit., 12.

25. When the parents of seventeen-year-old disappeared, Pablo Fernández Meijide recounted to police officers that the men who took away their son introduced themselves as being from the federal police, the reply was that it was not possible: police officers always wear uniforms. See Noemí Ulla and Hugo Echave, *Después de la noche: Diálogo con Graciela Fernández Meijide* (Buenos Aires: Editorial Contrapunto, 1986), 28.

26. "*si la cloaca es el destino de los desechos, las cárceles militares fueron la cloaca de nuestra historia.*" See Antonio Marimón, *El antiguo alimento de los héroes* (Buenos Aires: Punto Sur, 1988), 68. One of the most haunting images to illustrate the disappeared's double fall from life and history is of the military planes unloading their live "trash" into the ocean. And it was precisely the "Aeronautical Services" *(Servicios de la Aeronáutica)* that were associated with the task of disappearing people. Even the metaphysical, middle-class, and passive protagonist of Humberto Constantini's *La larga noche de Francisco Sanctis* (Buenos Aires: Bruguera, 1984) knows this: "You don't have to be any diviner to know what it means to say that the Aeronautical Services are going to pick up a man. . . . It means kidnapping, it means torture, it means . . . corpses hidden somewhere or thrown from an airplane" (54–55).

27. Ulla and Echave, op.cit., 48.

28. Ibid., 34. It is worth noting here that, rather than comparing her experience of her son's disappearance to the experience of a death, Graciela Fernández Meijide compares it to the sense of irreality she had when she walked out of the hospital after her daughter's birth and, proud and happy, wondered how the passersby did not stop to contemplate the miracle: "I had the same sensation of stupor—but then with a lot of anguish—when I went out after Pablo's disappearance, and the world had not stopped either" (14).

29. Alejandro Moreira, "A Past without History: Human Rights' Violations in Argentina," 1996 (unpublished paper). One of Moreira's main points is that the disappeared have prevented historical accounts of the period from stabilizing. The preoccupation with history and with what Beatriz Sarlo has called "the dissymmetry between the order of the real and the order of discourse" have characterized Argentinean literature due to support for this view by the dictatorship. See Sarlo, op. cit., 42.

30. This ironic twist of "history" clearly refutes the logic that the dictatorship had tried to impose, according to which, if someone disappeared, then they "deserved" it, for only those deserving disappearance disappeared.

31. In this respect it is interesting to note that there are relatively few documented instances of revenge, although most torturers are still at liberty to roam the streets.

12

Photo-
Resemblance

Charles Grivel

"Back! Hide yourselves in the broom closet! Put on a mask!
TEAR OFF YOUR RESEMBLANCE!
I recognize you, the son of that man, you, the father of that son!
Malevolent males. Psst! Psst! Glooh-ooh-glooh!"

It is a lady who thus greets her husband and son. She had been calm for
several days.
The sight of her family increased her delirium.
        —Albert Londres, *Chez les Fous*

1

THERE IS NO PHOTOGRAPHY, ACTUALLY, BUT PORTRAIT.[1] Whoever grabs a camera
gets ready to portray. Widespread perversion: the photographer is recognizable
("identifiable") in the picture he or she takes. This resemblance is an image,
with a supposed referent. It also is an act, which is to say a take, a casting and retrieval, just as the fisherman casts the bait with a quick flick of the wrist and
breaks the surface of the water. The photographer, miraculously, retrieves from
the bottom of the abyss other fish than those expected. Others and more:

An earlier version of this chapter appeared in French; see Charles Grivel, "La ressem-
blance-photo," in *Revue des Sciences Humaines* 210 (1988).

galoshes, old meaningless debris, doubloons or treasure, reality's rejects, that which does not figure, or badly so.

I note that the paper thing called "portrait" possesses an imposing air: it faces, it represents a body (at least the central part of this body), it is calm (even in the height of fury), it is fixed (even in the apex of a jump), as hanging on that sensitive point from where identity apparently escapes and will be applied—where the I photographer pushes the release and poses. I think that is where the decent, dreamy, melancholic yet authoritative air of people whose pictures are taken comes from: we recognize that they recognize us. Our eye desires the necessity of resemblance: a portrait resembles by definition, it is that of which essence is missing, yet not, since the image it constitutes replaces what it represents and does not catch it (resemblance, by definition, comes from elsewhere). This image is and is not what it shows. That person is and is not his or her veritable portrait. What I see, by identification, is not in what I see. It sure does resemble him or her though.

2

Nothing resembles. A resemblance is a lure produced by the more or less eloquent effort to reinstate what would be at the source. The photographic portrait suggests the presence-there of the represented individual; it captures this individual. This also is why photography, from the moment of its invention, became so popular: the inexpert customers wanted to look at themselves, but they could only do so by similitude, in the name of parity, as though they needed the sanction of this fact to dare consider their own face, bear the horrific violence of its appearance, accept that the indubitable sign of their imaginary animal-being is passing from the inside to the front of the head. I would be who I am outside of the image. I would represent my primary civil status. My body shown to be ordinary would unite in itself all of the aspects one can possibly *see* of it (not do with it). This whole assimilating body upholds, for whoever orders his or her portrait, the face he or she will receive on paper. All of the mimicry and all of the faces justify themselves without contradiction within a homogenizing model of basic individuality. Everything will "resemble" by necessity: photography, in this conception, intervenes secondarily: the model is brought to the photographer; how could one not feel repeated?

Of course, resemblance escapes a simple requisition of the model by the support: in the face of my own image, a doubt overtakes me, an insufficiency hits me; this portrait of myself, I do not accept, I remonstrate; something falters in the appearance it offers: *I am not he whom it represents.* On this point, the anecdotes told by Nadar in his *Quand j'étais photographe* concerning the experiences of his first clients are conclusive. For example, the man who perfectly recognized himself in the picture of a person he was not, or the gullible provincial who asked the photographer to send him his portrait C.O.D. because he just could not go to Paris to have it done on the spot. It represents anyway; it resembles anyway also, but badly or otherwise, "off" compared to what should have been reproduced. The portrait does not metaphorically double a person; rather, it extracts what is concealed outside of signification and oblivious to sight. *The portrait rather destroys its stock-individual.* "It shows" means that it positively destroys that (which) it shows. More than contradiction of portraits (if they are good), less than analogy. I am mistaken if I identify myself.

3

Identity, photographic lure of resemblance, is placed and is read *in the face*,[2] is inscribed in the reproduction of the face. Like something—and precisely at the point where physical reality springs forth (does the body not overflow its (jacket) sleeves, its (pant) legs, its (shirt) collar?)—that is shown, exclaimed, framed. Defined as such. Bare, unveiled, naked, if we refer to clothes, but prepared, mastered, if we think of the pose and everything that the *mise-en-scène* supposes (including the makeup), *of the identity-bound face as a naked mask*, photographically constituted in its double nature: immediate and fixed, true but composed. Remarkable thing, this picture's face tends to the objective as it tends to the one who beholds the image; it is not simply there, nor there for me, mine, concentrated (with violence) on the conviction that it holds to impose upon me: an "I am" seeks in advance to compensate the "wow! what a resemblance" of its user.

Thus as with all photographs, a portrait, perhaps initially conceived to resemble its original and suit one's appetite for recognition (and verisimilitude), identifies *what it is not.* One must understand it as a palimpsest figure of an object that it signalizes in itself, but beyond itself, abysmally, infinitesimally. At the same time it affirms (applies itself to affirming) the same to whoever considers it. It is the inexcusable otherness of this same that it denotes. It draws nearer, but it is already distancing. Identity, then, arises in one's eye from the photographic difference accomplished on the face of the other.

To resume: (1) specialization of corporal zones: it is the face's incumbency to inscribe the proper; (2) photographic fixture oversteps this desire for propriety and accomplishes it, by the pose, by chemical schematization; (3) it falls upon the shot's amenity (the famous smile) and its charm (that which is fit to be photographed and interesting to capture with the camera) to succeed in the communication of the proper (to make it desirable as spectacle); (4) the photo portrays to the extent that it aims at resemblance: it represents a resemblance, as well as the object of this resemblance, therefore an identity; (5) the portrait doubles photographic appearance, detaches it from reproduction. Before the photograph, the object is one; it lies in its concept and in its actual form (of which it is nonetheless a shadow). After the photograph, captured out of time, the object divides

into "thing" and the material reproduction of this thing—simulacrum and nature. It is, therefore, double, to be infinitely undoubled, *the same and the other*,
identifiable and different. Remarkably, the very machine that multiplies the self
accomplishes and does not accomplish its police identity.

4

The first photo—Niepce's, Talbot's—showed what the pyrotechnist could apprehend from his window. The photographs that followed aimed the view toward
the observer: from the watched to the watcher. The cards were dealt: photography was going to be able to think *who watches in the spectacle issued from its eye.*
Displacement of the subject, evasion, vaporization, transfer.

However, immediately as we know, police raids: photography was appre-
hended for the appearance of resemblance it procures, for the supposed automa-
tism of the production of this resemblance: it was summoned to identify. The
play of differences—Niepce photographing his photographic apparatus, Talbot
representing his technician asleep in his chair—gave way to those, more serious,
of universal probation: *You will be the one whom you resemble*, and only that one!
You will conform to your resemblance! Better, *you will resemble yourself.*

In connection with this it is helpful to recall exactly who conceived and
made, in the early 1850s, the first identity card as we know it, an amalgam of
words (the name, the determinants), of image (the three-quarter portrait), and of
traces (the signature, also the right-hand fingerprints) that works to bind the subject to its being, or in other words, to its representation (you will be one, you-
one, one-you, says the identity card): "It seems that a magician [*sic*] who went by
the name of Robin was the first to put such a system into practice in order to
ensure the surveillance of those who entered his establishment."[3]

We are thus inevitably led to speak of the "mainly repressive function" of
the portrait. The subject of the social portrait as conceived here displays the indubitable signs of its position and accession: to have one's portrait taken is, in
the golden age of photography, an effective means to notify one's standing. On
this, Charles Phéline writes: "The device is made to display an entirely civilized
being, who literally, from head to foot, from the hat to the tip of the shoes and
without forgetting the face's expression, is but the formal disposition of the signs
of its social integration."[4] Even if we see a touch of insanity in the excessiveness
of an apparatus that was to serve as a means to this integration,[5] let us recognize
the fact that what I distinguish of a photographic person is something like a coat
of arms; I consider the portrait by emblem: the pillar (broken), the curtain (we
are not at the theater), the volume (open or under the elbow), the plush (on all
visible furniture), the plants (artistically laced, colonial if possible), the armchair
(we are at home) or the chair (for madam), the ceremonial dress (with dickey,

medals, buttons, watch), and so on. My accessories certify what I am; my face is proper to all of this apparel: a cavalier resembles his riding whip, a cuirassier is the same as his helmet, and the lady is exactly like the gentleman she was given. It is amidst this hunger for self-celebration that the dream of a total policing of the nation arises. First step: know who is who; second step: detect, a priori, on appearance and "scientifically," by simple photographic application, the true nature of each being: to the one, captain-being, to the other, criminal being.

Photography opens the way to that very Lavaterian *phantasma* of the conformity between body and spirit: the new medium offers a means to "observation" and to the reproduction of adequate observation: it catches the "character" at the mere sight of the face (strictly speaking, only essences are "shot"). Photography, therefore, constitutes, in principle, appearance caught in the act (I am guilty of what I appear); it exposes "physical stigmas" forming evidence.

5

What we call identity is *nothing other than an effect of representation, that is, resemblance.* I reflect on a resemblance. That which identifies itself only figures as reproduced for its observer, and returned to him or her. A (photographic) image returns the subject *inside its eye,* and returns to it, as itself (as the one whom it must recognize). Integration to the subject of the subject by interposed images. Stases.

For instance:

1. He only sees "on the outside," always beside himself, this man;

2. He only minds himself in a reverse shot, backlash, retroactively, memorially, in sum (memory of the eye);

3. Photographic fixture confirms this movement by the paper: between the designated object and the subject, paper. Understand paper as the included middle—"objective"—of the me-world interface or exchange. The paper bears some "me" into the world, bears a "world" to the self, all the while dissimulating, for evident reasons of social tactics, this double transfer. How? By *paper-resemblance.*

6

I have not mistaken photos.

The portrait photograph, compared to the one that is only painted, offers the advantage of appearing undeniably real (the "it was there" does play its part) and true to what it is not (even if I do not recognize myself in my portrait, I must still stand corrected, for everyone knows that the more an operation is mechanical, the more it is reliable), the print's captivating power, compared to the line guilty of emanating, delayed and differentially, from a hand. However, this effect of reality with which we credit the photographic image strikes back, *before itself, in the observer's place,* he or she whom we so justly call its author. Take this meadow, this notch in this meadow at this place where the road rises over the embankment of the dike: northern Holland, late November, 1982, across from a receding sea. The image surely evokes the idea of the reality of this scene—out in the country, the specialists of green Europe, hiking enthusiasts. However, it especially calls attention *to the gaze that posed it,* from which it springs, *and to which it confers in return its own reality.*

7

Photo-paper. Paper is the outside skin of the person as shown in photography. It is a mask (or a bodysuit), torn off and turned toward the receiver, as the envelope and the letter it contains are turned toward the addressee who reads. In sum, the photo is a mirror; it represents—let us say—the gloomy landscape of Assamstadt at nightfall in Bade. Yet this mirror inverts an image that, in principle, I do not (voluntarily) recognize as mine. On the contrary, it represents a potato field just ploughed. Which is to say I know nothing (in principle) of the resemblance that it is nonetheless assigned to communicate to me, since I just as well only photograph impulsively, by "preference," obviously "that" which suits me, and nothing else. This resemblance of the paper-object, obscurely born out of the conjunction of the real and the eye, is felt as a pleasure. It is, I hope, a "nice" picture that I am taking here (does its "quality" conceal or justify what the photo—but by which necessity?—retains?). This skin detached from the originary mass exhibits a design whose nature escapes me, even though it is mine. The photographer is a headhunter and a hunter of skin bodies, capable of taking on any appearance one wishes—clear lawn under the lane's two rows of trees, policeman menu holders, truck spilling its load of fish, and so on. On this account, all photographs are *synthetic images.* The photographic vigil takes a shot the moment it hits him or her. The symptom of this connection denotes a resemblance at work.

Skin—or hood: the gaze pierces from the inside toward me, a self terrorized by the aspect of that which confronts it with an implacable gaze and which it does not recognize. Skin—or hood: the envelope of the foreign body filters through the holes a presence that gives me notice. It as well as I have a part in this misunderstood yet imposed resemblance. Let us consider its two aspects:

1. The photographic skin of the other is a trophy; it figures aggressively as a captured identity that I can savor on paper. My pleasure comes from a double substitution: the taking of the Other (in the name of the Same), the taking of the

Same (in the guise of the Other). Magical photographic operation: I stick my thumbtacks (in French, my *poupées-témoins*), which I take from my objective; I add some *Moi*; I take my fill of energy; I slash the world in order to extract, by some miracle, the proper that suits me. Of course, the more I gorge myself with photos, the more I become self-indulgent, and the more I exacerbate the schism inherently mine: the more there are, the more I do not have, the more I need. Insatiable me. Of drunkenness in photography.

2. The photographic object comprises the eye. The skin-face is an eye-face. This sighted eye returns seeing where it comes from: *I am thus the real picture of my picture*, thus here I am, myself photographed in my eye by the very *product* of my ocular activity—to the extent that the paper-object realizes it. The photographic portrait reproduces the photographing self.

8

The photographic portrait is nothing but a photographic portrait; the observer perceives only an image representing a portrait—not the one who posed, original for what did you say? We can reflect on the difference that this feigned representation exerts—see below for more—but we must admit that this difference, as its resemblance, is founded by the portrait *itself*, bottomless and without end, by my eye—full, complete, finished in its proper expression, however, *a portrait of nothing*, something in it obsesses by me or for me, demanding to appear. With no beyond nor hither, it is a slice inserted between my spirit and my spirit, myself and myself: nothing is reflected in it other than this place, this interval, this *scission* it occupies or produces. It does not therefore say: I resemble the one whom I represent, but only *I am wholly a resemblance*; true to my paper, you enjoy the untouchable view I offer, just like that conformity (the portrait succeeds: it portrays).

9

Difference, indifference, fatality of the flaw introduced by a movement of which everything suggested, on the contrary, that it would consolidate being and definitively bind, definitely as bourgeois individuality (what other word to use?), the face to the body, the meaning to the substance, *in kind*. Photography introduces difference at the heart of the same: I am not the same as my portrait; no one is themselves, exactly themselves, at the mere sight of the form they take on paper: I resemble myself, in sum, always too much, never enough.

To photograph is to set out on a quest for a self-resemblance that each picture revives. To buy one's photo, similarly, with the secret hope (but perfect anxiety) of being able to shout, if only once: "That is definitely me!" It also is the interest of the one who takes your portrait in the back of his or her store to orient your desire in this perspective. (It must nonetheless be said that the photo booth seriously cripples the myth: as soon as it becomes possible to take one's own portrait, immediately and without an intermediary, resemblance is no longer what counts, but only the speed at which the sign of identity is turned out.)

Everything indicates that the person wants resemblance. Indeed, fatal circle, each photo—and hereupon they can only proliferate—far from closing it back upon its image to assure it of the desired cohesion, *dispossesses* it of what gradually becomes the hollow shell of an appearance. In the reverse shot of the photo, me becomes, me becomes the other me, me insists on not becoming me. "I" do not adhere; on the contrary, "I" takes off. It is the other who arises in my place from what I am photographed—"caught on film," as they say.

10

Generalized insufficiency of the portrait; it depletes, and he or she who considers himself or herself in it is always taken *otherwise*. To examine things more closely, if only by the referent, we must admit that the face of a man (and when I say man, I embrace all women) does not hold. Nothing ages faster than a face, nothing endures the abuses of the weather less; blemishes, rashes, and moods devastate its disposition; a pathological being is constantly different from the one it was; it modifies itself to give free reign to expression, it grimaces at wanting to say, it folds, it wrinkles, and so on. The paper face, now, becomes livelier than its model. It is a fix that neither the pose nor the snapshot can really stop. For there arises, in its very rigidity or in the suspending of the mimic, something that comes across to contradict the impression it gives: the just *before*, the just *after* of the movement in which it has been seized, of the attitude it assumes; that which preceded (or followed) the form it gives to its smile, to its mouth, to everything that makes it appear as it is. This movement by which it takes place contradicts the actual fixity of the traits it gives itself, for the photo is not part of a mechanical ocular device but of a gaze, which is to say a system of reception-projection that is neither regular nor continuous, set to work within contingency, and of diverse intensity.

In addition, as there is never enough subject dealing with the subject, the portrait-self disappoints the portrayed-self for not having represented it sufficiently (even I do not resemble myself!).

In the same way, neither is it "her," never "beautiful" enough, or exact, or faithful.

I never recognize a portrait: time, undue time that the pose was supposed to eliminate, slips back in; my desire for the other slips in; it is "mediocre," or else "waisted"; how could it be otherwise? *By this same way.*

It falls upon the portrait to represent appearance *as it is missing*; it is therefore, so to speak, whether smiling or not, *fictitious*; imaginary would be an understatement, nothing but a "solution" I loathe, *visibly*, to face.

1 1

The portrait proposes the deformation of something that has never been seen, and cannot even be seen. It holds a monster (a factor of monstrosity). It accentuates, in any case, enhances, displays, unfolds, exhibits, exposes a mutilating excessiveness. It renders exorbitance: getting out of the eye socket. The person in the portrait is caricatural: the hooked nose of the cardinal bishop de Castelvetro at Urbino; the smile— or the moustaches!—of the Mona Lisa; the leguminous globes, in painting, derealize all appearance. Photography, as I see it, radicalizes the tendency: the only good photographic portraits are excessive. Witness those of Nadar, where each figure—at least the ones that turned out well—appears to implode. Witness those, quite close to us—but I am picking offhandedly—of Radisic,[6] the Algerian women of Marc Garanger,[7] madam Billot or madam Donzé by Gert Frost.[8] Looking closely at these images that take painting to its utmost,[9] something offends me: I am given what I asked and more than what I want to recognize.

Photography paints the infinite horror of the human face. I see it blend the faces, masticate the faces, finally open up to a world of smashed faces visibly held secret at the heart of our memories. Searching for what resemblance, which dissimilitude, and as to which, *by successive defacements?*

Photographic portraits deface what they represent: I see; it destroys what I see; what I see is the deformation of what I see. I am born disfigured, crushed against walls of flesh; I die having given myself, from this viewpoint, full satisfaction (many photographing dead people: this is why!). Photography aims for the systematic degradation of the traits of identity, aims for the ceasing of the "natural," ordinary, unified appearance of things. If I photograph, it is to twist. I have it in my field of view, and I implode it. I undo, I disassemble, seeking and producing the moment when the face disconnects, tires, becomes unsettled. I bring out the discord, the ruin—a wrinkle is my game, an abscess, a lesion, the most sensible marks of the unbalance. The strange (strangeness; better, the *strangement*) is the photographic object par excellence. I put into my camera, I take out of my camera the unexpected—but forced—expression, the non-meaning—but painful. Photography suspends all that x would signify and exposes the non-meaning as appearance. Ah, nothingness, ah, insanity! We photograph to strip a person of the apparent reason that he or she possesses.

A portrait of this kind no longer means to want to do anything (nor signify, nor resemble), except refusal, put to the face, facing, and which considers me, comes back to me, sticks to me, to please me.

1 2

This subject, of which only the interchangeability of its graphic manifestations on screen (page or paper—I am not counting the others here), is no longer held to resemble, to coincide with a model—"a father," an idea we would have of him: *unsuitable*, soft cell or gestating dough, fleeting and convertible. Contradiction no longer applies to it, but *disappearance*. The incessant rearrangement to which it is submitted in its particular world of simulation escapes negation: can a kaleidoscopic figure be denied by another kaleidoscopic figure? Of a subject with variable geometry, modifiable wings, light, filmy—a *motion picture*.

The photographic portrait, and the photograph as portrait, is therefore inscribed in the process. *To photograph is to displace the subject*, to make it seen to be there where it was not before, to flatten it out, to give it a flat existence, infinitely, piled up and forwarded—always on the surface. We make it alternately slip in and out of its appearance; we successively dress it with all the cheap finery imaginable (and more); we experiment sliding out and throwing in; we bring into being *that which it has not been*.

Of photography as an attempt to *exhaust* subject-appearance, shuffling and dealing anew the cards of this appearance: this appearance is a form, this form is a path—like the form it is, we blow it up or thin it out, we stop it, prepare it, or blow it each in turn. Manipulation: *I make as I want with you, including something other than you.*

Of photography as a paper-contradiction, paper-displacement, paper-transfer of the face's features, as a dissemination: I undo while approaching, I undo while backing away from the objective. Generalized symbolizer: photographed reality serves everything I desire, willingly or not, to make it say. *My camera is an oneirograph*—a machine that records dreams.

Of photography as an intervention upon the face: I cleanse what I see, I break what I see in the depths of my camera, I subject it to the now-warm, now-violent fire of the overcharges. A face, I grate it, I twist it, I empty it; I remove it layer by layer—I develop it—pernicious appearance, I see you! What it gives me to see, I detach; what it makes me see, I excoriate. I go too far on one side, I leave cold on the other: the relations, distorted, leave the represented abysmally dealt with: it is visible within, it is a frame made to scrutinize. From appearance, here develops *transparency*. I empty, clear away: [of] resemblance *by abstraction* carefully composed! "Zoom," "City," "Woman": all the magazines say this. By suspension, over- or under-focusing of particulars (in any case, exorbitances), by washing the quick, washing out, watering down, fading away, and erasure! Thesis: photography retakes the identification-bound sign on the face where it was supposed to figure and which it was supposed to seize. *Photography says that it no longer resembles anything.*

The photographic face is therefore partial; it has undergone a shock; a mutilation inflicts it; I consider it broken, wrecked, representing above all its proper degradation, the crack that can be read in it, decline or worsening, a process in any case in which denaturalization is at work. I photograph a loss, a face without substance, without character, without anything; I photograph *the face of a photograph, I photograph in the making the resemblance of no object.*

For example, Medusa, fallen from the pediment of the temple at Didyma and broken horizontally across the middle, at the base of the nose, which now only represents, on the picture taken, the bar of scission of her head: unless Medusa is just that, *a ravaged face augmented by a fragmentation that comes out.*

For example, the ornamental figure of the northern fountain—man or monkey?—of Dubrovnik's Plaça, as it comes out in my camera, from where the water flows and which now only represents the irreversible monstrosity of an off-center spout that its mouth contains with difficulty.

For example, Man Ray's listless wheelbarrow woman who,[10] in her padding and on paper, now only signifies the cadaverous transport she gives rise to: the content is the container! the padding is the load! I am pushing what she would have been!

1 3

Photographic meditation (1): How to realize an image? Calvino, "The Adventure of a Photographer."[11] (1) This is the story of someone who desires the real. (2) This is the story of photography's fulfilling the desire for the real. (3) First observation: one leaves home to photograph. Having photographed, one returns with the game. This little shot is used to signify that it has taken place. It has taken place: sigh of satisfaction. (4) A father will not rest until he photographs his progeny. *I am the daddy of my photos.* (5) Beautiful, it was not; photographed, it becomes. There is no reason for ceasing to take the picture of—take!—what is there: this makes it bearable to us. (6) Only the multiplication of photos is liable to guarantee their truth. But visibly at work in this principle also is the negation of this principle. (7) One must only avoid choosing what one photographs and how one photographs it (shooting away at one's object, aiming once more for the opposite of that of which it gives the impression). (8) The setting into the past that the photographic shot produces is compensated by the multiplication of views ("to believe that the snapshot is more *true* than the posed portrait is a prejudice"). (9) One will choose to prefer the pose; one will devote himself or herself to the genius for artifice. One will prefer the old-fashioned portraits of the nineteenth century—because they suspend their expression—to contemporary photos, which cut into the quick and therefore *miss the mark.* (10) The only way I really see this person—singularly, this woman—is through the objective that I aim toward her. (11) I would search in vain for the "unique" picture of her, the one that would resume all the others and render them unnecessary. The view is missing that would look onto her. I will not see her through a picture, and yet she is perceivable only there. (12) Upon the lack of such a photo that would supplant all the others, I can only obtain, targeted by it, the mask of the real of the person she is, that is, *her other image*. I can only photograph her mask. I can only, photographing her, mark the pertinence of this mask. (13) Cast off anyway into the past: the photo inexorably returns me to the antecedents; the pose stops the flux before I make up my mind (memory secures everything that is good for it). How, then, can one really photograph *in the present*? (14) Photographing demolishes congruities. I learn through photography that only disproportion and excessiveness are likely to produce the desired effect of reality— I do not describe, I do not record, I do not give a sensible image of the world. (15) The photographer sets his sights on this woman in order to provoke her self-disclosure. He desires to get *the* answer directly from her—violence paid back for violence done. (16) Dream photography. I seize, I do in the camera that it metamorphoses. Oneirography. The things that metamorphose also are those that instill fear in us. (17) She is a body. The body is truly (really) fit to be photographed only if the clothing accomplishes its *ceremonial*. Show the display. The dress, in the lens, must be husky and the body spring, by the shoulder and the neck, from an unfathomable décolleté. It falls upon photography to realize that appearance, this emanation of a substantial invisible *out-of-time*. (18) The photographer has it, this complete nude, detemporalized, become real, of the woman's body. Then he loves the woman of this body. (19) This love demands the snapshot. The lover in photography needs only to take this body unceasingly into view. Cast-realized gaze always, rape always. The multitude of this woman to take on the image is part of the wonder that I feel from her: "Identity fragmented into a powder of images." There is no end to the photographic act (as with orgasm): "Photography has a meaning only if it exhausts all possible images." (20) The program of a total photography of she whose love I am. This program supposes that I also photograph her without being seen by her and even *without seeing her*, in such a way as to catch her in her being-there. I desire of her the most perfect *invisibility*. (21) Out of shot, in extreme cases, to photograph *nothing*, her departure, her absence, the content she occupied the moment before, the seam or the contour from where she issued, her detail, her interval, her *not*. (22). Suppose that I have lost sight of her; suppose that I am now only photographing that nothing which remains after she takes leave; suppose that I discover a certain charm, for that very reason, in news photography (nothing exchanging nothing, any photo appearing compatible); suppose, therefore, that I tear up all the pictures I could have possibly taken of her. (23) I discovered what photographing really was: to effectuate by photo the relating of both the object, reduced to pieces, of the most intimate desire (this woman stuffed in her images, broken and kneaded, reduced to the paper's proper substance) and, to the same extent, of the newspapers' everyday imaginary (the great flat emptiness of the world reduced to its dramaturgic perfection). On one side, the nullity of the fragment with which I am forced to content myself when I take her, and on the other, all of the ceremonial agitation of the coronations, the conferences, the visits and the sessions, the incidents, the accidents (this world), and by the same stroke, in one release of the shutter. *To photograph-view nothing and all at once,* x just as much as that which denies it, in front, behind, inside, outside, publicity in the resolutely private. Such a photo contains the trace of both randomness (its passage) and necessity (the geographical present). It represents, without representation of course, and in a single stroke, the will to see accompanied *by the non-desire that it engenders:* yes and no by the extremity of the index. (24) Lesson: *One would only know how to photograph photographs.* (25) Lesson: Photography brings into sight a new hybrid: two disorders in one same order (her and not her, positivity and negativity), two insufficiencies in one sufficiency. *To photograph, of course! is to realize the real.* (This lesson is as true as the preceding one.)

14

Photographic meditation (2): How to make a random portrait? Take the photo that represents, in a certain disposition, a ladder, a floor, and the head of a woman with her mouth open and eyes closed. This portrait is faulty with respect to the degree of the subject's eventual recognizability. However, the insistence of this applied face, flattened, contrasts with what we can know of it: it appears that its imperfection measures the meaning that it carries. But where does this "imperfection" come from, and how to describe it? Everything suggests, of course, that it does not come from the model, but from the process: we are facing the process; *it is the process that has been photographed*—but photographed as a face. This picture, and this face it carries, coincides with the manner in which it was executed: it is a portrait of the *manner*.

I therefore describe its manner: You have to repaint your bedroom. You place a plastic drop sheet on the floor. You take a ladder, your can of paint, your brushes, and you start painting. Then you notice that the color—which by no coincidence is called "Gobi," a kind of indefinable pale yellow between beige, bistre, and brown—trickles down the container and smears the top of the ladder. A little later, but not too late, you cover it with a newspaper. This can be any newspaper. You just choose newspaper. You do not look at it. You only absentmindedly lay it out, in its place, turned over onto the open side of the fold, so it does not slide, that is, in sum, face to the ground. You place your instruments on the newspaper. You continue calmly to paint the room *while the portrait comes into making*. A nice yellow appears. You disregard what appears. The work finished, you let the walls dry and leave the brushes and the can in their place. You go to bed. The next morning, with renewed enthusiasm, you start cleaning up. You tear the newspaper off the plasticized step—and you discover her: her face is there looking at you, bursting, radiant and horrified, come in the night, through the support, indistinct from this support, transposed, unexpected, enigmatic. Who is she? Which opacity constitutes her on the dreary appearance of a floor that is no longer what it was? You then realize photographing her as she has arisen: *the apparition she is*, the asymbolic wavering she is—she in her original picture form and she suspended in the *chambre claire* of your eye.

A photo that comes from a photo deposit. A being arises from the photographic resemblance that it was. The portrait of this woman was not where you put it, nor where it was. Truly speaking, it is nobody's portrait—the transposition makes it nobody's portrait—yet its resemblance is *absolute*. Especially the mouth, those dead eyes, that slant of the forehead, by the love expressed.

The deposit contains: (1) the nature of an absent woman; (2) the picture at the agency's disposal; (3) the thread into which the newspaper transcribes it; (4) the tearing unto which the page has been submitted (with its effects of deformation, of blindness—a portrait of this nature can only be obtained *contingently*); (5) the palimpsestic reading operated by my eye in the objective that it applies to it, the photo of the photo expressing the invisible tear from which the face comes forth. This portrait, I *alone* have been able to make it, and this woman *alone*, able to consider it: the picture of her apparition is a unique individual product; this picture is mine *proper*, and I myself also figure the view to which it could have been exposed. Plotinus: "In general, the soul is and becomes the thing of which it remembers." And I add that it only remembers it photographically: *to photograph is to remember by the eye*. My soul is an album. What I see of which I remember arises by photography, by threading, by tearing, and as if this was not yet sufficient, by passage to the photocopier. An appearance is irradiated. An imaginary portrait escapes from its initial reality. Filtered, muted, passed from code to code so as to cease to be exact, *it finally possesses the unavoidable sign of its truth and its resemblance*. An identity has been destroyed. The relation to the origin has been destroyed. The very material that has taken in this origin has been destroyed. Photography has been instrumental in this triple passage. At the end of the process, pure, visual, oneiric, raw material: I have perfectly adapted what I see—this feminine face—to my eye. I have cut it exactly to the measure of the demands proper to me—*I really see what I want*.

1 5

Quickly, *on the principle of photographic decomposition*. To photograph entails a loss. On the one hand, the object ceases to respond simply to its nature of being-there; it goes through simulacrum and becomes confused with the given representation. On the other hand, the photographing subject ceases to occupy the comfortable place of the observer; he or she passes from the side of the eye, from the side of the seen, *facing*, and becomes the site of an unceasing transport, mutable and monstrous, capable of assuming all appearances with equal pertinence. This subject is constantly recognizable by the infiniteness and randomness of the forms it takes. Unstoppable, it *circulates*. Decomposing but decomposed but recomposed but decomposed *from an image the other*.

Photographer, you are what you can shoot—you depose, you arouse, and singularly the feminine figurine abundantly introduced in the objective. Photographic anality: the destruction to which you resort is so total that nothing is left to indicate it. Possible portrait resembling her to you held in the depths of this automatic eye with which she is bestowed. Possible and always otherwise.

Translated from the French by François Desaulniers.

NOTES

1. The author plays upon the ambiguity of *photographie*, which can mean both "photography" and "a photograph." I have translated the French word *portrait* by "portrait," but it also means "face" (n). Readers should constantly keep this double meaning in mind. [Tr.]

2. The author use the word *figure*, which also can mean "figure." [Tr.]

3. Charles Phéline, "L'Image accusatrice," in *Les cahiers de la photographie* 17 (1985): 22. The patent is dated 1866.

4. Ibid., 27.

5. On the power of clothes in a naturalist regime, see my "L'Appareil de représentation naturaliste," in *Le Naturalisme*, edited by Pierre Cogny (Paris: Presses Universitaires de France, 1978), 197–228.

6. In the exhibition catalogue *Identités: De Disdéri au photomaton* (Paris: Éditions du Chêne, 1985), 133.

7. Ibid., 48–51.

8. In *Couchaton* (Berlin: unknown, 1981), 25–26.

9. But the height of photography also exists in painting, in Bacon.

10. See *Minotaure* 10 (1938): 44.

11. Italo Calvino, *Difficult Loves*, translated by William Weaver, Archibald Colquhoun, and Peggy Wright (San Diego: Harcourt Brace Jovanoich, 1984).

13

Utopian

Legacies

Memory, Mediation, Cinema

Johanne Villeneuve

ROLAND BARTHES STRESSED THE EXTENT to which "reading" a photograph "is implicitly, in a repressed manner, a contract with what ceased to exist, a contract with death."[1] Ever since the emergence of a culture of moving images with the invention of the film projector, the question is whether life has sealed this "contract with death" drawn up by photography. The flow of life seems to loom from the dimension of mortality itself, and death, from the utopian dimension of an invaluable presence. Photographs, as Ron Burnett more recently reminded us, do not perfectly correspond to what is generally called an *image*: "images cannot claim the autonomy of photographs. Images can never be separated from vision and subjectivity (in other words, photographs can be put into an archive while images cannot). . . . Images operate within the realms of perception and thought, conscious and unconscious."[2]

In addition to the moving images of cinema, photography itself is currently swept up in the whirlwind of novelty and advertisement. The speed with which it circulates no longer confines it to a mere archival role. Archives themselves—in the sense of documentary evidence, records, and chronicles, as well as the institutions charged with housing them—have been set in motion, blending into the images of our lives and filling our dreams. Though images remain just that, we are now so saturated with them that even our lives are defined by the speed of their circulation, by the certain illumination and impression that they endlessly afford. In this way, our surroundings lead us to confuse image and photograph, everyday aspirations and *clichés*.

In his movie, *Level Five*, French filmmaker Chris Marker incorporates archival footage from the turn of the century, in which a reckless flying man is shown leaping from the top of the Eiffel Tower. Temporarily pausing the film, Marker freezes one particular image: that of the man's gaze, as he realizes he can no longer turn back and must jump, now that he is caught on film. This visual reciprocity between viewer and flying man is the means by which the archive suddenly takes wing in the flow of time, thereby disclosing the subjective power of the image: as their eyes meet, the flying man is *shot* by the being-to-come (that other-in-time), while that gaze is simultaneously transformed into his archive and image. Much as the butterfly only spreads its wings with the death of the chrysalis, this reciprocity makes visible at last how much the viewer owes his or her own becoming to that death. The being-to-come recognizes in the man of the past the sacrifice of the present.

In their film, *Chronicle of a Genocide Foretold*, Danièle Lacourse and Yvan Patry thread their way through the events of the Rwandan genocide. Their chronicle is all the more disturbing for allowing survivors and witnesses their say upon returning to the site of the events, much as Claude Lanzmann did for the Holocaust. But unlike Lanzmann, who chose deliberately not to present archival images, the producers had no archives to speak of at their disposal.[3] Indeed, the film shows indiscriminately events preceding the genocide with those in its aftermath and those during. It is well and truly a "chronicle." Although the producers are careful to help viewers with the chronology of events, it is impossible to differentiate, on a material basis, between archive and film itself. The chronicle, which is itself shot in video, confounds images chosen by the producers with amateur video taken by a Belgian soldier with the peacekeeping forces of the United Nations (UN). Such a leveling effect, made possible by the medium of video, has important consequences for the memory of the events and their mediation.

First of all, this leveling effect allows us to understand how little what are called "archives" or records, in the realm of images, have to do with the material aspect of images alone. This material aspect has continued to change over the course of the twentieth century, as filmstrips themselves are prone to aging and erasure. Meanwhile, the technology of the medium has continued to progress: just think of the various applications and transformations of color, of film and television pigmentation, of the speed and efficacy of the equipment, of the improvements in sound technology—all of which allow us to date images and stamp them with the seal of the age. Until now, wear and tear and the development of new technologies have enabled us to almost naturally date film and television archives. Likewise, the rapid evolution in fashion and the gradual transformation of everyday objects and technology in the areas of transportation, labor, and communication have greatly fostered this chronological proclivity. Today, however, advances in the medium seem to have the opposite effect. While visual technology appears to outstrip reality, more than ever offering that feeling of immediacy that characterizes hypermediatization, the medium itself, far from facilitating chronology, levels the temporal dimension of events, even to the point of enabling the live mediatization of war.[4] Video, to a certain extent, brings crimes against humanity into the cozy space of the family den (and the banality of home movies) in a startling way.

In the second place, the leveling effect that Lacourse and Patry achieve in their film through video seems to efface the subjectivity of the images; to put it another way, they *shoot* the image, more than ever restoring to the reality of genocide a semblance of immediacy. We are among these people, framing the terrified gaze of witnesses, hearing their desperate cries, just like the Belgian soldier preparing to leave and who knows that, by leaving, he condemns them to certain death. Paradoxically, this "nearness" produces an uncanny effect. There are no longer any images at this point, only an intensity as real as it is unreal: real, because painful; unreal, because these people, though already dead to us, still gaze at us as though from the *other side of sacrifice*. Now, unlike Marker's image of the flying man, the sequence does not capture the gaze of a dead man in the cinematics of life; rather, it captures the last *sight* of the living in the midst of death itself. Nothing, if not the opacity of their gaze, guarantees the relay that goes on between the condemned and ourselves. In the viewer's eyes, this gaze appears as the last avatar of cinema in the midst of death; it says: I am in hell on earth, prisoner of this unbearable and timeless communication. Only the eyes of the condemned, by their terrifying cinematics, can elucidate a reality so flat: a reality without depth, since everything here is profound; a reality both banal and without relief, because nothing seems to escape the obscene efficacy of the means of communication. The eyes alone still recall the troubling dimension of life and its mediation and restore depth to the leveling media coverage of world news. A threshold where images are born and death is overcome, the human eye is indeed the *anima* whose force and fragmentation are ever intensified by melancholy.

By making room, in the heart of a hypermediatized age, for mediation between the living and the dead, Marker's work provides an example of this melancholy. The testamentary film, *Level Five*, focuses on a lesser-known episode from the end of the Second World War, the Battle of Okinawa, in which inhabitants of the island killed their kin and took their own lives, rather than surrender to the enemy. Over archival footage, Marker voices his thoughts on sacrifice, mourning, the power of images, and memory. In addition, the film relates the dialogue between a woman friend of the director and a computer—the vestigial presence of the man she loved and recently lost. Using computer commands, and following in the mnemonic tracks of the beloved, she must play out the Battle of Okinawa as one would a game. Through various media (archives, photographs, films, video games, texts, multimedia), the film raises the question of mediation in connection with an *ethics of loss*. Though wary of the hypermedial character of our age, and of the way in which media err and preclude mourning, Marker draws nonetheless on the figure of mediation as a *utopian legacy*. What is bequeathed is the *image*. Only on the basis of the image, and not montage, does experience again fully become the experience of mediation. Not that Marker denies the importance of montage, but the latter relies, first and foremost, on the power and fragility of a single image—one that, insofar as it is memorial, remains inexhaustible. The relation to this other-in-time is born of a single memory, a single image, in an epiphany. If Marker's images are more oneiric than they are iconic, this does not make them "unreal," for all that. They do have a fluid texture, though, and because they cannot be grasped except in flux, at their vanishing point, as they disappear, these images do not solicit the gaze; they solicit *sight*: a defocusing of the gaze, an absentminded, epiphany-like appreciation for the decomposition of light and forms. This flicker of images can never be cumulative, one image added to another, but rather the pursuit of a single, forever inaccessible, ever desired image. In short, Marker's images are made of that fragility and power, held and concentrated in the eye of he who, in Lacourse's and Patry's film, holds us witness to his own death. What holds in this eye, like the flickering flame of life itself, takes the form of an image in Marker's films. In a utopian way, the eye gazes over the surface of a world, all the while revealing that which disappears from its sight.

This revelation shares the structure of ritual itself: it is at once integrated and autonomous, and like ritual, finds its meaning and persistence not in its objective contents but as a force of renewal in the very heart of habit. In his testamentary film, *The Sacrifice*, Andrei Tarkovsky depicts a small boy and his father preparing to plant a tree in the very spot where the world will soon come to an end. To save the world, the father tells his son, it would suffice that someone carry out the same action every day, at the same hour, someone coming to water the tree each day, at the same time.

This is indeed what ritual is all about. Tarkovsky's modest tribute to ritual is echoed in the concerns of Marker, who sees in the loss of ritual the negation of human experience: the negation of memory, but equally the negation of that which memory cannot do without—forgetting. In Tarkovsky's film, a mailman—mediator *par excellence*—arrives on bicycle to tell one of the 284 anecdotes that he collects. The anecdote is actually a photograph, taken in 1960, of a woman with her son, a son, however, who died in 1940 at the Front. What can we make of this photograph, if not precisely an "image," in which the meeting of other-in-time and memory, in other words what we call "ritual," is so accurately revealed?

I would like to further develop these thoughts on memory and the mediation of images with the help of Marker, since cinema, for Marker, is just such an unexpected *time sharing*, a collective working through memory and forgetting by which the living contact the dead in a unique actualization of human experience. This is the impetus behind Marker's life's work and hence his autobiography. But like the father in Tarkovsky's film, Marker's legacy communicates the following: Ritual is nothing but the daily fulfillment of existence; and it is by this gesture of *presence to life* that human time, that is, past and future together, *immemorial*, is held responsible. A single memory, in and of itself, is of no great importance; nor is any project for the future. What matters is the motion, the cinematics, which galvanizes memory and hope. As Marker suggests in the film *Sans soleil [Sunless]*, one must endeavor to trace those signs that are soon to be erased, to make them manifest in disappearance, to sketch the blueprints of a world that will be wiped clean by time. Marker operates at the limits of photography and the image; the moving images of cinema likewise create their own "archival effect." With utmost care and attention, Marker explores this threshold, this blurred boundary between archive and life, between the traces of the dead and imagination. In the Markerian world, there is no pure photography without image; even the Rwanda video would assume this memorial aspect within the reified form of the image, thereby forcing us to question its *immediacy*.

AUTOBIOGRAPHY, OR THE MEMOIRS OF CHRIS MARKER

Marker's iconoclastic, multimedia work seems ever to follow the thread of a single thought. The notion of "thought" should be taken in Hannah Arendt's ethical sense of the word, that is, of a "gap between past and future," of a "treasure" passed on by time, but "left us by no testament."[5] In the course of a unique body of work—from the 1949 publication in France of his novel, *Le Coeur net*, to his recent CD-ROM, *Immemory*—Marker has explored the possibilities presented by various media: books, photo novels, documentary and feature films, television, video clips, multimedia installations, and collaborations on collective artistic projects. Just as wide ranging are his subjects. They include the documentary analysis of political events and debates: on the 1962 student strikes in France, in *Le Joli mai [The Lovely Month of May]*; in *Zapping Zone*, a multimedia installation bringing together documents dealing with, among other things, Ceaucescu and Berlin between 1985 and 1990; the 1969 film on torture in Brazil; in *Le Fond de l'air est rouge [Grin without a Cat]*, a chronicle of the Left around the world, filmed between 1967 and 1977. Then there are the reflections on and tributes to filmmakers, artists, and intellectuals in *L'Héritage de la Chouette [The Owl's Legacy]*, a televised series produced in 1989, in which philosophers are given their say, and in articles and films on Hitchcock, Medvedkin, Christo, Tarkovsky, Giraudoux, and Django Reinhardt. Also, along the way, there have been projects that focus on specific sites (Africa, Peking, Siberia, Cuba, Tokyo, Paris, Okinawa, Mexico,

Chile, and Iceland). But it is as a filmmaker, particularly of the cult science-fiction film *La Jetée [The Pier]* that Marker is best known.[6]

A single question, however, inexorably recurs throughout this diversity: How are memory and the future interwoven in the spiral of time? As I see it, over time, Marker has tried to bequeath to the memory of our times just such a testament as Arendt described. This testament can only be utopian: the testament of thought throwing itself into the gap between past and future.

With Marker, documentary and poetry form the warp and the woof that make up the fabric of a life lived in images: "images of the century," captured from the four corners of the world, ever mindful to register the memory of different cultures; "images of the century," marked by the personal experience of time, by the necessity to provide testimony at once to one's own life, as well as to the life of cultures. What Raymond Bellour writes in regard to the CD-ROM *Immemory* aptly summarizes Marker's work as a whole and its testamentary value: it is the "repository of an œuvre and life which have taken this century as a memory palace for all the world's memory."[7] Personal images of happiness and the image-memories of the century intersect along an analogous course. This course is always Marker's own, but one in which his audience finds itself doubly invoked, as the personal dimension of human experience combines with the historical and utopian dimension of a changing world. It is almost as though Marker leafs through this world like a family album and, like a sensible storyteller, whispers in the viewer's ear: Behold, this is the stuff of your experience, the experience you believe escapes your grasp because it is made of noises, images, and the evanescent; in reality, it is truly yours, for it concerns a memory and a future from which you cannot escape.

Can we call Marker's work autobiographical though? "The Marker 'I'," critic Olivier Kohn objects, "is never introspective." What is more, "the fact that 'I' never explicitly designates 'Chris Marker,' but a borrowed, anonymous identity, also separates it from the 'personal diary.'"[8] Marker's name is itself a pseudonym, making the figure of the filmmaker all the more enigmatic. Very little of his private life is ever revealed. What events and relations form the fabric of his existence? Only by the recurrence of familiar images from places visited (for instance, the cats and owls glimpsed up a Tokyo street), and in the meandering of a thought bordering sometimes on dreaming, does anything personal indeed appear.[9] If we define autobiography as "consciousness turned back upon itself," then Marker's work hardly fits the genre, and so Kohn believes, preferring instead to speak of "consciousness" as a "dream of action," a "field of possibility," as "action" through images.

In point of fact, there is still a certain ambiguity regarding the autobiographical nature of an œuvre inspired by a secret identity. However, in contrast to Kohn—albeit, following in the wake of his reflection—I would nonetheless like to insist on this autobiographical aspect. Not by evoking "reflexive consciousness," but on the grounds of the testamentary value of the work. In a culture where mediatization and the immateriality of information become the *subject matter* of human experience, the notion of "autobiography" itself must actually undergo considerable modification. The subject no longer "reflects" on its own existence, interiorizing speculative discovery through writing; rather, it discovers the *proof* of a life (in the double sense of that which is *put to the proof* and the *photographic proof*), the proof of a life made of images, vision, and the evanescent. The legacy of this double proof is what constitutes Marker's testament and lends it the aspect of *memoirs*.

The idea that autobiography is first and foremost "the introspection of an I" is thoroughly undermined in the culture of images, not because of the "disappearance of the subject," but precisely because subjectivity is significantly inflected through exposure to image media. The notion of "introspection of an I" loses all relevance in describing subjectivity once the subject recognizes itself henceforth in "images of the world"; it loses its pertinence as soon as the subject recognizes some correspondence between the unfolding and packaging of images in cinema and the movement of its own reflecting consciousness.

In Marker, subjectivity is shot through with those images of the world that intrinsically tie all narrative identity to historical discourse: the individual gaze influences memories, just as historical discourse influences collective memory; it is just as easy to delve into the dreams of passengers on a Tokyo train (as Marker does in *Sunless*) as it is to manipulate history through the power of images. In each case, however, the *images* yield a truth of sorts: the truth of pain and hope. To that extent, the inchoate and indestructible core of Marker's autobiography is that need, ever so important since the end of the Second World War—the need to "bear witness."[10] Nothing reveals the irreducible truth of pain and hope like the experience of war and cataclysm.

UTOPIAN LEGACIES

Like the film *Level Five*, *Immemory* seems indeed to present the utopian testament of an artist whose work of remembrance began in the wake of the camps and war's end.[11] Marker's path, between 1949 and 1998, blurs the line between fiction and documentary, poetry and political analysis. It combines an ethics of the word, in the form of "speaking up" and "testimony," with the figuration of action (the treasure of images holding the promise of a future). In a complex undertaking that draws on images and sounds from around the world, and scorns neither chance encounters nor well-known current events, Marker nevertheless insists on leaving the mark of contingent subjectivity. In the end, these images, passing events, and encounters are traces of a subject—the strain of its voice and vision. These traces constitute a particular memory.

We cannot overemphasize how indebted the notion of "narrative identity" is to the enormous efforts of reflection in the aftermath of the disasters of the twentieth century. The traumas of the two World Wars produced a shock wave so great that it completely upset the relationship between history and experience. The obligation to remember, along with our responsibility unto others, engenders a different idea of experience. It was on this basis that Paul Ricoeur elaborated the notion of narrative identity, drawing more, in the process, upon Lévinas than on Heidegger. Above all, Ricoeur borrows from Arendt the idea that to pose the question "Who?" means opening the door to narrative—that one tell the story of a life.[12] Thus the issue of identity shifts from the self-reflexive task of the subject to the consideration of what narrative "bestows." What this indicates is that events have compelled the subject to understand his or her own alterity as a duty unto an other: oneself as an other, the other as oneself, that is the motto Ricoeur follows. Alterity, however, also is the aporetic feature of time, since time is never present to itself, but is always, by definition, *other*. The same goes for identity, which remains unstable, since it is wound around the distaff of time, continuously modified in transit between past and future.

Marker's work is not unaffected by the way identity unfolds in time and time coils back upon itself. It offers a keen experience of vision and exchange with others, shot through with memories and the knowledge of forgetting: travel memories; archives of conflicts, wars, and revolutions; enigmatic faces furtively surprised up a street, at the marketplace, on a subway car seat; the indolent goings about of an animal oblivious to human history, but showing, in its supreme insouciance, the very vulnerability of everything around us, everything that humans risk destroying. Alert precisely to memory as it shifts with the images of the century, to the least fibrillation of the camera as "singular witness" to the times, his work brings about a formidable synthesis, a melancholy mediation, between personal vision and the history of our times, between the countless faces of oblivion and the personal pursuit of happiness.[13] But one would doubtlessly have to acknowledge yet another stake in autobiography, one different from what Ricoeur understood by the "closed circle," or the full and finished life, of narrative identity. The circle is never closed, and the filmmaker is only ever present as a vision perpetually overwhelmed by the exuberance of life and the movement of collective memory. He does not tell "the story of his life" but the spectacular unfurling of a world remade in images, the sudden epiphany-like appearance of faces conjured up in memories, as ancient as they are intimate. Narrative identity, as Ricoeur conceives it, is inadequate to define autobiography in this sense. We must resort to the notion of *utopian testament*, for the twofold aspect of memory and utopia, of travel memories and the unfurling of images, breaks the placid circle that Ricoeur draws about identity. "Moving images" cannot answer the question "Who?" by simply recounting the story of a life; they continue to draw other circles, other frames and spaces where untold moments join and intermix. These moments, far from being the smallest units of time, trace the outlines of time as it flashes up and fades away.

The different perspectives, the many playful identities that make up Chris Marker, whose name is but a pseudonym, ultimately converge in the course of a tenacious, even intractable preoccupation with "time." Indeed, his work is given over to "time," to grasping time and its grip on us, as it is to seizing how time eludes our grasp, loses us in the thick of things and the movement that leads all things to death and oblivion.

Ever since his collaboration with Alain Resnais on *Les Statues meurent aussi [Statues Also Die]* in 1950, and on *Nuit et brouillard [Night and Fog]* in 1955—the one dealing with the destruction of indigenous memory in the appropriation of African arts by European museums, the other, with the Holocaust and Nazi concentration camps—Marker has been preoccupied with collective memory as it is refracted through the prism of a personal experience of time. In his recent *Immemory*, he conflates two clichés of modern memory: By asking "What is a Madeleine?" he combines the Proustian experience of the *madeleine* with Hitchcock's ruse, which consists of naming the enigmatic character of *Vertigo* "Madeleine"—she who is at once object and subject of a fixation on the past. In each case, the Madeleine is the key with which human memory enters the vortex of time. In his personal obsession with Hitchcock, Marker tirelessly takes up the thread of *Vertigo*, from *The Pier* and "the story of a man fixated on an image of the past," through *Sunless* and *Level Five*, to *Immemory*.

Vertigo is the story of a man obsessed with the identity of a woman he will ultimately lose through his own fault. The woman, Madeleine, is herself obsessed by the portrait of a dead woman with whom she identifies. This story becomes Marker's own—the story he tells, under another alias, between the 1965 film *Le Mystère Koumiko [The Koumiko Mystery]* and *Sunless* (1982). As critic Terrence Rafferty remarked when *Sunless* premiered, if *The Koumiko Mystery* was inspired by an obsession with a face (that of a young Japanese woman), *Sunless* is the diary of a trip back, of a return to places evoked seven years earlier, in the course of which Japan itself assumes an enigmatic face. Shortly thereafter, Marker himself would assume the features of an enigma: "In a sense," Terrence Rafferty writes, "*Sunless* is *The Koumiko Mystery* remade as *The Marker Mystery*."[14] It is not surprising, then, that Marker is fascinated by Hitchcock's characters, caught up as he is in the differential recurrence of time that film and multimedia make possible. The uncanny mystery of a face reincorporates the familiar thread of personal memories, transforming documentary into a private album.

In his films, Marker dwells upon the at-once memorial, present, and utopian aspect of the gaze: everywhere in Tokyo, the mass is subject to the prying eyes of gargantuan voyeurs, looking down from giant billboards. Other eyes—fearful, furtive, curious—gaze back at us relentlessly from the ubiquitous television screen and return in dreams to haunt the sleep of subway workers. Are these the dreams of the keeper of images—the filmmaker Marker invents, the filmmaker he is—or are they part of some gigantic oneiric screen on which the city is merely projected? The thought occurs to the narrator of *Sunless*, as she reads the filmmaker's letters aloud. The collective dream of all those asleep on subway benches, as Marker puts it, would be the ultimate film, his dream film.

Does Marker not show, by interweaving the collective dream of subway sleepers with scraps of last night's television, the extent to which narrative and our most personal images converge in a utopian way with the scaled-down visions of today's world? In *Dimanche à Pékin [Sunday in Peking]* (1955), the film-maker begins with a childhood memory—an engraving from a children's book—only to wind up transported to monuments of the Ming dynasty. The child is haunted by the engraving, and so too is the man, before he finally sets off: "Without knowing it, I was dreaming of Peking. In my mind's eye, I could see an engraving from childhood." Obsession with an image (the mode of memorial spectrality) and projection (the mode of utopia) are leagued together.

As we see, with Marker it is customary to travel the world as we would our own lives, from childhood images to cultural monuments, as though toward a utopian testament—utopian, because it is a message "delivered" in a child's dream, one that is, at the same time, the dream of a world. In characterizing the autobiographical nature of Marker's work, one must first understand that, under the regime of images, narrative identity introduces the variable perspective of the present—the *now* of a palpable actuality responsive to memory. As Ernst Bloch might say: We must understand autobiographical memory as a *processive reality*, a knowledge turned toward the *transformation of the world*.[15] Autobiography, then, becomes "panorama," a living collection of images and voices, a tender knot out of which personal stories unwind, along with stories of the end of the world, like those Marker loves to spin in *The Pier* and *Sunless*. Are not those ages in which utopia rises from its own ashes—those times obsessed with births, origins, and emergence—the same ages in which images of "the end of the world" (cataclysms, epidemics, and catastrophes) flourish? At such times, narrative identity unravels, surviving in the hollows, vertiginously, in bits and pieces. History then assumes the form of a particular expressivity: the expressivity of time grasped in its material consistency, in its actualization. It is an expressivity that belongs to the modern experience of shock, and the fragmentation of experience that Benjamin described in connection to melancholy which, for him, goes together with utopia.

This actualization involves the necessity to rethink questions of alterity and temporality. We must grasp time, as much in its actualization as in its illusory immobilization in images. It is not only a duty of memory but a duty to the future. As Hans Jonas observed, the subject redefines itself on the basis of its self-imposed duty to others, while the present redefines itself on the basis of its self-imposed duty to the future.[16] The question Marker raises is the following: How do we "bestow" something of actuality to that other-in-time which is the coming humanity?

The answer quite literally expands the concept of narrative identity: the other-in-time, the being-to-come, who is always also the being that haunts our own death, can only be depicted in terms (or "images," more appropriately) of "oneself." Marker films memory as one would the future; he films the future as one would memory. Here, testament assumes its full meaning, which never fails to recall an everyday aspect of utopia—the daily ritual of hope.

As we know, the image media cannot employ the past tense (present perfect, present continuous, past perfect, or simple past); perforce, they set time in a "present" endlessly differentiated by the repetition of images. Their memorial function is none the lesser for all that, but it changes the nature of this function. While Marker is still preoccupied with memory and time, with the strain between memories and their obliteration, circumstances dictate that past, present, and future will collide in the same frame. For in this time frame, past and present converge in the gaze, out of which the epiphany of the future flashes up. Cinema has always done so. Think of the ever-departing workers of the Lumière factory: in a single time frame, an action unfolds and reveals in images of the past, not "past images," but the passing of time itself. In realizing as much, the viewer recognizes the irruption of becoming within her or his own present. It is not only that "tomorrow" is coeval with "yesterday" and "today," as Olivier Kohn maintains,[17] but that "tomorrow" takes form wholly within the utopian *presence of the past*. For Marker, this is the significance of the spiral of time that we see unwinding from the center of the eye, in the famous opening to *Vertigo*: the gaze itself is what sets the vertigo of time in motion.

THE EXPERIENCE OF MEDIATION

As a documentary filmmaker, an archaeologist of images, and a philosopher of the cutting room, Marker is careful to register a sense of subjectivity at work: the hesitation of the camera, the interference of images, and the speed with which they follow one after the other are some of the many ways in which Marker emphasizes the fleeting, multifarious character of a reality ever apt to undermine the bases of the enunciatory subject. Running commentary accompanies his films: the narrative voice-over in *The Pier*, a woman's voice reading letters from a filmmaker friend in *Sunless*, the epistolary exchange, again, in *Lettre de Sibérie [Letter from Siberia]*, Marker's own voice and the dialogue between a woman and her computer in *Level Five*. Each of these voices provides the thread of thought, as though "words always link together the images and carry the arguments."[18] Each film allows us to see and hear the question of transmission and mediation.

And yet, each film records the resonance of one voice in the absence of another, reverberates with a singular, often impossible destination. The labor of reflection assists the images in spreading doubt and stripping away all but the
essential. Essential, in this case, does not mean a "world of essences" but the
recognition of the very evanescence of things and beings, and of the necessity to
rethink mediation. Poetry provides a final recourse for thought, a last resort in
the face of the aporias of being and time. And seeing as the normative distinction
between documentary and fiction has never been applicable in Marker's case, it
is not surprising to find poetry and *logos* imbricated in his work. Whether made
from images he himself shot or ones gathered from archives, Marker's films en-
courge such a reading, so that, when trying to tackle the question of time and
memory, the poetic intent of thought cannot dispense with questioning what we
commonly call "mediation."

In this respect, Marker's work is particularly sensitive to the paradox of mediation, or the way in which the medium effaces itself by its own efficacy: the
more effective the medium, the more it tends to disappear. Marker appears un-
willing to reconcile himself to this disappearance; rather, the film medium, it
seems, is only unveiled in the flash in which it disappears. As the voices jog
memory, haunting the recollection of images, they remind us that there is nothing inherent to images (no meaning, no signification) save the absence or lack
that they disclose.

But what becomes of the film medium if, like Pasolini, we define its language as "life itself"? Life long ago invented cinema, Pasolini reminds us—the
cinematic being finally no more than the gestures and expressions of everyday
life, the language of the body, of things, and of landscapes whose signs we have
always been able to decipher.[19] Gestures, looks, the rustle of leaves, the play of
shadow and light, the body falling, the commotion of crowds, all are imprinted
in us. Inchoately, they summon other gestures, other looks. In their endless play
of repetition and difference, they score the film of our lives and give form to our
ways of being. In this way, cinema is life, and life is intrinsically cinematic, which
is to say that, even in the midst of communicating after its fashion, "life itself"
ceaselessly unveils that which it still lacks, that which is still absent. From the outset, life is "filmic," and because it is ever mediated, it is tied to technology. Thus
we begin to appreciate just how paradoxically mediation and the disappearance
of the medium go together.

It is prevalent in film criticism to view cinema either as a continuation of, or
a break with, literature and orality. Cinema, so it goes, takes its "sense of story"
from literary and oral narrative. Venturing to paraphrase Pasolini and Ricoeur in
one stroke, I submit, rather, that literature and story borrow from cinema. They
borrow, to the extent that life is already a cinematic communication. But they
borrow, above all, in that this cinematics of "life itself" already always possesses a

narrative inchoation, an "appeal" to story. It is there in the gaze that calls for a story, in the brutality of an event that calls for testimony, in the grief of mourning, or in the suffering of war, which imposes a duty to remember. In his films, Marker focuses this luminous ray in which life and mediation form part of the same experience—making the communication of "life itself" visible, while rendering the experience of mediation equally palpable and difficult.

Before the emergence of the culture of literacy, traditional cultures were masters of this experience of mediation, for in such cultures, the oral transmission of experience (as Benjamin noted in his essay on the storyteller) is fully a part of ordinary experience. In other words, since all experience, for traditional culture, is tied from the outset to the community and the perennity of its *memoria*, living is the same as transmitting.[20] Only with the culture of literacy is experience itself cut off from the conditions of its transmission. As Wlad Godzich reminds us, the book and, above all, its reproducibility, confer a new autonomy upon experience, making the question of its mediation that much more pointed. For Godzich, the concept of mediation is more strictly applicable in the context of technical reproduction, where knowledge is no longer *directly* transmitted.[21] In some sense, I would add, the medium called writing—and, even more significantly, its reproducible version—ends up reversing the previously instituted relation between mediation and experience, between legacy and praxis: it transforms what, to traditional culture, was *the experience of mediation* into *the mediation of experience*. This reversal has, of course, important consequences for the meaning of collective memory.

It would appear necessary to reconsider the hypermedial tenor of our times in light of this relation between mediation and experience. Does the culture of image media in fact not oblige us to redefine this relationship? The solicitation of the gaze, along with all that there is to see; the sway the cinematic holds over experience through force of habit, compounding the "life itself" effect of which Pasolini spoke; the daily exposure to the steady stream of images; the media cacophony that resounds even within the innermost reaches of our lives; that deep confusion between the materiality of the world and its immaterial expressivity—does all of this not undermine the various shapes that human existence assumes between birth and death, what Ricoeur called "the story of a life"? Clearly the mediation of human experience, as well as human experience in and of itself, has reached the heights of equivocacy. We can no longer think simply in terms of a *mediation of experience*, forced as we are to ponder in "life itself" the flow of these images not only surrounding us but now making up our lives. Is modern experience, from the start, not, by definition, the experience of media? Propelled by the movie camera, and intensified by television and the "society of spectacle,"[22] the experience of media is not one "of motion, which we can render simply in a spatial sense as that of covering a certain distance," to use Alain Menil's terms. It is, as he says, "the very essence of all mobility, which is becoming."[23] But once beyond the *mediation of experience*, are we back, for all that, to the *experience of mediation*? Can the efficacy of contemporary media be compared to the capacity that traditional societies had to explain, at once, both experience and mediation?

The parallel is deceptive, for while the hypermedial environment of today implies an *experience of mediation*, the latter can only be lived paradoxically, if not traumatically, as an experience of dereliction and vertigo. In reality, the *mediation of experience* to which the culture of literacy has accustomed us, is coupled with the *experience of mediation*, as though the two relations were drawn into an abyssal structure of self-reference, or *mise-en-abyme*. It would be illusory to regard the hypermedial turn in contemporary culture as an unexpected, revolutionary return to a mediation freed, finally, of all instrumentality—a kind of return to the traditional experience of mediation within our own medial environment. Hypermediality has its source as well in the culture of reproduction. Nevertheless, if instrumentality has not been eradicated, it has taken on a new dynamic, accentuating, now more than ever, the paradox of mediation. On the one hand, the media have never been so apt to efface their own materiality, confounding the impression of immediacy with the immateriality of their expression. On the other hand, the impact of media has never been so hotly debated, to the point of promoting a pseudo-critical attitude toward the media—a healthy form of skepticism upon which citizens count to defend themselves against the "omnipotence" of the media. Such skepticism can sometimes be dumbfounding, as in the case of one student who, thinking he knew all about the media and their impact, candidly proclaimed that the conflict in Kosovo could be explained by the need to increase viewer ratings among the television networks of the West.

Never has the average citizen been so aware of the mediatization of experience by the profusion and diversification of media; never has this citizen, though, been so inclined to see this as the result of immediacy. Contemporary experience of mediation throws the Pasolinian notion of cinema as "life itself" into a hypermedial vertigo. Whether or not we call it "postmodern," as some indeed prefer, our age is no longer simply the age of reproduction, but of recycling and the prepackaging of images and communication. This is characteristic of hypermediality. If the age of reproduction heralded the advent of technology, today's culture is one of images mediatized by images, sounds mediatized by sounds, that is, of a further and further disguised technology. "Life itself" now becomes inseparable from its own mediatization. Paradoxically, this removes that very mediation which is the foundation of culture and any rapport with memory from the sphere of experience. "Mediatization" is what I would call this traumatic and paradoxical aspect of mediation, which is specific to contemporary experience: mediatization translates an experience that is already always defined by mediation; it does so, however, in the twofold and paradoxical negation of both the materiality of the medium and its disappearance. As much as we would like to believe that reality is right to hand, without any mediation whatsoever, we also suspect that we are only ever dealing with *mere images*. We must therefore distinguish between *mediation* and *mediatization*: while our society permits the out and out mediatization of death (the corpse is a constant screen figure), it has forgotten the knack that traditional societies had for mediation with the dead. The various figurations of death in the former, verge on the recycling of death; in the latter, mediation with the dead perpetuates the very meaning of shared memory.

It is therefore no longer the task of thought to examine the "contents of experience" but to take the ambiguities of mediation itself for the contents of experience today, whether personal or collective. Chris Marker's work is devoted, in part, to just that. Unlike Dziga Vertov, his acknowledged mentor, Marker does not keep personal experience out of camera shot; he is not the "man-with-a-movie-camera," that revolutionary android commemorating the technological wonder of the age. Rather, he shows how the cinematic has infiltrated all experience, *even our dreams*. Experience has become cinematic to the power of two since, in addition to the cinematic that Pasolini spoke of, that of "life itself," there is the *cinematic of images* now making up the panorama of our lives. Siegfried Kracauer had an inkling of this reversal as early as 1927, when he attributed to photography already such an ascendancy over culture: "For the world itself has taken on a 'photographic face'; it can be photographed because it strives to be absorbed into the spatial continuum which yields to snapshots."[24] Where Vertov celebrated the revolutionary advent of technology in the mobility of the man-with-a-movie-camera, Marker reveals, rather, the vulnerability of technology and the frailty of the human eye. The materiality of experience is thus subjected to the vertigo of a particularly personal gaze—a gaze that cannot escape the ambiguities and equivocations of mediation today. Happiness itself lies in the very fragility of the image, in the vulnerability of beings and the gaze, and in that entirely human hesitation to see and be seen—that hesitation to film, which belongs not to Vertov's man-with-a-movie-camera but to the gaze that takes things in as if for the first and last time. "Mediation" no longer appears, except in fragmentary forms. In Marker's films, for instance, it is figured anew, but it is always "filled" with the loss unveiled in mediation. Images of happiness are always those that fade and abide in the oscillation of memory.

In a famous essay, from around the same time as Kracauer's work on photography, Maurice Halbwachs worked out a sensible distinction between the memories we encounter in dreams and collective memory.[25] Dream memories are fragmentary, he maintained, because they belong to a closed world, an individual construct; because there is in them no "surrounding memory," what Halbwachs rightly calls "social frames of memory," it is impossible to have a nonfragmentary memory in dreams. The more the social frames of a society crumble, and the more a society loses the unity and coherence of its memory, the more memory is individualized, even fragmented. Things and beings no longer seem to belong to any world. The question then becomes whether the media constitute a new form of "surrounding memory" or an extraordinary expansion of "fragmentary memory." Walter Benjamin discovered a memorial path by which the modern eye is led into the twin dimensions of collective memory and fragmentary experience: "precisely in that which is newest," he reminded us in his *Arcades Project*, "the face of the world never alters."[26] Utopia and memory meet where experience and the fashioning of images become one, where modern identity is constructed and reconstructed in the shock and solicitation of things to see. Under the reign of images and speed, "recalling memories" necessarily means surrendering to the epiphany-like flash and fade of a materiality in motion. Before the Second World War, when neither Shoah nor Hiroshima had any resonance within experiential consciousness, it was still possible to pair, as did Benjamin, the fragmentation of modern experience with the memory of the world. From his utopian perspective, Benjamin saw, in the frenzy of Modernity, the fragmentary memories of dreams intertwine with that collective memory of which Halbwachs spoke—as if a society, like a child in its room, dreamt itself asleep and awake. According to Halbwachs, though, cultures can only dream at the expense of losing their social frames, which is to say that, once carried along in the fragmentary flux of memory, they become amnesic. "Mediatization" describes this loss and flux quite well, for it is indeed a fragmentary and productive dream, modeled on the individuation of experience, that nonetheless fills the gap in social frames. This mediatization, however, is not the same as the rich impression of Modernity described by Benjamin. Rather, mediatization seems to impoverish experience, as Benjamin indeed noted at the close of the First World War.[27]

How then can we reconcile this fragmentary experience of medatization with the responsibility to a shared memory? Can we revitalize the social frames of memory, once we are subject to the shock of mediatization and its "perpetual hemorrhage of action and meaning," as Jean Louis Schefer put it?[28] Schefer too invokes dreams in order to explain the emergence of cinema: starting with Romanticism and early-nineteenth-century fantasy, Western Modernity produced an "incredible dream catalogue," he writes. "The formation, in this way, of an 'oneiric continent' at the outset of the modern world, by weaving an impalpable tunic of shadows, of ghostly parts, abruptly reveals to the dreamer, the poet, the storyteller his terrible situation: dreams have no author. Nobody signs a dream, and anybody can be its subject."[29] This "nobody," this "anybody," are they not telltale signs of the collapse of social frames described by Halbwachs? And yet, even in the midst of terror and dereliction, the melancholy dreamer never loses *sight* of the memory of the dead. These dead have always been a concern of Marker's. He transforms the faces of strangers around the world momentarily, fragmentarily, into so many masks—death masks and primal faces of women. These faces ever call to mind the same face: the face, familiar but now lost, of the mother or beloved. A face that is familiar, *because lost*, and thus always *recovered* in the multitude of images. It is then in full media frenzy that mediation once again becomes possible. For Marker, mediation appears precisely in the form of what is lost and, *because lost*, unfailingly recovered from the shattered fragments of images. Marker's "imaginary news" are not imaginary because false or fictional but because they are expressed in "images" and registered as such in an ever-fragmentary memorial itinerary. The catastrophes of the last century, and those especially of the Second World War, have undeniably compelled us to acknowledge the fragmentary character of memory. But not as the dialectical face of history in revolution, as Benjamin believed, rather, as that which calls for an ethics of loss.

Translated from the French by Brian Neville.

NOTES

1. Roland Barthes, *The Grain of the Voice: Interviews 1962–1980*, translated by Linda Coverdale (New York: Hill and Wang, 1985), 356.

2. Ron Burnett, *Cultures of Vision: Images, Media and the Imaginary* (Bloomington and Indianapolis: Indiana University Press, 1995), 53.

3. No archival images, save, appropriately, those of the Holocaust which are shown at the outset of the film to signify the horror of recurrence: we said "never again," and only forty years later the abominable recurs, forewarns the film.

4. This is true not only of video; cinema has equally created a certain confusion since it began "imitating" the moving images of the past and thereby producing archival effects.

5. Arendt borrows the idea of an *inheritance left us by no testament* from René Char. Under the Nazi occupation, contends Char, those in the Resistance found liberty, as action and thought came together, beyond the sadness of a private life "centered about nothing but itself." For Arendt, thought turns toward the lost treasure of revolution and resistance; "the trains of thought, of remembrance and anticipation, save whatever they touch from the ruin of historical and biographical time." Within each of us, a bond unites the capacity to think with the capacity to judge good and evil; a bond on which depends the possibility of resistance to evil in periods of moral crisis. Thinking, for Arendt, is thus a veritable memorial duty on which the future depends. See Hannah Arendt, *Between Past and Future: Six Exercises in Political Thought* (Cleveland and New York: Meridian, 1954), 3–15.

6. Hollywood has recently drawn on it for the filmscript of *Twelve Monkeys*.

7. Raymond Bellour, "The Book, Back and Forth," in *Qu'est-ce qu'une Madeleine? A propos du CD-ROM Immemory de Chris Marker*, translated by Brian Holmes (Paris: Yves Gevaert, 1997), 124.

8. Olivier Kohn, "Si loin si proche," in *Positif* 433 (1997): 79 (my translation).

9. The owl and the cat are Marker's pet fetishes, veritable film logos that amount to trademarks for all of his films. In *Sunless*, a Tokyo billboard advertises "Hotel Utopia," which is immediately associated with cats; an owl is used for an advertisement, and then another owl appears. The same images will be used in other films and in the CD-ROM, ceaselessly reminding us that the images Marker shoots always record his own individual experience.

10. See Stéphane Bouquet, "Chris Marker, dans le regard du chat," in *Cahiers du cinéma* 522 (March 1998): 59. "Chris Marker belongs to those two or three generations of artists and thinkers who believed (wanted to believe) that, in the history of humanity, Auschwitz or Hiroshima were events one could not get over. To cite examples from France and from film alone: Resnais, the Straubs, Godard, Duras, Daney. Obviously, they are not totally naive, for all that. All are well aware that Auschwitz will fade from memory, just as the trenches of 14–18 no longer speak to us (I mean viscerally speak to us). It is this contradictory understanding—that Auschwitz is at once essential and doomed to oblivion—which no doubt explains, like an open wound, the obsessive relationship these artists and thinkers share with memory" (my translation).

11. See Bellour, op. cit., 118–19: "Perhaps he started *Immemory* at the moment when he chose to write and to film; at the time when memory, after the war and the camps, became *his* problem, almost his sole subject. He entered *Immemory* as soon as he began to remember, to remember that he remembered, and to accumulate—in the increasingly disproportionate treasure of his archives where he keeps 'everything'—the traces of his life refracted in so many others' lives."

12. See volume 3 of Paul Ricoeur's *Time and Narrative*, translated by Kathleen McLaughlin and David Pellauer (Chicago: University of Chicago Press, 1984–1988), as well as Hannah Arendt, *The Human Condition* (Chicago: University of Chicago Press, 1958).

13. On Chris Marker, intermediality, and melancholy, see my "L'Ordinateur de Chris Marker: Mélancolie et intermédialité," in *Protée* 28:3 (Hiver 2000–2001): 7–12.

14. Terrence Rafferty, "Marker Changes Trains," in *Sight and Sound* 53:4 (1984): 286.

15. See Ernst Bloch, *The Principle of Hope*, translated by Neville Plaice, Stephen Plaice, and Paul Knight (Cambridge, Mass.: MIT Press, 1986).

16. See Hans Jonas, *The Imperative of Responsibility: In Search of an Ethics for the Technological Age*, translated by Hans Jonas, with David Herr (Chicago: University of Chicago Press, 1984).

17. Kohn, op. cit., 81.

18. Robert A. Rosenstone, *Visions of the Past: The Challenge of Film to Our Idea of History* (Cambridge, Mass.: Harvard University Press, 1995), 154–55.

19. See Pier Paolo Pasolini, "The Written Language of Reality," in *Heretical Empiricism*, edited by Louise K. Barnett and translated by Ben Lawton and Louise K. Barnett (Bloomington: Indiana University Press, 1988).

20. See Walter Benjamin, "The Storyteller: Reflections on the Works of Nicolai Leskov," in *Illuminations*, edited by Hannah Arendt and translated by Harry Zohn (New York: Schocken, 1969).

21. See Wlad Godzich, *The Culture of Literacy* (Cambridge, Mass.: Harvard University Press, 1994), esp. "After the Storyteller," pp. 96–105.

22. See Guy Debord, *The Society of Spectacle*, translated by Donald Nicholson-Smith (New York: Zone Books, 1995).

23. Alain Menil, *L'écran du temps* (Lyon: Presse Universitaire de Lyon, 1991), 10 (my translation).

24. Siegfried Kracauer, "Photography," in *The Mass Ornament: Weimar Essays*, edited and translated by Thomas Y. Levin (Cambridge, Mass.: Harvard University Press, 1995), 59.

25. Maurice Halbwachs, *Les cadres sociaux de la mémoire* (Paris: Albin Michel, 1994).

26. Walter Benjamin, *The Arcades Project*, translated by Howard Eiland and Kevin McLaughlin (Cambridge, Mass. and London: Belknap Press/Harvard University Press, 1999), 544.

27. See Benjamin, "The Storyteller," op. cit.

28. Jean Louis Schefer, *Du monde et du mouvement des images* (Paris: Cahiers du Cinema, 1997), 66 (my translation).

29. Ibid., 49.

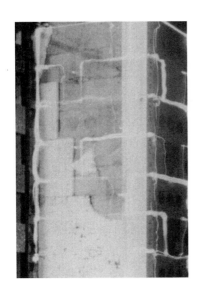

14

ˢcrypt

Memory Building

Gordon Bleach

ˢcrypt
. . . more than a building and no more of a building

as
soon as,
in a second,
the first stroke of
a letter divides itself,
and must indeed support
partition in order to identify itself, there are nothing but post cards,
anonymous morsels without fixed domicile,
without legitimate addressee, letters open, but
like crypts. Our entire library, our entire encyclo-
paedia, our words, our pictures, our figures, our secrets,
all an immense house of post cards.[1] Only a very small part
of architecture belongs to art: the tomb and the monument.[2] The
camera is a portable tomb, you must remember that.[3] Finiche! Only a
fadograph of a yestern scene.[4] (this is—writing/written on the frame)[5]
sewing and patching that betrays, exposes what it should hide, dis-simulates
what it signals . . .[6] Transpose . . . to discompose; agitate; disturb mentally. *Rare*[7]

figure   scrap-heap of epigrams (post Loos and Smithson)[8]

PRIMER

ˢCRYPT FIXATES ON AND EMBODIES THE INTERMINABLE FABRICATIONS—memory *buildings*—of an archival *corpus*. Initialized in 1989 on the Wallace Memorial Library construction site at the Rochester Institute of Technology,[9] ˢcrypt proliferates as a viral archive through auditoria, books, bricks, computer bits, continents, individuals, installations, museums, notepads, paint flecks, photographic grains, and so on.[10]

Inˢcryption, the earliest ˢcrypting, was a publicly visible para-site archive that mimicked official library procedures. Stenciled by a nocturnal archivist-painter, the words comprising this borderline fabrication were emblazoned across the I-beam frame of the L-shaped extension to the host library block.[11] In time, the erection of the external brick façade around the building's frame archived the superficial word–set in an interstitial space where (at the time of this writing) it still remains.[12]

Inˢcryption also masked its successor, the supplemental stage of buildingˢcrypt. In this, a cluster of small geographic and architectural pathologies (*building walks, spurious artifacts*) materialized in the interim arenas of the construction site. Artifacts took on material form via the after-hours "loan" of library building materials. Through s-lavish transposition of "thought at work in architecture" gleaned from the writings of Jacques Derrida, Adolph Loos, and Aldo Rossi, the artifacts performed as a grafted filiation of "material" aphorisms. Flashlight traces recorded in long-duration photographs exposed the makeshift operations. Since the aberrational structures were traced, built, dismantled, and returned *during* photographic exposure, they are only *partially* legible in the final images. Ceaseless motion of the archivist-builder during exposure rendered him invisible. The spurious artifacts are now dispersed across the official building and the borrowed material-units encrypted in their proper place.

ˢcrypt has gradually amassed a southeastern track of building installations throughout the United States and into Africa. *Memory Building*, an installation/resumé in the finished library extension during 1991, has been followed successively by six "spurious artifact" photographs wall mounted in *In/sight: African Photographers, 1940 to the Present* at the Guggenheim Museum in New York, the floor-scape "\ backslash" that landmarked *CROSS/ING* in the Museum of African American Art in Tampa, and the split-plinth "cityˢcrypt" reflecting on the *2nd Johannesburg Biennale's* monumental Electric Workshop housing and inner-cityscape surrounds.[13]

In this conjoined write-up and image bank, only two aspects of ˢcrypt (that is, Inˢcryption and buildingˢcrypt) are to be reprised. This cursory reprisal is a further night shift, sited in a certain sense between a brick and a hard place. It seeks on the one hand to *project* these dual components to readers without simply reifying them as "architectural projects" (topics to be memorialized, diagrammed in retrospect). Yet it also is an obsessive *maintenance*, enacting the prophylactic role of the archivist. In this latter guise, the reprise dotes on the indexical (evidential) properties of the photographic image while asserting the filiations (institutional and otherwise) that render the indexical illusory.[14]

Iɴˢᴄʀʏᴘᴛɪᴏɴ: ᴀɴ ᴇxᴘᴏsɪᴛɪᴏɴ

Inˢcryption worked over an official archive, building a double that was visibly out of place. Body-length word-forms (transparent plastic sheeting approximately six feet long with stenciled letter incisions) were used to spray-paint a set of surface words on the structural I-beam girders. This exteriority underlined the presence of the *internal* archive—even as that "proper" archive was doubly walled (encrypted) by the extension enfolding the original building. As an exhibitionist archive, Inˢcryption functioned as a billboard: a superficial mimic of modest means, advertising the official corpus within. It flaunted a word-set that could at first glance be mistaken for a gaggle of Dewey headings; a slim collection of surface words that, upon further reflection, were never quite consolidated into proper order or placement. Moreover, the words formed an incongruous match with other framing inscriptions and myriad hieroglyphs chalked in by official builders, which all combined as a rather desultory linguistic surface rust to sign the building's frame.

Topos, Aʀᴄʜɪᴠᴇ, Tʜʀᴇsʜᴏʟᴅs

What is it that constitutes the archive? Allan Sekula terms the photographic archive a "territory of images" and claims that it is primarily the impositions of ownership that construct the (spurious) unity of the archive from an amorphous aggregate of constituent elements.[15] Derrida notes that the term *archive* devolves from the Greek *arkheion*—the residence of the superior magistrates: "It is thus, in this *domiciliation*, in this house arrest, that archives take place." From this recognition, Derrida entrains in his inquiry these nested words: shelter, law, document, classification, and institutional rites of passage from private to public. He then elucidates a cartographic linkage between territorial space and imposed order: "[T]he documents, which are not always discursive writings, are only kept and classified under the title of the archive by virtue of a privileged *topology*. They inhabit this uncommon place, this place of election where law and singularity intersect in *privilege*."

But not only is it required that

> the archive be deposited somewhere, on a stable substrate, and at the disposition of a legitimate hermeneutic authority. . . . [It] must also be paired with what we will call the power of *consignation*. . . . *Consignation* aims to coordinate a single corpus, in a system or a synchrony in

which all elements articulate the unity of an ideal configuration. In an archive, there should not be any absolute dissociation, any hetero-geneity or *secret* which could separate . . . or partition, in an absolute manner.[16]

Taken in light of Derrida's and Sekula's observations, the surface pattern-language mapped primarily the guardian "artistic persona" that created it. How-ever cursorily, it held additional intimations of anonymous work production at the steel mills, on the building, and in the official archive within. In^{s}cryption's sputtering growth, errant structure, and superficial location sought to stress the latent fractures in the ideological bracings of every archive (Derrida's consigna-tion); in other words, it was to exemplify the ruptures in access and meaning that occur despite the policings of ownership. If one recalls the epigram "this is—writing/written on the frame," then the library building performed as In^{s}cryption's frame while, simultaneously, In^{s}cryption framed the building of the archive. Furthermore, if one follows John Tagg and takes framing to mark "the never settled threshold at which a legitimized discourse is allowed to begin," then In^{s}cryption posed a working space between two already accom-modated modes of public art on the campus: institutional identity logo and high art. In general, then, In^{s}cryption was to act and be enacted on the framing of three apparent publics: art, architecture, and archive.[17]

In^{s}CRYPTION: INVENTORY, SIGNATURE, ALIGNMENTS, DURATIONS

What words comprised this exteriorized archive growing wrongly in the dark, and how were they configured? Approximately thirty were chosen according to a split-toned requirement. Deemed accessible to a campus audience due to their resonance with connotations from "everyday life," the words were, simultane-ously, sonorous in theory (continental philosophy, art and architectural history, cultural studies, etc.). Their official entombing—the brick shuttering—encapsu-lated a stockpile of words that not only enjoyed an affective and a vernacular *grav-itas*, but also indexed a trajectory within academic discourse, a trajectory that diagrammed In^{s}cryption's own genealogy (a self-referential slice of academic life, shuttered in deadpan imitation of the photographic decisive moment).

Words were not conjoined as slogans, morals, phrases, or sentences. At first glimpse, they appeared as isolated units, internally riven by double-colored let-tering. Under certain lighting conditions at night, subwords dis/appeared as one walked by the library façades, hallucinating the night-shifted archive:

ME within MEMORY, WE within POWER, CULT within CULTURE, . . .

Although the individual words performed as construction units (*à la* bricks), they were spatially networked in order to index and insinuate larger structures (linguistic, spatial, institutional, etc.). For example:

• IMAGE was the first word and IMAGE the second. Positioned on diago-
nally opposite frame corners, these counter-signed the official building. Spray-
painted stenciling reprised, with ironic and retentive interests, the capitalist
graphic of the painter's signature and ghostwrote the architect's signature-space
in the process. The building, yoked into double service, inadvertently performed
the supplementary man-oeuvres of In^scryption.

• POWER was indexed on a vertical frameline that flowed down from the
library then angled out across a horizontal landscaped space to enter the bronze
tiger testicles of a monumental sporting icon. Undeflected in transit through the
mascot, the line emerged from its conventional snarl to ricochet up the shaft of
Building One—the institutional power building and tallest of course, housing
the upper administration, of course. Not quite incidentally, it was from the lofty
vantage point atop Building One that official permission had originally been
given for In^scryption to be performed on the library.[18]

In^scryption exposed temporal as well as spatial concerns; it developed according to multiple time scales, with visible intersections between official and
insubordinate building schedules. Daily construction continued unabated, per-
ceptibly changing the material context for the fitful nocturnal additions to
In^scryption. The paint-writer, moonlighting from jobs as assistant lecturer in
math and computer science and as teaching assistant in photography, kept a
sporadic work pattern. Tactics employed by the night shift were cognizant of
the symbiotic relation to the official day and explicitly reactive to its program.
One example—reinforcement through reiteration—is notated in what follows:
MEMORY.

MEMORY was centered, horizontal, in white/silver on the north façade: a
site adjacent to the preexisting library entrance and in close proximity to pedes-
trian traffic passing below. MEMORY was visible for only a single night before
being covered over—as a normal part of official building procedure—by a
scumbly gray skin of fire retardant. The next night, in an almost osmotic return,
MEMORY was resprayed, directly over its previous gestation, in the color of dried
blood on the retardant (MEMORY building MEMORY). Two divergent treatments
of "the space of memory" are juxtaposed here: "Psychoanalysis recognizes the
past *in* the present, historiography places the one *beside* the other."[19] First, the
covert MEMORY returns, reddened (as psychoanalytic agent of history). In addition, one MEMORY tails another; memory beside itself (as historiographic interpretation ingests and redeploys the archive to fabricate "History"[20]). As one
faced the MEMORY, the proximities were dual: superimposition (the reiterated
word) and abutment of two façades (the library's official entrance wall shoring up
the construction to its right).

In^scryption was built into closure through the basal routine of official construction. Brick tier upon tier, the exterior façade gradually enveloped words,

steel frames, and interstitial concrete walls alike, forestalling not only the sequence of nocturnal painting operations but also foreclosing on the overall diorama. Thus as official building took its natural course, the adjunct In⁵cryption
was quietly shuttered—rendered both subcutaneous and photographic. With the
"original" word–set consigned to the latency of light-tight storage until some future reexposure, the activities of the painterly archivist have been displaced onto
other image-language banks, such as this chapter and its accompanying figures.

AFTERWORD ON MODERN FORMS

If the external impetus to In⁵cryption's closure was the brick overlay, there was
nevertheless an intimation from within the ⁵crypted *quorum* that the makeshift
word string was headed toward an impasse. This was indexed by the final stencil
made under the guise of In⁵cryption. Top dead-center on the north wall I-beam
and shrouded by a thicket of scaffolding, the barely visible terminal mark was ap-
pended at a time when the brick façade had risen mostway up the wall, blocking
out **MEMORY, HISTORY, FANTASY,** and **FORM** in the process. A discreet foursome
sprayed in rusted red primer formed the finishing sequence, taking shape from a
cutout comma stencil as follows:

,, ,,

This silenced sound bite, a close quotation symbol directly preceding its
own opening, lends itself to divergent interpretation. It can be taken as closing
on In⁵cryption before opening immediately onto as-yet-unnamed successors,
both on the building and off (as here, perhaps). Another plausible scenario is to
read the quotation line as circumnavigating the building, quietly incorporating
library word stacks and In⁵cryption. The language referent is itself undecidable:
read in German, for instance, the quote is immediately curtailed in a linguistic
beheading.

Clearly, this small and quadra–comma'd mural can be made to speak to relations between linguistic, painterly, and architectural inquiry. In addition, it en-
gages, partly by default, the venerable history of capitalized headings emblazoned
on buildings of substance (libraries, museums, courthouses, etc.). Unlike those
headboard entries—injunctions, exhortations, mere listings (generic "Great Men
and Muses," Bruce Nauman's neon frieze *Vices and Virtues*,[21] etc.)—it blanks out
and apparently fails to deliver onto anything other than the building's structured
surface. In swearing off linguistic presentation, the sprayed marks divert the spectator to other art-architecture scenarios projected on and around buildings: at a
minimum, the suburban houseworks by Rachel Whiteread, Dan Graham, and
Gordon Matta-Clark and the disparate monumental makeovers by Krzysztof
Wodiczko and Christo.[22]

If one turns to the linguistic edge of the matter, treating the inscription "it-self"—as though pared off the beam and shorn from the disheveled construction signage—then Blanchot's pulverizing rumination on the singular alterity of the quote is apposite. Namely, "If quotations, in their fragmenting force, destroy in advance the texts from which they are not only severed but which they exalt till these texts become nothing but severance, then the fragment without a text, or any context, is radically unquotable."[23] The quotation symbols on the façade seem to enact the Blanchot injunction almost by refusal, deferring and deflecting the force of severance and exaltation through ambiguous length and line of action, and the makeshift paradox of the close-open quotes backed into each other is almost caricatural—outlining "nothing but severance" while they mark, simultaneously, the deferring indeterminacies.

The spray-painted commas can of course be yoked to more than questions of non/severance. In a slightly expanded field of inquiry, the vestigial marks can be trammeled into service as a glottal pre-speech act, in the fashion of Derrida's *plus* effects in "+R (into the Bargain)." Here Derrida is working to forestall the impetus of writers "on" painting that he purports to be as follows:

> As for painting, any discourse on it, beside it or above, always strikes
> me as silly, both didactic and incantatory, programmed, worked by the
> compulsion of mastery, be it poetical or philosophical, always, and the
> more so when it is pertinent, in the sight of what, at a stroke *[d'un
> trait]*, does without or goes beyond this language, remaining hetero-
> geneous to it or denying it any overview.[24]

Defraying the pertinence of his own writing, whose nominal concern remains Valerio Adami's painting, Derrida attempts to play down the discourse-graphic duel by detouring through a musical space in which both he and Adami are displaced amateurs. Repeated prefixings such as *gl* or *tr* ("+r *effect*. Consonant plus r.") are called on to do some of the grunt work, dislodging the mellifluous coherency of poetic-philosophical overviews.[25] (Although such attempts to cede mastery are laudable, Derrida's strategy remains embroiled in a "+D" effect—the drawing power of intellectual *maestro* status inevitably colors the sonogram, conferring a blue-chip bargaining power.)

Vexations implicit in this duel also haunt the later *Chora L Works*, Derrida's collaboration with Peter Eisenman, a "star" architect of theoretical bent. Having enthusiastically imbibed aspects of Derridean thought with a view to their architectural transcription, Eisenman not unreasonably calls on Derrida to relinquish the strictly linguistic domain and "draw." Derrida proffers the vestigial sketch of an oblique loom-lyre-sieve sculpture accompanied by a written prescription that the piece "figure as detached pieces—neither fragments nor ruins." Sometime later, provoked perhaps by Eisenman's intimations that he is not being sufficiently challenged, Derrida draws back: a meticulously polite postscript disinters Eisenman's vogue philosophical soundings. In return, Eisenman manages only to reiterate the alterity of architecture and philosophy before latching onto the Deleuzian fold for alternative philosophical support.[26] Thus in an all-too-standard gesture, the reinscriptions of disciplinary competency intone the lapsing of the collaboration.

In a somewhat droll sense, the tensions plying these borderline art, architecture, and philosophy maneuvers are reprised in the anonymous banalities of In⁵cryption's headline-endnote on the I-beam. Nevertheless, the stakes and competencies in this final quotation *motif* (and across the marked-up library building in general) are modified by the following duplicity: the performative act is at one and the same instant a mundane painterly self, spraying the stenciled score, and a prosaic writerly self, inscribing a set of commas. Although this contiguity defers certain problems of "pertinence" that Derrida notates, these inevitably haunt later image-writing bifurcations. Writing gets retrospective purchase—as here—in its line-by-line (brick-by-brick) archival constructions; "spatial arts" make a comeback when, despite being out-flanked by titles, signatures, and so on, photo-graphics fabricate mute testimony of "the thing itself" in this chapter, on gallery walls, and in other illustrative arenas. Brick-by-brick allusions return, bit by bit, in the computer-graphic formulations of ⁵crypt, lodged deep within the architectures of this mini-tower "personal" computer. Additionally, numerous belated and makeshift amalgams of image and linguistic matter exist such as ⁵**CORE**, an image-text piece deposited in the Rochester Institute of Technology (RIT) Library archives. Despite the links organized by the artistic personage that initialized it (and even in spite of the subjective insistence that it be marked by heterogeneity), In⁵cryption, therefore, signifies an archival production at odds with itself across space and time.

Even if the spray-written quotation doublet figures as an unusually succinct node for these word-painting questions and corollaries, there is, inevitably, more at stake than word and painting. The close-open quote spattered across an example of late-modern brutalist architecture bleeds into another interminable *topos*: modernist signifying practices. Here, Fredric Jameson's commentary on well-intentioned formal language games proves especially apt. Although the theoretical terms invoked (Venturi's, Scott-Brown's, and Izenour's Long Island duck—the "building-becoming-sculpture," Barthes' "connotation") are somewhat *passé*, Jameson clearly and economically illuminates the propositions made by the master prototype to its retro-surrounds:

> The monumental duck of the International Style, it will be recalled—
> like Mallarmé's *Livre*, like Bayreuth, like *Finnegan's Wake* or Kandinsky's
> mystical painting—proposes itself . . . as a radically different, revolu-
> tionary, or subversive enclave from which little by little the whole sur-
> rounding fabric of fallen social relations is to be regenerated and

transformed. Yet in order to stage itself as a *foyer* of some kind, the "duck" must first radically separate itself from that environment in which it stands: it thereby comes slowly, by virtue of that very inaugural disjunction, that constitutive self-definition and isolation, to be not a building but a *sculpture:* after the fashion of Barthes's concept of connotation, it ends up—far from emitting a message with a radically new content—simply designating itself and signifying itself, celebrating its own disconnection as a message in its own right.[27]

Star architects have, of course, attempted to take on the modernist formal legacy via quotation strategies, albeit with mixed success. Here is Marxist architectural historian Manfredo Tafuri's critical reinforcement of James Stirling's work, posed in terms of strategic withholdings:

> Withdrawn from the public, the forms return to the same archeological universe from which they were excavated. . . . Stirling liberates the architectural language from the duty of alluding, speaking, expressing; he condemns it to meditating and to being—by the very act of its appearing—artifact, evidence, exhibit.[28]

Despite the generosity implicit in Tafuri's reading, the very interiority—encrypting—of the Stirling maneuvers remains vulnerable to Jameson's basic critique, reiterating, by design, precisely the disconnection that he diagnoses.

If the products of the high and mighty are mired in solipsistic declamation, what of ordinary architects and their output? To sketch too briefly and unprofessionally, star architects (typically white male) of modern and nominally postmodern ilk remain anachronistic icons of a profession increasingly constrained by a decrease in construction, an excess of newly qualified architects, territorial encroachment by related professions, the motility of contemporary capital, homogenization of designer *motifs*, and so on.[29] Contemporary architecture, often reflexively aping the diagrammatic models of the masters (which, as Beatriz Colomina's work on Le Corbusier and Mies van der Rohe has shown, often were more publicity shots than mattered bodies[30]), has proved both less and more verbose than originally projected.

Even if, as Jameson indicates, the earnest message never quite reaches its intended (*pace* Lacan, the letter-brick never arrives), this does not imply that the buildings are merely mired and mirrored in their own presumptions. On the contrary, they are continually texted, spoken for and speaking awry. Here the quotation doublet reprises, with a twist, Derrida's injunction that

> [d]espite appearances, the "presence" of an edifice does not refer only to itself. It also repeats, signifies, evokes, convokes, reproduces and cites. It *carries* towards the other and *refers* to itself, it divides even in its *reference.* Of the inverted commas in architecture.[31]

Powerhouse speech acts are, therefore, to be heard from the buildings by long-suffering beholders, even though the designer semiotics of modernist forms often have proved as privatized as Jameson claims. A typical example is furnished by the Rochester Institute of Technology, where two unquenchable rumors pertaining to its trademark brick-bunker building style are in circulation. The first is that the administration in the late 1960s bought cut-rate plans for a campus in Arizona and simply transferred the diagram to Rochester, New York, with makeshift modifications for winter climate control. The second is that the bulwark building *motif*, punctuated by massive access portals, is a formal consequence of 1960s' administration siege mentality—a campus enclave configured to forestall student riots. Both images indicate how the ornamental repressions of "formal innovation" have turned out to bark a less-than-attractive message of social control.[32]

DIVULGING THE BUILDING ^{S} CRYPT

Transposition: . . . *Med.* Abnormal location of an organ . . . *Surg.* Transplantation of a flap of tissue without severing it entirely from its original location until it has united in the new place.[33]

Each grafted text continues to radiate back towards the site of its removal, transforming that too, as it affects the new territory.[34]

ON BUILDING WALKS

A series of "building walks" projected into the interior spaces of the construction site formed a territorial precursor for building ^{s} crypt. In each walk, the nocturnal carto-graphic artist tracked out an arbitrarily selected triangular floor pattern, compulsively pacing the angular spoor throughout the performance. Why was the designated motivic cell triangular?[35] To access the fabulous archive of *tri*allusions, embracing *inter alia* these cartographic inclinations: triangulation, triangle (ruled space-enclosing figure), tripod, index,[36] pyramid, Alberti, Bermuda, Freud, and so on.

The time line of each traversal was photographically prescribed: silver saturation mandated that the camera imbibe the dimly lit scenes for nearly an hour. This labored accretion of evidential tracings means that the photographic prints divulge, belatedly, the presence of the builder-body only as a virtually illegible smear: a slow-motion painterly wash rendered hauntingly transparent by movement during exposure.

What *is* startlingly evident in cold print is a glittering array of gestural light traces. Each has emanated, in due course, from a flashlight held facing the camera throughout the triangular walk. During the long exposure, this innocuous, near-automatic, and rudimentary procedure laces the image with a patchwork of unsettling graphic effects. The mental map of an ideal triangular path at uniform height

FIGURE 14.1 "Building Walk 2," Gordon Bleach, ˢcrypt

is modulated in the indexical trace of the light signal by the rhythmic waveforms of walk and turnabout. While these imprintings of the singular body in motion solicit the locomotor refrains of the putatively scientific photographs of Edweard Muybridge and Etienne-Jules Marey, the body motions in the "building walks" are not restricted to the plane parallel to the lens.[37] The three-dimensional specularities are absorbed here into the flatness of the negative picture plane, only to resurface in the photographic prints as if canted up, oblique triangles refracted off the horizontal planes that they actually index. Decoding reflexes, based on the artifice of perspectival convention triggered in the viewer, remain confounded. Such disorientation recalls the signposts to the viewing subject given in a Derridean *envois* (and, differently delayed, by Marcel Duchamp and Sigmar Polke):

> While you occupy yourself with turning it around in every direction, it is the picture that turns you around like a letter, in advance it

deciphers you, it preoccupies space, it procures your words and gestures, all the bodies that you believe you invent in order to determine its outline. You find yourself, you, on its path.[38]

A brace of building walks was performed in an interim verandah space
looked down upon by RUIN, MEMORY, MAP, DESIRE: a quadrangular and
totemic In⁵cryption angled inward rather than out from the building. Within
this local vista, words and their allusions mesh easily with the representational
paradoxes that the long-duration photographic traces make manifest. These
conjunctions, captured around dusk, are resonant with a Benjaminian refrain:
indexical glints of history and its reprisings. One recalls, with Hannah Arendt,
that "for Benjamin, to quote is to name, and naming rather than speaking, the
word rather than the sentence, brings truth to light."[39] The unsettled angulari-
ties of graphic spoor, poised against a backdrop of linguistic matter, spar at the
hallucinatory epigram for ⁵crypt from early in the *Wake*: "Finiche! Only a fadograph of a yestern scene."

In circumscribing an individualized territory, the wavering fixations of these
walks relate peripherally to the work of English artist Richard Long. Unlike
Long's characteristic mark production, these are not vestigial incursions ruled
into "exotic foreign" landscapes but internalized in a nondescript urban construction space.[40] These local withdrawals are prompted, in part, by an awareness
of the colonial loadings incurred when one walks into territorial possession. In
Valentin Mudimbe's characterization,

> *colonialism* and *colonization* . . . derive from the Latin word *colere*,
> meaning to cultivate or to design. . . . [T]he colonists (those settling a
> region) as well as the colonialists (those exploiting a territory by dom-
> inating a local majority) have all tended to organize and transform
> non-European areas into fundamentally European constructs.[41]

The building walks attempt an allegorical disassembly of cartographic procedures. *Locale* is rendered photogenic, but the long-exposure artifacts snipe at
the evidential pretensions of the image. Territorial inscription is maintained
only in the filmic negative and its reproductions, never quite precipitating out
as concrete settlement. The jittered image of the boundary is not the ruler-
straight linear design inscribed from intercontinental distance but one stumbled
through *in situ*.

BUILDING⁵CRYPT: THE SPURIOUS ARTIFACTS

Enfolded within In⁵cryption during its public broadcast were privatized "spurious artifacts." Whereas the former enclosed the building frame and disclosed the
archive through individual word-units, these internalized artifacts enacted building and library loan procedures (to issue, recall, reshelve, move stacks, etc.) on the

construction material-units themselves. In^scryption and building^scrypt can thus be succinctly linked: surface-building—material-buildings.

Production procedures for the artifacts were modest and relatively banal:

- Materials awaiting installation as well as site detritus were borrowed to construct the artifacts. Fabrication was exclusively a folding, stacking, and balancing act, the artifacts reliant on friction and gravity for stability. In some cases, the construction procedure was merely nominal—assigning ready-made status to the material.

- Artifacts reprised in their configurations the prime sculptural forms of modern architecture (skyscraper, tower block, apartment complex, temple, triumphal arch, pentagon, etc.). These recollected forms were, however, shrunk to fit the scale of individual material-units (brick, cinder block, window frame, walk-through scaffolding, etc.). The resulting structures ranged typically in scale from one to fifty feet.

- Most of the artifacts were sited within the unfinished library extension. This almost-empty interim space was bounded by construction materials on the exterior (plastic sheeting, concrete blocks, etc.) and by broken-up library walls on the interior.

- Artifacts were photographed by "available light" (dusk, incandescent construction lamps, library fluorescents, halogen streetlights), using long exposures of up to an hour.

- The expanded possibilities of the hour-long photographic "moment" were exploited by outlining the artifact using a flashlight and/or dismantling it *during the exposure*. The selfsame light-tracing procedures also were used to notate selected artifacts as ready-mades. In a few cases, light drawings were simply traced across an open night vista, framed by the building. Here, the library was, in effect, transformed into a museum/gallery. These images—marred and melded gestures of graphics *plus* writing—ventriloquized Duchamp and Cy Twombly *motifs* in "an effect of scribble and scrypt."[42]

- Once each artifact had been dismantled and the camera shutter had closed, all materials were carefully returned to their prior positions, readied again for official library building.

WORKING THROUGH BUILDING^sCRYPT

To take stock, prematurely: in building^scrypt, materials were selected, loaned, posed (small buildings, crypts), photographed (scrypted), returned, and fixed (encrypted) in and out of place. The artifacts could, in the first instance, be thought of as "heaps of material language,"[43] disseminated through the larger building:

FIGURE 14.2 "Spurious Artifact 22," Gordon Bleach, ^scrypt

proper configurings in the former were improper in the latter, and vice versa. The official text continued, apparently uninterrupted, but marginal buildings also took place. This "taking place" suggests a deconstruction of modernist architectural forms in a quite precise sense explored later. First, however, buildingˢcrypt is considered something of a minor material literature, derived in part from Loos, Jameson, and Rossi read, almost, to the letter.

The Loos epigram: "Only a very small part of architecture belongs to art: the tomb and the monument" was doubly enacted. Pedantically and ironically, a miniscule fraction of the banal edifice was diverted to the art-ifact during its brief solo stand. In a dogmatic and sardonic truth to materials, the minimalist material construction unit (brick, window frame, etc.) morphed into monumental structural form (tower building, temple, triumphal arch, Pentagon, etc.): sheer, uninhabitable, and alluring at micro-scopic scale. In this transformation, the artifacts appeared as gargoyles and misprogrammed mutations on the intestinal and external surfaces of the library, thereby flaunting a perverse refusal of Loos' injunctions against ornamentation.[44]

Over time, the spurious artifacts coursed through the proprietary building as pathological offspring; excretions prized illicitly from the proper thing and then, apparently unmarked, patched officially and unremarkably back in to extend the host. Simultaneously and more generally they were effigies for the social grandstanding of the exemplary modern form. In this guise, they reprise the Jameson remark, noted earlier in the context of Inˢcryption, that "the 'duck'. . . comes slowly . . . to be not a building but a *sculpture*: . . . simply designating itself and signifying itself, celebrating its own disconnection as a message in its own right."

Although the artifacts can be perceived as "architectural models" in some conventional sense (e.g., as material pinups for a future project), they were not tailored to the task, and their standing in for this function is, therefore, potentially misleading. Rather than denied, these deceptions were incited by photo-graphic strategies that feint at standard gambits in architectural drawing. The glinting gestures forming the flashlit outlines, for example, mimic architectural sketch plans and elevations. Despite these intimations, the artifacts fall short as proper models in that they were neither a program for the extended library within which they are encrypted, nor a visionary prescription for an architecture still to come. In a sense not unrelated to Jameson's observation, they project only themselves.

One projection doubles another when the artifacts are considered fashion models. Playing up the desire for the architectural signature look, the artifacts were set to preen for the lens, voguing in the diorama of construction dis-repair. In the wake of Warhol's maxim, these private, hour-long sittings held out the promise that every little upstart building would fall into its fifteen minutes of fame. Thus the photographs of the spurious artifacts reprise and play up the following shift in architectural thought-practice. Refusals that characterized Loos'

FIGURE 14.3 "Spurious Artifact 5," Gordon Bleach, *crypt

injunctions on photography—that the best of his complex architectural interiors necessarily escaped photographic representation—have morphed into their inverse: the active production of architectural exteriors whose "best side" is designed exclusively to solicit and be fully revealed to the voyeuristic look of the magazine camera.[45]

building*crypt, then, acts out by design a precarious and parasitical fidelity to Loos' prescriptions under the moonlit impetus of its professionally unsanctioned architect, and to persist with the vision of Loos' thought-patterns is inevitably to be led to the writings of one of his more salient heirs, Aldo Rossi.[46] In a set of autobiographical *dicta* written in the wake of a certain modernism, Rossi muses on *Forgetting Architecture* and draws this distinction:

> I have always thought that the term *teatrino* was more complex than
> *teatro*; it refers not just to the size of the building but also to the private,

specific, repetitive character of all that is fiction in the theater. . . .
Teatrini were also simple, temporary structures. [. . . They] were fragments and opportunities, though perhaps they failed to anticipate
other events; their dramas made no *progress*.[47]

Parasitic relationship with the library notwithstanding, building^{s}crypt often
is in tangible accord with Rossi. Both the ebb and flow of the makeshift structures from their interstitial enclaves and the rudimentary construction algorithms
rupture and repeat the im-material plot lines. Dysfunctional progress in these
minor dramas can perhaps be divined in this triple cessation: the artifacts were
reified in the photographic dioramas, piled back into place by the ghosted interventions of the director and, still later, dispersed and locked into official service
across the library. These connectivities, dispersed across the space-time continuum of the site, hark back to Benjamin via Rossi's remark: "The object, whether
part of the country or the city, is a relationship of things . . . and in the end the
artist can write, in Walter Benjamin's words, 'Therefore I am deformed by connections with everything that surrounds me here.'"[48]

The above sketch of building^{s}crypt's modern architectural referents has
drawn on three diminishing returns (Loos' art fragment in architecture, Jameson's
wizened sculptural communicators, and Rossi's fictional condensations in the
teatrini) to portray the artifacts as a late-breaking articulation of modernist architecture, palpably more viral than virile. Spurred by the ghosted interventions of
its director-constructor, building^{s}crypt passes through the ruling theoretical motions at wayward speed and distance-time scales, scarcely supported by the legitimating fable of evocative power. Also, the host library from which this work is
extruded is itself an extrusion, an exemplary brick block replicating the campus
grand *motif* (brick bunker performing as motivic cell).

Additional textual formulations are now grafted on to building^{s}crypt's material formation. The "materiality" of the spurious artifacts is of course inconceiv-
able outside of photographic, linguistic, and other textual representations. Two
Derridean lines of inquiry are invoked and ranged across the spatial granularity
of the intimate and frangible edifices. In the first of these approaches, the spurious artifacts are treated as "material" aphorisms. Construed as terse and somewhat dogmatic fragments, they thus perform as unsettled precipitates from
proprietary systems of philosophical and architectural writ.

The motivating term is rendered here in condensed form as a^{for_s}i'm, imbuing
the standard *motif* with the cryptic sense of Derridean *fors*[49] and, less coherently,
with the radiance of Barthes' intemperate insistence on the "evidential force" of
the photograph.[50] When a^{for_s}i'm is daubed as a logo onto the artifacts, Derrida's
fifty-two aphoristic injunctions made in the pretext of a foreword are perforce
entrained. Extracts from these aphorisms, which concern philosophy and architecture proper (habitation, form, system, monument, ruin, totality, etc.), are

FIGURE 14.4 "Spurious Artifact 24d," Gordon Bleach, ˢcrypt

proffered below, pock-marked by ellipses (and it is as trite as it is accurate to point out that the period in triplicate, which forms an ellipsis, is reprised as the three cylindrical voids in the standard institutional brick: bricks that formed artifacts and blanketed ⅃n^{s}cryption):

1   The aphorism decides, but as much by its substance as by its form, it determines by word play. Even if it speaks of architecture it does not belong to it. . . .

40   Leaving the aphorism on the threshold. There is no inhabitable place for the aphorism. . . .

41   . . . one does not inhabit an aphorism. . . . The aphorism is neither a house nor a temple, . . . nor a tomb. Neither a pyramid nor above all a *stadium*. . . .

43   . . . Architecture in the most philosophical form of its concept is neither a pure interruption, nor a dissociated fragment, but a totality which claims to be self-sufficient, the figure of a system (according to Kant, the architectonic is the art of systems). . . .

46   Despite their fragmentary appearance, [. . . aphorisms] make a sign towards the memory of a totality, at the same time ruin and monument. . . .

48   Contrary to appearances, "deconstruction" is not an architectural metaphor. The word ought and will have to name a thought of architecture, it must be a thought at work. . . .

50   . . .The baseless ground *[le sans-fond]* of a "deconstructive" and affirmative architecture can cause vertigo, but it is not the void, it is not the gaping and chaotic remainder.

51   . . . A still unnameable filiation, another series of aphorisms.[51]

The spurious artifacts—the a$^{for;s}$i^{s}tic filiation under consideration here—cannot be reduced to mere outtakes from Derrida's list. They are not simply projected from the published paper archive (scholarly works cored in the RIT Library) and concretized in the enfolding construction space. Nevertheless, it can be conceded without loss that the a$^{for;s}$i^{s}ms find themselves, on occasion, playing out his words. (Other enactments occur as a matter of course: as he himself notes, his words are at all times outmaneuvered, but not necessarily in linguistic form.) Leading off from the fortieth aphorism, for instance, one recalls that the a$^{for;s}$i^{s}ms were posed in two stop-gap spatial arenas. The majority came into being in the interstices between the working library and construction exterior, and the final few were poised precariously on the edge of the external brick cladding as it rose to close over ⅃n^{s}cryption. So they were positioned to work the shifting spatial thresholds during the interim time of official building; premature monuments that never properly settled into the official structures. Of course, the work space radiates throughout the building from which the a$^{for;s}$i^{s}ms were prized and through which

FIGURE 14.5 "Spurious Artifact 6," Gordon Bleach, ⁵crypt

they were eventually disseminated.[52] With a certain slipshod *gravitas*, the aᶠᵒʳ;ⁱˢms both comprised and notated a "working thought" of architecture[53] in their hysterical and haunted concocting of towers, arches, ruins, monuments, and so on from the proprietary project.

BUILDINGˢCRYPT *in camera*

The self-referential purview of aphorism two charts a reified and a-systemic prophetic power: the aphorism "prophesies, . . . proffers that which will be, stops it in advance in a monumental form, certainly, but anarchitecturally."[54] The aᶠᵒʳ;ⁱˢms are most closely aligned with this clairvoyancy through the aberrational fidelities of their flashlit tailings. These lightings seem at times to mask and preempt the object, as if proposals made for and to it. Simultaneously the trace weaves an indexical skein within and around the object, lying together with its lumpen material presence, and yet the traces are assuredly belated, replete in the privatized black box of the camera only after catastrophic dismantling has taken place. Thus is generated a distended photographism; a freeze-frame movie in which the slurred and washed-out builder blindly disinters the edifice while tracing its ex-outline for completion in the negative. This procedure seems infused with loss and mourning, even and especially in its most constructive acts.[55]

The conceptual and sensual effect of this graphism is indissociable from the specifics of the photographic materials that were used. Polaroid "positive/negative" film yields this duality: a singular black-and-white print as well as a fine-grain negative from which other prints (markedly distinct from the singular positive) can be made. In a deliberate refusal of proper archival treatment, the "original" prints of the spurious artifacts have never been fixed (Polaroid provides a clear, gelatinous varnish to be brushed across the photographic grains—goop that hardens in lumpy strokes and smells, a revealing odor of historical fixture[56]). Left to their own entropic devices, the prints rapidly mutate: grays blotch to yellowed age, and silver migrates upward to pool as an iridescent surface. In short, the coherent image recedes into an oddly polyglottal flotsam. Print enlargements from the negative (these are *not* the singular prints discussed above) were made on color paper and filtered in tones from bronze to puce to sepia in emotive reference to early photographic codes. (ˢcrypt began to take place during photography's "official" 150th anniversary, the dating of which obliterated the first eight-hour captures made by Nicéphore Niepce in 1827, to celebrate the gleaming machinations of Louis Daguerre and French expansionism that went public in 1839.) This Polaroid negative film has the signature characteristic of a painterly bleed as framing edge, albeit an edge that indexes chemical process rather than the overt topic of the photograph. (As noted earlier, movements recorded within these photographic frames index painterly washout as much as decisive moment.) Icy conditions in the unfinished building caused negative emulsions to tear from their corners in, ripping additional spatial allusions into the colorized prints. Epigrams trip in circulation once again: post cards, stacked decks, niched building, monumental fadographs of yestern scenes, ruptured frames, and patched exposures, the smell of graft and transposition.

For Freud, recovery from loss is typically characterized either in terms of introjection (successful mourning, digestion) or alternatively as incorporation (incomplete mourning, the melancholic state in which the other remains within one like a foreign, living, dead). Despite the marked differences between these dual trajectories, "half-mourning" has been coined as an index of Derrida's complex relation to metaphysics (Geoffrey Bennington: "One cannot formulate everything in a logic, but at most in a *graphic*").[57] If one seeks a counterpart at the scene of building'crypt, one recognizes that the artifacts were both incorporated (as whole entities within the building) and introjected (consumed, digested after dismantling), and it stares one in the face that reification and eviscerations pervade the photographic documents that show and show through the buildings— and are themselves shown up in the act (photographic realism internally fraught and frayed, flatly divulging its conventional disquiets). It seems clear that building'crypt can be taken as a half-mourning—but for what exactly? Perhaps not for one singular loss but for photography as evidence, for the neutrality of the archive, for modern architectural form, and for the flamboyant figure of the signature artist-architect. A prophetic aspect of the a^{for}i^{s}ms would then be to signal the demise of certain trains of thought while entraining operations constitutive of them. In reinforcement of this remark, one could insist on the spurious artifacts as post cards heavy and light, and as material writings/written on the frame of proper structure.[58]

MEMORY BUILDINGS

In the guise of a^{for}i^{s}ms, the "spurious artifacts" have been seen to lend themselves to a line of inquiry concerning the aphorism. Latent throughout has been a second refrain: that trademark Derridean singularity, deconstruction. As he and many others have pointed out, widespread circulation of this term in American institutions of higher learning has inevitably resulted in caricature: deconstruction as formulaic project and method. Thus "worn to transparency and beyond" in Stephen Melville's apt characterization, deconstruction seems an increasingly thankless *motif* to invoke: too readily assimilated and yet inapprehensible.[59] Despite this, explicit attention to deconstruction is spurred here by the following observations at least. The obsessively worked banalities, small affirmations, and virtual anonymities that are part and parcel of ^{s}crypt seem an apt fit with Derrida's recent remark that "deconstruction, in the manner in which it is utilized and put to work, is always a highly unstable and almost empty motif."[60] Furthermore, building'crypt forms one of many complements (and/or antidotes) to the signal collaborations of Derrida with master architects

(Bernard Tschumi, Eisenman, etc.) that have been the favored provenance of "deconstruction in architecture" to date.[61]

As in the case of the aphorism, the invocation of deconstruction as a *motif* is not merely an importation from the linguistic arena in order to stack the material deck of buildingˢcrypt. The conviction is rather that deconstruction grows in buildingˢcrypt in ways that exceed inventory in the linguistic realms in which deconstruction first became manifest. And, as a corollary, *this* commentary (by the builder-cameraman returning as sentence-writer) should not be treated merely as retrospective mastering, but as *building* ˢcrypt's production scenes.

Among points of entry to Derrida's variegated statements concerning deconstruction are his aphorisms forty-eight and fifty, associating deconstruction with a "working thought" of architecture and spurning associations to "the gaping and chaotic remainder." Elsewhere, he has delimited a work zone thus, "the messy and tense area left between determinacy and indeterminacy, where odd things happen, is where deconstruction is at work."[62] The workday is necessarily of sporadic and untimely duration, since "deconstruction takes place, it is an event which does not wait on the deliberation, consciousness or organization of the subject, nor even of modernity."[63] Significantly, reinscription is key to linkages between architecture, deconstruction, legible memory, and archive:

> Now as for architecture, I think that *Deconstruction* comes about . . .
> when you have deconstructed some architectural philosophy, some
> architectural assumptions—for instance, the hegemony of the aes-
> thetic, of beauty, the hegemony of usefulness, of functionality, of liv-
> ing, of dwelling. But then you have to *reinscribe* these motifs within
> the work. You can't (or you shouldn't) simply dismiss those values of
> dwelling, functionality, beauty and so on. You have to construct, so to
> speak, a new space and a new form, to shape a new way of building
> in which those motifs or values are reinscribed, having meanwhile
> lost their external hegemony. . . . Deconstruction is not simply for-
> getting the past. What has dominated theology or architecture or any-
> thing else is still there, in some way, and the inscriptions, the, let's say,
> *archive* of these deconstructed structures, the archive should be as
> readable as possible, as legible as we can make it.[64]

In the wake of all of these, however, brevity mandates that one brandish Derrida's "single definition of deconstruction, one as brief, elliptical, and economical as a password," namely, "*plus d'une langue*—both more than a language and no more of a language."[65] And if buildingˢcrypt is to be worked through as an excessive transposition or transference from this curt citation, then by alluding to:

    the abnormal space-time intervals of ˢcrypting—the grafts across conventional procedures;

    the loaned material organs, their brief existence as "autonomous" entities and disappearance—integrated into official building;

the deployment of photo-graphic practices to unsettle conventional subjects of the "medium";

one password to building^scrypt becomes (another heading, taken from the top, to end):

^scrypt . . . more than a building and no more of a building

NOTES

1. Jacques Derrida, "Envois," in *The Post Card: From Socrates to Freud and Beyond*, translated by Alan Bass (Chicago: University of Chicago Press, 1987), 53.

2. Adolph Loos, "Architektur," in *The Architecture of Adolph Loos*, exhibition catalog, edited by Yehuda Safran and Wilfried Wang (London: Precision Press, 1985), 108. Also quoted in Beatriz Colomina, *Privacy and Publicity* (Cambridge, Mass.: MIT Press, 1994), 68; see her notes 1, 7, 8, 23.

3. Robert Smithson, "quoting" the Mexican god Tezcatlipoca; see *The Writings of Robert Smithson: Essays with Illustrations*, edited by Nancy Holt (New York: New York University Press, 1979), 95. The name Tezcatlipoca ("Mirror that Smokes") refers to the clouding of the black obsidian mirror when used by magicians for seeing into the future. See C. A. Burland, *The Gods of Mexico* (New York: Putnam, 1967), x.

4. James Joyce, *Finnegan's Wake* (New York: Penguin, 1976), 7.15.

5. Jacques Derrida, "Parergon," in *The Truth in Painting*, translated by Geoffrey Bennington and Ian MacLeod (Chicago: University of Chicago Press, 1987), n. 14, 73. Footnote reads: "*Ceci est—écrit sur le cadre*: "*écrit* is also "a piece of writing."

6. Gayatri Chakravorty Spivak, "Acting Bits/Identity Talk," in *Critical Inquiry* (summer 1992): 795.

7. *Webster's New International Dictionary*. 2d. ed. (New York: Merriam Webster, 1940), 2694.

8. Robert Smithson, "A Heap of Language," pencil drawing, 1966. Note also his remark that, "My sense of language is that it is matter and not ideas—i.e., "Printed Matter.'" See *Robert Smithson: The Collected Writings*, edited by Jack Flam (Berkeley: University of California Press, 1996), 61.

The triangular configuration recalls Loos' definition of architecture: "If we find a mound in the forest, six feet long and three feet wide, formed into a pyramid shaped by a shovel, we become serious and something within us says, 'Someone lies buried here.' This is architecture." Quoted in Colomina, op. cit., 68. The slump-stack formation of these epigrams also points forward to the construction methods for the "spurious artifacts" presented in the latter half of this chapter.

Loos and Smithson are implicitly juxtaposed perhaps via Smithson's post card photo of Dan Graham posed in front of a pyramidal tombstone in a Newark cemetry, 1970. Reproduced in Dan Graham, *Rock My Religion: Writings and Art Projects 1965–1990*, edited by Brian Wallis (Cambridge, Mass: MIT Press, 1993), vii.

"Post" draws throughout on Derrida's *Post Card*, hence, post card relays to Loos and Smithson.

9. A five-story, 65,000-square foot L-shaped extension made around the south and east walls of the original library building during the period 1989–1991. In view of the importance of photographic representation to ˢcrypt, it is not irrelevant to note that Rochester, New York, is indelibly associated with George Eastman and Eastman Kodak. There is, of course, a key photographic archive housed in the International Museum of Photography at the George Eastman House.

10. The sense of the "viral" and the "para-site" invoked here is indebted to Derrida's discussion in "The Spatial Arts: An Interview with Jacques Derrida," in *Deconstruction and the Visual Arts: Art, Media, Architecture*, edited by Peter Brunette and David Willis (Cambridge: Cambridge University Press, 1994), 9–32, esp. p. 12. Note also Spivak's remark concerning Derrida's work from around the time of *Glas* and *Truth in Painting*: "This is not postmodern practice. There is none of that confident absolute citation where what is cited is emptied of its own historical texting or weaving. This is a citing that invokes the wound of the cutting from the staged origin." See Spivak, op. cit., 795.

11. See *The Alphabetical City* pamphlet for a post–Pound cataloguing of the ABC's (and I's and L's . . .) of early twentieth-century American architecture in gridded cities. Holl's epigram, coincidentally, is from Smithson, and it reads: "A word outside of the mind is a set of dead letters to be looked at." See Steven Holl, *The Alphabetical City, Pamphlet Architecture #5*, 2d. ed. (New York: Princeton University Press, 1980), I:11–14, L:39–40. See also Ezra Pound, *ABC of Reading*, 1st ed. (New York: New Directions, n.d.).

12. One precursor for the Inˢcryption exposure/covering procedure was Kate Ericson's and Mel Ziegler's "House Monument" of 1986, in which the wooden materials for a suburban house were painted with remarks concerning housing. The results were exhibited in Los Angeles before being sold and built up as a conventional house, the writings being obliterated in the process. See Patricia Phillips, "Out of Order: The Public Art Machine," in *Artforum* XXVII:4 (December 1988): cover, 92–97.

13. *In/sight: African Photographers, 1940 to the Present*, at the Solomon R. Guggenheim Museum, New York City, June–September 1996. See the catalogue essay by Okwui Enwezor and Octavio Zaya for a reading of the ˢcrypt photographs that attends particularly to the ghosted body tracings in the images: "Colonial Imaginary, Tropes of Disruption: History, Culture, and Representation in the Works of African Photographers," in *In/sight: African Photographers, 1940 to the Present* (New York: Guggenheim, 1996), 17–48, esp. p. 42; image reproductions, 158–63; *CROSS/ING*, curator Olu Oguibe, Museum of Contemporary Art, University of South Florida, and Museum of African-American Art, Tampa, Florida (September–October 1997); *2nd Johannesburg Biennale: Trade Routes: History + Geography*, "Alternating Currents" Exhibition, Electric Workshop, co-curators Okwui Enwezor and Octavio Zaya, October 1997–January 1998; Catalogue (Johannesburg: Greater Johannesburg Metropolitan Council and Prince Claus Fund for Culture and Development, the Netherlands, 1997).

14. On the relations between seeing and evidence (both rooted in *videre*) in Michel Foucault's work, see John Rajchman, "Foucault's Art of Seeing," in *October* 44 (spring 1988): 88–117. Particularly germane to ˢcrypt are the relations between seeing, space, fiction, and history introduced from pp. 91–96ff.

For photographic particulars, these remarks by John Tagg are key: "The indexical nature of the photograph—the causative link between the pre-photographic referent and the sign—is therefore highly complex, irreversible, and can guarantee nothing at the level of meaning."
"Histories are not backdrops to set off the performance of images. They are scored into the paltry paper signs, in what they do and not do, in what they encompass and exclude, in the ways they open on to or resist a repertoire of uses in which they can be meaningful and productive. Photographs are never "evidence" of history; they are themselves the historical." See John Tagg, *The Burden of Representation: Essays on Photographies and Histories* (Minneapolis: University of Minnesota Press, 1994), 3, 65.

15. Allan Sekula, "Reading an Archive," in *Blasted Allegories*, edited by Brian Wallis (New York: New Museum of Contemporary Art and Cambridge, Mass.: MIT Press, 1987), 114–27, 116.

16. Jacques Derrida, *Archive Fever: A Freudian Impression*, translated by Eric Prenowitz (Chicago and London: University of Chicago Press, 1996), 2–3.

17. Rather than accepting Kantian notions of framing, Derrida envisions "[a] reflective operation [. . . of] writing on the frame or have itself written on the frame (this is—writing/written on the frame)." And as the frame *works* (with difficulty) rather than being stably located and easily self-effacing, parts of what is framed become *structurally* open to intersecting with other networks. See Derrida, "Parergon," op. cit., 73; "To Speculate—on 'Freud,'" in *The Post Card*, op. cit., 273. Tagg provides an exemplary consideration of Derrida's work in the strained circumstances constitutive of, and peculiar to, art history. See John Tagg, "A Discourse (With Shape of Reason Missing)," in *Art History* 15:3 (September 1992): 360.

18. "Power has its principle not so much in a person as in a certain concerted distribution of bodies, surfaces, lights, gazes; in an arrangement whose internal mechanisms produce the relation in which individuals are caught up. . . . The Panopticon is a marvellous machine which, whatever use one may wish to put it to, produces homogeneous effects of power." (Note that the panopticon is a machine to induce particular subject configurations, not a metaphor for a specific building profile.) See Michel Foucault, *Discipline and Punish: The Birth of the Prison*, translated by Alan Sheridan (New York: Vintage Books, 1979), 202, 205.

19. Michel de Certeau, *Heterologies: Discourse on the Other*, translated by Brian Massumi (Minneapolis: University of Minnesota Press, 1986), 4.

20. "The same century invented History and Photography." Roland Barthes, *Camera Lucida*, translated by Richard Howard (New York: Hill & Wang, 1981), 93. See John Tagg's lucid investigations around the "twin capitals" of this phrase in his "The Pencil of History," in *Fugitive Images: From Photography to Video*, edited by Patrice Petro (Bloomington and Indianapolis: Indiana University Press, 1995), 285–303; see esp. pp. 286–88, 296–300.

21. Bruce Nauman, "Vices and Virtues," (1988). See also David Joselit, "Lessons in Public Sculpture," in *Art in America* (December 1989): 130–35.

22. Rachel Whiteread, *House* (London: Phaidon, 1995); *Rachel Whiteread: Shedding Life* (New York: Thames & Hudson, 1997); Graham, op. cit.; see pp. 194–203 in Graham on the work of Gordon Matta-Clark (*Splitting*), and note the photograph on p. vii of Graham by Smithson (see note 8). See also Jeff Wall, *Dan Graham's Kammerspiel* (Toronto: Art

Metropole, 1991); Krzysztof Wodiczko: "Teaching buildings to speak . . . metaphor of the body . . . you project desires onto built forms," public lecture, Rochester Institute of Technology, March 22, 1990. See also Ewa Lajer-Burcharth, "Understanding Wodiczko," in *Counter-Monuments*, exhibition catalogue (Cambridge: MIT Press, 1987), n.p.

23. Maurice Blanchot, *The Writing of the Disaster*, translated by Ann Smock (Lincoln: University of Nebraska Press, 1986), 37.

24. Jacques Derrida, "+R (into the Bargain)," in *The Truth in Painting*, op. cit., 155.

25. Somewhat hokey musical allusions are rolled out, invoking the spirit of the piano duet and the humdrum sing-along, with all-too-accessible musical hooks to aid the part-time participant. The relation between Adami's paintings and Derrida's writings is complicated by the fact that Derrida's own words are quoted in the painted spaces by Adami, miring Derrida as designated commentator in an unusual case of pre-echo. See ibid., 174.

26. Jacques Derrida, "Why Peter Eisenman Writes Such Good Books," translated by Sarah Whiting, in *Restructuring Architectural Theory*, edited by Marco Diani and Catherine Ingraham (Evanston: Northwestern University Press, 1989), 99–105, 102. See also Derrida, "A Letter to Peter Eisenman," in *Assemblage* 12 (1990): 7–13. Note especially the postscript on pp. 12–13. Eisenman's reply follows in "Post/El Cards: A Reply to Jacques Derrida," in *Assemblage* 12 (1990): 14–17. These and other texts are collected in *Chora L Works: Jacques Derrida and Peter Eisenman*, edited by Jeffrey Kipnis and Thomas Leeser (New York: Monacelli, 1997).

Derrida's recent remarks on his collaborations in the "spatial arts" appear in "The Spatial Arts: An Interview with Jacques Derrida,"op. cit., esp. pp. 9, 27. For a reading of Derrida's contribution to *Chora L Works* that attends to new technologies, the relation of theory to practice, and the relation between the local and the global, see Gregory L. Ulmer, "Gadget Goes to Florida," interview with Laurence Rickels, in *Artforum* (January 1996): 68–71, 106, esp. 71.

27. Fredric Jameson, "Architecture and the Critique of Ideology," in *Architecture Criticism Ideology*, edited by Joan Ockman (Princeton, N.J.: Princeton University Press, 1985), 83. For the definition of the duck, see Robert Venturi, Denise Scott-Brown, and Steven Izenour, *Learning from Las Vegas: The Forgotten Symbolism of Architectural Form*, rev. ed. (Cambridge, Mass: MIT Press, 1985), part II, esp. pp. 87–90. See also Geoffrey Bennington, "The Rationality of Postmodern Relativity," in *Legislations: The Politics of Deconstruction* (New York: Verso, 1994), 172–95.

28. Manfredo Tafuri and Francesco Dal Co, *Modern Architecture/2*, translated by Robert Erich Wolf (New York: Rizzoli, 1986), 380.

29. An inventory of gender inequities in the U.S. architectural profession is succinctly noted in "The Strictly Architectural," in *Assemblage* 16 (December 1991): 70–71. Racial inequity is indicated by an anecdote from the *Village Voice* to the effect that only two of all of the buildings south of 95th Street in Manhattan are designed by African Americans.

On orthodox strategies for generating a successful career in architecture, note Rob Wellington Quigley's thumbnail sketch: "The time-honored method (which I recommend to students) is to graduate from a high-profile school, train under an elite 'star' or mentor, create a well-connected network through teaching, reject the mentor, invent a highly manageable stylistic signature, and repeat that graphic signature with each built project until enough material exists for a book." See "Framing the Fit," in *Reflections on Architectural Practices in the Nineties*, edited by William S. Saunders (New York: Princeton University Press, 1996), 170–75.

30. Colomina, op. cit., 42.

31. Jacques Derrida, "Fifty-Two Aphorisms for a Foreword," translated by Andrew Benjamin, in *Deconstruction: The Omnibus Volume*, edited by Andreas C. Papadakis, Catherine Cooke, and Andrew Benjamin (New York: Rizzoli, 1989), 67.

32. There is a danger that the case against formal architectural motivations may overstate the case against the institution of RIT as a whole, and against its faculty, employees, and students in particular. My purpose in this section is to indicate links between late-modern architectural form, a certain inclination in architectural pedagogy and practice, the "appropriate" image for an institute of technology, and the instance of the archive. My work at RIT could not have been carried out without explicit, committed, and sustained support from specific members of the RIT administration, faculty, library staff, campus employees, construction workers, and fellow students. Despite the reiteration of the typical campus style, the new library extension represents a marked improvement on the norm, in that it has extensive fenestration on more than the ground floor.

33. *Webster's New International Dictionary*. 2d ed., op. cit., 2694.

34. Jacques Derrida, "Dissemination," in *Dissemination*, translated by Barbara Johnson (Chicago: Chicago University Press, 1981), 287–366, 355.

35. The sense here is of a *motif*: the "shortest intelligible and self-existent melodic or rhythmic figure," according to *The Concise Oxford Dictionary of Music*, edited by Michael Kennedy (New York: Oxford University Press, 1980), 431. Although the same entry cautions against the adjective "motivic" as being "an invention of analytical writers, functional but ugly and better avoided," motivic cell is preferred here for the architectural—as well as analytical—allusions it invokes. Michel de Certeau's remarks on the linguistic and psychoanalytic loadings in cartographic inscription link the rhythmic motion evoked by the motivic cell and the autobiographical compulsions echoed in the darkened nocturnal tracings. In the wake of Jules Verne, de Certeau considers the questions posed by "writing the sea": "The navigational colonization inaugurates an operativity by providing it with a place of its own: the map, which replaces beings, 'calls' them to the linguistic network which situates them in advance in a field of human history. . . . Undoubtedly, the indefinite act of naming, of circumscribing and delimiting units, of thus dragging oneself out of maritime indeterminacy, is also the narrative path followed by a relation to maternal differentiation . . . names must be carved out of it [the ocean] relentlessly (islands, submarines, 'floating apparatuses'), outlets for meaning must be engineered in it, the dotted lines of a paternal symbolic system must be inscribed upon it, one must attempt to *leave*, to be born, to walk. Navigations in a primal cavern, where one must mark out names and places. Voyages simultaneously within and without." See de Certeau, "Writing the Sea: Jules Verne," in *Heterologies: Discourse on the Other*, op. cit., 144.

36. Signpost: Geoffrey Bennington, "Index," in *Legislations*, op. cit., 274–95.

37. Etienne-Jules Marey, "Man dressed, for photographic experiment, in black costume with white lines along limbs," 1883. Reproduced in Hollis Frampton, *Circles of Confusion: Film·Photography·Video Texts 1968–1980* (Rochester: Visual Studies Workshop

Press, 1983), 45. See also François Dagognet, *Etienne-Jules Marey: A Passion for the Trace* (New York: Zone Books, 1992) and Marta Braun, *Picturing Time: The Work of Etienne-Jules Marey* (1830-1904) (Chicago: University of Chicago Press, 1992).

38. Jacques Derrida, back cover supplement to "Envois," November 17, 1979, op. cit. See also the entry on *envois*—and "invoice"—in the translator's "Glossary," xx–xxi. Germane here are the recent "alchemical" experiments of Sigmar Polke, whose complex celerities might be thought of as "delays in paint" after the fashion of Duchamp's "delay in glass." Installations of ^{s}crypt at RIT ("Memory Building," 1991) at the Museum of African-American Art in Tampa, Florida ("\ backslash" 1997) and in the 2nd Johannesburg Biennale ("city^{s}crypt" 1997–1998) expand *inter alia* on the questions of Duchampian delay. See Rosalind Krauss, "Notes on the Index: Seventies Art in America," in *October* 3 (1977): 68–81; John Caldwell, "Sigmar Polke," in *Sigmar Polke* (San Francisco: San Francisco Museum of Modern Art, 1990), 12–13, plates 48–55, 65–69.

39. Hannah Arendt, Introduction, in Walter Benjamin, *Illuminations*, edited by Hannah Arendt and translated by Harry Zohn (New York: Schocken Books, 1969), 49.

40. Herman Rapaport's reading (following Heidegger and somewhat *contra* Derrida) of Richard Long's work in Nepal seems unduly generous. Long's walks, erasures, and photographs in locations that Rapaport calls "worlds utterly remote from our experience" redeploy, all too uncritically, discursive practices that have been constitutive of European (neo-) colonialism for a well-established international art market niche. Thus it seems implausible that Long's work is quite so easily "devoid of nightmare, hallucination, and phantoms" in its "clear[ing]" the way for the return of the aesthetic," as Rapaport suggests. See "Brushed Path, Slate Line, Stone Circle: On Martin Heidegger, Richard Long, and Jacques Derrida," in *Deconstruction and the Visual Arts*, op. cit., 151–67, esp. 164–66. The "nondescript" RIT construction site rests on land that has a complex colonial history. New York State stole the land from the Iroquois Confederacy, despite U.S. government assurances of Confederacy sovereignty. See Christopher Vecsey and William A. Starna, eds., *Iroquois Land Claims* (Syacuse: Syracuse University Press, 1988).

41. V. Y. Mudimbe, *The Invention of Africa: Gnosis, Philosophy, and the Order of Knowledge* (Bloomington and Indianapolis: Indiana University Press, 1988), 1.

42. Marcel Duchamp, *The Bride Stripped Bare by Her Batchelors, Even*, typographic version by Richard Hamilton of Marcel Duchamp's *Green Box*, translated by George Heard Hamilton (Stuttgart, London, and Reykjavik: Edition Mayer; NewYork: Rietman, 1976), section on the sieves, funnels, dust, and photograph, n.p. See also Harald Szeeman, ed., *Cy Twombly: Paintings, Works on Paper, Sculpture* (Munich: Prestel, 1987); Derrida, "Scribble (writing-power)," translated by Cary Plotkin, in *Yale French Studies* (1979): 58: 124.

43. Smithson, op. cit. His deferential attention to entropy is not of primary concern here.

44. Colomina charts the sexism and homophobia in Loos' definition of "modern man," biases that underpin his injunctions against ornamentation in modern architecture, op. cit., 37–38. There is a danger in Colomina's work that the dominant image of the "genius-architect" is, paradoxically, reinforced by her concentrated attention to prototypical figures such as Loos and Le Corbusier, even though her work serves as an important *exposé* of their actions. In this regard, see Sylvia Latvin's remarks on Eileen Gray, in "Colomina's Web: A Reply to Beatriz Colomina," in *The Sex of Architecture*, edited by Diana Agrest, Patricia Conway, and Leslie Kanes Weisman (New York: Abrams, 1996),

242   W a s t e - S i t e   S t o r i e s

183–90. Note also Karen Burns' considered attempt at an "other than oppositional" reading of commentaries on Loos' model house for Josephine Baker, in "A House for Josephine Baker," in *Postcolonial Space(s)*, edited by G. B. Nalbantoglu and C. T. Wong (New York: Princeton Architectural Press, 1997), 53–72.

45. Colomina, op. cit., 42–43, 64–65. Certain contemporary architectural firms design specific aspects of their buildings with the primary goal of creating a photogenic signature look, all of this in hopeful anticipation of the architectural magazine cover shot. For more on photographic representational practice in the architectural profession, particularly in the "glossies" (architectural trade journals), see Greig Crysler, "Universal Pictures: Grand Style Photography and the Simulation of the American City," in *Afterimage* 19:1 (summer 1991): 4–7. See also the remarks on fashion and boutique architecture by Elizabeth Padjen, "The Shaping of Architectural Practice," in *Reflections on Architectural Practices in the Nineties*, op. cit., 26–35, 31.

46. Attention here is primarily to Rossi's earlier work, most notably his Cemetry of San Cataldo (Modena, 1971–1984), with Gianni Braghieri, the floating *Teatro del Mondo* (Venice, 1979), and to a lesser extent the *Funerary Chapel* (Brianza, 1981), with C. Stead. Later projects, nominally drawing on historical Italian memory *motifs* but deposited in international sites, are more vulnerable to criticism, despite the complexity of the questions raised. Rem Koolhaas' stupefaction at the "horribly beautiful" face of globalization in architecture manifested in Rossi's Fukuoka hotel is pertinent. Rossi's considered response to these questions, drawing from Alberti and Michelangelo, is given in his interview with Bernard Huet, "A Conversation," in *Aldo Rossi: Architect*, edited by Hans Gerhard Hannesen and Helmut Giesert (London: Academy, 1994), 15–27, see esp. pp. 19, 23–24; Hans Gerhard Hannesen, "Cara Architectura," ibid., 42–44, 62; see also 88–90, 104–11; *Aldo Rossi: Buildings and Projects*, compiled and edited by Peter Arnell and Ted Bickford (New York: Rizzoli, 1985), 88–101, 220–37, 260–61; Rem Koolhaas, "Architecture and Globalization," in *Reflections on Architectural Practices in the Nineties*, op. cit., 235–37.

47. *Forgetting Architecture* is offered as a "more appropriate title for this book": Aldo Rossi, *A Scientific Autobiography* (Cambridge, Mass.: Oppositions Books, MIT Press, 1984), 28, 29. The *teatrini* add, of course, to the tri-allusions listed earlier, and Rossi addresses map, topographical elements, and triangulation as follows: "I came across Opicino De Canistri's map. In this map human and animal figures, sexual unions, and memories are confounded with the topographical elements of the relief; it demonstrates the different directions which art and science take at times. . . . I read the geometry of the monuments at Cuneo and Segrate as derived from complex sources, even though others emphasized their purism and rationalism. . . . whenever I draw a triangle I always think not only of the difficulty of closing it, but of the richness implicit in the error" (81).

48. Ibid., 19. For more on the links between Rossi, Benjamin, and Aby Warburg, see Christine Boyer, *The City of Collective Memory: Its Historical Imagery and Architectural Entertainments* (Cambridge, Mass.: MIT Press, 1994), 195–201.

49. "*for, fors, fort* are homonyms. . . . (Fors . . . describes the paradoxical nature of the crypt as something secret and open, inner and outer, perhaps like a crypted letter whose message is as private and public as that on a post card.)" See Alan Bass, "Glossary," in *The Post Card*, op. cit., xxii.

50. Roland Barthes, *Camera Lucida*, op. cit. Despite the allure of Barthes' phrase "evidential force," I share the reservations expressed by John Tagg in "The Pencil of

History," op. cit., 285–304. See also my "Home Movies," in *Nka: Journal of Contemporary African Art* 3 (fall/winter 1995): 42–44.

51. Derrida, "Fifty-Two Aphorisms for a Foreword," op. cit., 67–69.

52. Derrida, "Parergon," op. cit., n. 14, 73. Recall also the second epigram in the latter half of this chapter, taken from *Dissemination*: "Each grafted text continues to radiate back towards the site of its removal, transforming that too, as it affects the new territory."

53. "When I speak of thought at work in architecture, as could also be said with respect to painting or the fine arts, I am making a distinction between thought and philosophy." See "The Spatial Arts: An Interview with Jacques Derrida," op. cit., 24–27.

54. Derrida, "Fifty-Two Aphorisms for a Foreward," op. cit., 67.

55. Rossi's remarks on drawing are germane: ". . . a type of drawing where the line is no longer a line, but writing. Hence this form of writing which lies midway between drawing and handwriting fascinated me for a long while, even if at the same time it made me peculiarly uneasy." See Rossi, *A Scientific Autobiography*, op. cit., 44. Note also Derrida's phrase "absence like the shadowed sound of the voice" made in the following context: "This question of history, as the history of spacing of time and voice, does not separate itself from the history of visibility (immediately, mediate), that is to say, from all history of architecture." See Derrida, "A Letter to Peter Eisenman," op. cit., 9.

56. "History-as-odor," Roland Barthes, *Roland Barthes by Roland Barthes*, translated by Richard Howard (New York: Noonday Press, 1977), caption to the fourth photograph, n.p.

57. Bennington, "Derridabase," in Geoffrey Bennington and Jacques Derrida, *Jacques Derrida*, translated by Geoffrey Bennington (Chicago: University of Chicago Press, 1993), 147–48, 286–91, 287.

58. "The thick support of the card, a book heavy and light, is also the specter of this scene." See Derrida, "Envois," op. cit., back cover. Recall also the first and fifth epigrams, from "Envois" and "Parergon," respectively.

59. Stephen Melville, "Color Has Not Yet Been Named," in *Deconstruction and the Visual Arts*, op. cit., 33–48, 34. In recent synoptic remarks on Derrida's work, Bennington excludes "deconstruction" from the headings under which his accounting is made. See Bennington, "Derridabase," op. cit., xiii–ix.

60. Jacques Derrida, "Remarks on Deconstruction and Pragmatism," translated by Simon Critchley, in *Deconstruction and Pragmatism*, edited by Chantal Mouffe (London and New York: Routledge, 1996), 85.

61. The work of Jennifer Bloomer is one such complement. See, for example, her "Tabbles of Bower," in *Deconstruction and the Visual Arts*, op. cit., 228–47.

62. Jacques Derrida, *Of Grammatology*, translated by Gayatri Chakravorti Spivak (Baltimore: Johns Hopkins University Press, 1976).

63. Jacques Derrida, "Letter to a Japanese Friend," translated by David Wood and Andrew Benjamin, in *A Derrida Reader: Between the Blinds*, edited by Peggy Kamuf (New York: Columbia University Press, 1991), 273–74. The quote is preceded by: "It is not enough to say that deconstruction cannot be reduced to some methodological instrumentality, to a set of rules and transposable procedures. It is not enough to say that each 'event' of deconstruction remains singular, or in any case as close as possible to something like an idiom or a signature. We should also make clear that deconstruction is not even an act or an operation."

64. Jacques Derrida, "Jacques Derrida in Discussion with Christopher Norris," in *Deconstruction II*, edited by Andreas Papadakis (London: Academy Editions, 1989), 9. See also Bennington's "Deconstruction Is Not what You Think," in *Deconstruction: The Omnibus Volume*, op. cit., 84.

65. Jacques Derrida, "Mnemosyne," in *Mémoires: For Paul de Man*, translated by Cecile Lindsay, Jonathan Culler, Eduardo Cadava, and Peggy Kamuf (New York: Columbia University Press, 1989), 15.

Contributors

ALEIDA ASSMANN became Chair of English Literature at the Universität Konstanz in 1993, after obtaining a doctorate in English and egyptology from Heidelberg and Tübingen Universities. A Fellow of the Essen Kulturwissenschaftliches Institut, 1992–1993, and the Institute for Advanced Study in Berlin, 1998–1999, she is the co-editor of a volume on forms and functions of memory, *Mnemosyn: Formen und Funktionen des kulturellen Erinnerung* (Fisher Verlag, 1993). Her most recent publications include *Zeit und Tradition* (Böhlau, 1999) and *Erinnerungsräume: Formen und Wandlungen des kulturellen Gedächtnisses* (C. H. Beck, 1999).

STEPHEN BANN is Professor of Art History at the University of Bristol, and is a Fellow of the British Academy. His most recent books are *Under the Sign: John Bargrave As Collector, Traveler and Witness* (University of Michigan Press, 1994), *Romanticism and the Rise of History* (Twayne, 1995), *Paul Delaroche—History Painted* (Princeton University Press, 1997), and *Parallel Lines: Printmakers, Painters, and Photographers in Nineteenth Century France* (Yale University Press, 2001).

CHRISTINE BERNIER holds a Ph.D. in comparative literature from the Université de Montréal and works at the Musée d'art contemporain de Montréal. As Director of Educational Services, she has organized the international conference series *Definitions of Visual Culture*, which began in 1994 with *The New Art History*, followed by *Modernist Utopias* and *Art and History*, in 1995 and 1997, respectively, and *Memory and Archives*, in 2000.

GORDON BLEACH was Assistant Professor of Photography in the Department of Art at the University of Florida, Gainesville. He first obtained a Ph.D. in applied mathematics from the University of Cape Town, before pursuing graduate work at the Rochester Institute of Technology and a second doctorate in art history, from Binghampton University on American and European film, photographic and cartographic representations of Africa. He had exhibited extensively over the last two decades, in both Africa and Europe, as well as in North America, where he participated in the Guggenheim Museum group exhibition, *In/sight: African Photographers, 1940 to the Present.*

WOLFGANG ERNST has taught media studies at a number of German universities since his doctoral work on neo-classical collections of antiquities in Britain, published as *Historismus im Verzug* (MRM Verlag, 1993). He submitted his habilitation at Humboldt-Universität—*In the Name of History: Collecting, Storing, Narrating.* Among his many publications on the archaeology of media, he edited *Die Unschreibbarkeit von Imperien: Theodor Mommsens Römische Kaisergeschichte und Heiner Müllers Echo* (Verlag and Databank für Geisteswissenschaften, 1995).

WLAD GODZICH is Dean of Humanities at the University of California, Santa Cruz. The former co-editor of the *Theory and History of Literature* series (University of Minnesota Press), he also is the author of many essays and two books, *The Emergence of Prose: An Essay in Prosaics* (University of Minnesota Press, 1987), with Jeffrey Kittay, and *The Culture of Literacy* (Harvard University Press, 1994).

CHARLES GRIVEL is Professor of Romance Languages and Literature at the Universität Mannheim. He has published several essays on popular culture and literature, photography, and art. He is a specialist on Dracula, having edited a collection of essays on the subject (Cahiers de l'Herne, 1996). In 1990, he published *Précipité d'une fouille* (Antigone), but is better known for a celebrated book on fantasy, *Fantastique-Fiction* (Presses Universitaires de France, 1992).

DAVID GROSS is Professor of History at the University of Colorado, Boulder. He is the author of *The Writer and Society: Heinrich Mann and Literary Politics in Germany, 1890–1940* (Humanities Press, 1980), *The Past in Ruins* (University of Massachusetts Press, 1992), his influential study of history and memory, and most recently, *Lost Time: On Remembering and Forgetting in Late Modern Culture* (University of Massachusetts Press, 2000).

HANS ULRICH GUMBRECHT is Albert Guérard Professor of Literature in the Departments of Comparative Literature and French and Italian at Stanford University. He is the co-editor of the *Writing Science* series (Stanford University Press) and several essay collections, most recently, *Materialities of Communication* (Stanford University Press, 1994). His publications in English include *Making Sense in Life and Literature* (University of Minnesota Press, 1992) and *In 1926: Living at the Edge of Time* (Harvard University Press, 1997).

SUSANNE HAUSER teaches at Berlin's Humboldt Universität, where she received her habilitation in 1999. A Fellow of the Institute for Advanced Study in Berlin, 1995–1996, she has worked with a number of European and American research institutions. She has taught at various departments of anthropology, urban history, and cultural sciences, including, most recently, the Department of Architecture, Urban Planning, and Landscape Planning at the Universität Gesamthochschule Kassel. She has quickly become a leading cultural historian in Germany on the social discourse of waste and artistic practices of recycling.

ÉRIC MÉCHOULAN is Professor of French Literature in the Département de littérature française at the Université de Montréal. He is co-editor of a collection of essays on memory, *Zeit des Ereignisses—Ende des Geschichte?* (Fink Verlag, 1992). As an editor, he has been published in the journal *Substance*, and he is the author of *Le corps imprimé: Essai sur le silence en littérature* (Les Éditions Balzac, 1999).

WALTER MOSER is Professor at the Département de littérature comparée and the Département de langue modernes at the Université de Montréal. Head of the research group *Les Recyclages culturels*, he has published widely on contemporary aesthetics, hermeneutics, and German literature. He is the author of a study on Novalis, *Romantisme et crises de la modernité* (Éditions du Préambule, 1989) and co-editor of the collective volume *Les Recyclages culturels: Économies de l'appropriation culturelle* (Les Éditions Balzac, 1995).

BRIAN NEVILLE is an independent writer and translator, living in London. In addition to his professional work, he has written on Walter Benjamin and he is co-editor of *La Mémoire des déchets: Essais sur la culture et la valeur du passé* (Nota Bene Éditeur, 1999) Among other projects, he is currently writing *On the Horizon*, a critique of aphorism.

VALERIA WAGNER teaches comparative literature and English at the Université de Genève. After publishing widely on the concept of action in literature and philosophy, she published a book-length study on the subject, *Bound to Act: Models of Action, Dramas of Inaction* (Stanford University Press, 1999). She is presently elaborating the themes of her contribution to this volume into a book.

JOHANNE VILLENEUVE is Professor at the Département d'études littéraires at the Université du Québec à Montréal, where she teaches literature and film studies. She is co-editor of *La Mémoire des déchets: Essais sur la culture et la valeur du passé* (Nota Bene Éditeur, 1999), and has written extensively on the discourse of intrigue in modern culture. Her current projects include a monograph on French filmmaker Chris Marker.

Index